GUNS OF FEBRUARY

T0345565

GUNS OF FEBRUARY

Ordinary Japanese Soldiers' Views of the Malayan Campaign and the Fall of Singapore 1941–42

Henry Frei

NUS PRESS
SINGAPORE

© NUS Press
National University of Singapore
AS3-01-02, 3 Arts Link
Singapore 117569

Fax: (65) 6774-0652
E-mail: nusbooks@nus.edu.sg
Website: http://nuspress.nus.edu.sg

First Edition 2004
Reprint 2007, 2016, 2023

ISBN 978-9971-69-273-5 (Paper)

Typeset by: Scientifik Graphics (Singapore) Pte Ltd
Printed by: Markono Print Media Pte Ltd

Contents

List of Illustrations

About the Author

HENRY FREI (1947–2002) was a native of Switzerland. He earned a PhD in history from Sophia University in Tokyo, and was Professor of Asia Pacific History at Tsukuba Women's University in Japan. His special area of interest was Japan's historical relations with other countries of the Pacific rim, and his first book was entitled *Japan's Southward Advance and Australia: From the 16th Century to World War II* (Melbourne: Melbourne University Press and Honolulu: University of Hawaii Press, 1991). Other publications include articles in academic journals such as *Monumenta Nipponica*, *Australian Historical Studies* and *Kokusai Seiji*, as well as chapters in several books on the Asia Pacific Region.

While teaching Japanese history at the National University of Singapore in the early 1990s, he developed a strong interest in the fall of Singapore during the Pacific War. On behalf of the Singapore Oral History Centre Project he interviewed a number of Japanese soldiers and civilians, as well as Australian soldiers, who had seen action in the Malayan campaign and experienced the fall of Singapore in 1941–42. In addition he carried out lengthy interviews with surviving members of the *kempeitai* (military police) who, following the British surrender in Singapore, were involved in the purge of overseas Chinese in the city, and also with Chinese residents of Singapore who survived the purge.

After returning to Japan, he took part in a five-year project, sponsored by the Toyota Foundation, to gather materials on the Malayan campaign and the Japanese Military Administration in Malaya, joining some of Japan's foremost military historians including Akashi Yoji and Hata Ikuhiko to assemble a major archive of interviews and documentation on the occupation of Malaya and Singapore. Much of this material is being published in Japanese. One collection of articles written by project participants was published in *Nippon Senryoka no Eiryo Maraya/Shingaporu*, ed. Akashi Yoji (Tokyo: Iwanami Shoten, 2001); an English translation is planned for 2004. Another of Henry Frei's projects, a translation of the published memoir of Onishi Satoru, a *kempeitai* officer quoted in the present book, will be published at a future date.

Biographical Notes

(Prepared by Yoji Akashi)

Arai Mitsuo, Warrant Officer (b. 1912)
Drafted in 1937 and fought in China, Malaya, and Burma on the staff of the 114th Regiment command, 18th Division. Repatriated from China in 1947. Published a memoir entitled *Singapore senki* [A Battle Record of Singapore] because information about the regiment's role in the assault of Singapore was scanty in the official history of the Malayan campaign published by the National Institute for Defence Studies, and because a publication entitled *Detailed Battle Record of the 18th Division*, written by a staff officer, contained erroneous accounts of the 18th Division.

Fujiwara Iwaichi, Lieutenant Colonel (1908–86)
Graduated from the Military Academy in 1931 and from the War College in 1938. He was assigned to the Strategy Section of the General Staff, and in October 1941 was sent to Bangkok as an intelligence agent to deal with Indian affairs. As chief of the "F Kikan" Fujiwara helped organise the Indian National Army, using Indian soldiers who surrendered to the Japanese during the Malayan campaign. In March 1943 Fujiwara became an intelligence staff officer with the 15th Army and took part in the Imphal campaign. Subsequently he served as an instructor at the War College, and then as a staff officer of field armies in Japan. After the war, he was arrested by the British and given a military trial, but was found not guilty. He joined Japan's Self Defence Force in 1955, and retired in 1966 with the rank of Lieutenant General. He published a memoir of "F-Kikan" and an autobiography (*Ryukonki*). Fujiwara wrote these books to make known the patriotic activities of his former comrades who worked for the Japanese cause in India, Malaya and Sumatra.

Ochi Harumi, Captain (b. 1918)
Drafted in 1939 to the 11th Regiment, 5th Division and fought battles with the 11th Regiment in China, French Indochina, Malaya, and New

Guinea. From February to December 1942, Ochi was stationed at Port Dickson for garrison duty, and then was deployed to Wewak in New Guinea where he remained until June 1945. After Japan's surrender he was sent to Singapore and interned on Rembang Island until his repatriation to Japan in 1946. Ochi published two volumes of memoirs, *Malay senki* [A Battle Record of the Malayan Campaign] and *Kyoran Do Singapore* [Singapore Upside Down].

Omori Kichijiro (1911–94)
After graduating from Tokyo College of Commerce (now Hitotsubashi University) in 1931, Omori was employed by the Senda Trading Co. After spending four years in Calcutta and Bangkok, he was transferred to the firm's Singapore office in 1935. When war broke out, Omori was interned in Changi and then at a camp in New Delhi. He returned to Shonan (Singapore) in August 1942 and worked for Senda Trading Co.'s Singapore office until the end of war. He went back to Japan in 1946.

Onishi Satoru, Major (1903–94)
A graduate of the Military Police Training School and of the Military Police Academy, Onishi was appointed to the Second Field Military Police Unit in 1941 and took part in the Malayan campaign. Following the fall of Singapore, he commanded a Special Police Unit that fought the Malayan People's Anti-Japanese Army until the end of war. After the war he was indicted and sentenced by a British military court to life imprisonment for the massacres of Chinese in Singapore carried out in February and March 1942. He was released in 1947. He published his memoirs, *Hiroku Sho Dan Kakyo shukusei jiken* [An untold record of the massacres of Chinese in Singapore] because he wished to preserve an account of the *sook ching* massacres and the mop up campaign against the MPAJA for posterity.

Tsuchikane Tominosuke, Sergeant First Class (b. 1920)
Drafted in 1941, Tsuchikane served in the 4th Regiment, Imperial Guards Division and took part in the Malayan campaign between December 1941 and February 1942. From March 1942 until the end of war he was stationed in Sumatra. After Japan's surrender, he was interned along with other "Japanese surrendered personnel" by the

British Army and engaged in forced labour until his repatriation in 1947. He published a two-volume memoir, *Singapore he no michi* [The road to Singapore] to preserve the stories of individual soldiers who fought in the battle.

Tsuji Masanobu, Colonel (1902–68)
Tsuji Masanobu Graduated from the Military Academy in 1924 and from the War College in 1931, with honours in both cases, and held various staff positions with the General Staff and the China Expeditionary Army prior to 1941. He was senior operations staff officer of the 25th Army from September 1941 to March 1942. After a period as a staff officer for armies in the Southwest Pacific and China, he was appointed a staff officer of the Burma Area Army and the 18th Army in Thailand from 1944 to the end of war. After the war, Tsuji was sought by the British for war crimes and went underground to avoid arrest. After hiding in Thailand, French Indochina, and China, he returned to Japan in May 1948. Cleared of war crimes charges in 1950, he was elected to the House of Representatives in 1952 and the House of Councillors in 1959. In April 1961, he travelled to Southeast Asia and disappeared in Laos. Tsuji was officially declared dead in 1968. He wrote *Unmeino'tenkart* (translated as *Singapore 1941–42*), presenting the Japanese version of the Malayan campaign, and *Sanju tai ichi* (regarding Japan's disastrous Burma Campaign in 1943–5).

Yamashita Tomoyuki, General (1885–1946)
Graduated from the Military Academy in 1905 and from the War College with honours in 1916. After having served in various important posts in the War Ministry and with field armies in Korea, China, Manchuria as well as foreign missions during the 1920s and 1930s, he was appointed commanding general of the 25th Army in November 1941. His forces conquered Malaya and Singapore in 70 days between 8 December 1941 and 15 February 1942, a feat which gave him the sobriquet "Tiger of Malaya". In July 1942 he became commanding general of the 1st Area Army in Northern Manchuria. In September 1944 he was transferred to the Philippines as commander of the 14th Area Army. After Japan's surrender, Yamashita was tried in connection with atrocities committed by his troops defending Manila. He was found guilty, and was executed on 23 February 1946.

Acknowledgements

THE maps that appear in this volume were published in 1978 by the Mainichi Shimbun in their series *Nihon no Senshi*, vol. 7, pp. 126 and 169. They have been redrawn by Mrs. Lee Li Kheng, and translated into English. The photographs are from the same source. The publisher is grateful to the Mainichi Shimbun for permission to reproduce these materials.

Dr Greg Clancey of the Department of History and Dr Mika Toyota of the Asia Research Institute at the National University of Singapore, and Professor Hara Fujio of Nanzan University, provided assistance with the Japanese terms. Professor Yoji Akashi provided the biographical notes.

Preface

HENRY FREI died of cancer in 2002. At the time of his death the manuscript for *Guns of February* was nearly finished. He planned to check the material one last time, but considered this labour of love, which had been ten years in the making, ready for publication.

I write this introductory note as his editor and publisher, but Henry was also a colleague and a personal friend. We had discussed his work on several occasions, and the excitement he felt about seeing this book in print was palpable. He wanted the world to understand the Japanese army as he did, as human beings rather than automatons blindly serving the emperor, or as inhuman fighters lacking emotion and compassion for their enemies. He was acquainted with many former soldiers, and they differed widely in their feelings about the war. Some saw the advance through Malaya as a great adventure, others as a terrifying ordeal, but for all of them it was an experience marked by death and suffering. Many of the soldiers he knew, by now old men living out their days in a world that had changed beyond recognition, felt deep remorse for the actions taken in their country's name, and for things they themselves had done. Henry crafted his book in an unusual way, presenting the material with an immediacy that is rare in academic works. The account reads like a historical novel, but Henry took pains to emphasize that every word he quotes, every expression of feeling, every description of place, comes directly from accounts by the Japanese who participated in these events, and these sources are carefully identified.

Henry did not complete an introduction to the book. His files contained some tentative beginnings, but he had much more to say because he wanted to position this book very carefully for its readers, to let them know what kind of work it was and what he intended it to accomplish. After giving the matter much thought, I decided that the best way to introduce the book is to reprint an article that Henry wrote while this volume was in preparation about the memoirs that provide its content. The piece appeared in a publication

I edited under the title *Malaya and Singapore during the Japanese Occupation*,[1] and has been slightly modified for the present book.

Some of the actors who appear in this volume are likely to be unfamiliar to most readers. Professor Yoji Akashi, a scholar with whom Henry worked closely, kindly prepared biographical information on the key figures. In addition, Dr Brian Farrell of the Department of History at the National University of Singapore checked the military and geographical information in the book, correcting a number of points of detail, and wrote an appreciation of the study.

Henry would certainly want me to conclude with a word of gratitude to his wife Kyo. She contacted me not long after his death to say that she very much wanted to proceed with the publication of Henry's manuscript, and she provided considerable assistance as the publication took shape. Kyo saw this book as a tribute to her husband's dedication to understanding Japan and the Japanese people, and she wanted to ensure that his work was not lost. Henry considered it a contribution not only to academic scholarship but also to international understanding, a grand ambition, but not too grand for the eloquent book Henry Frei left behind as his legacy.

Paul H. Kratoska
Managing Director, NUS Press

---

[1] Singapore: *Journal of Southeast Asian Studies*, Special Publications Series No.3 (1995): 148–68.

Foreword

STUDENTS of the Second World War in Asia and the Pacific who do not read Japanese have long been disadvantaged by not being able to exploit the very large literature produced by Japanese participants, observers and scholars on their national wartime experience. Lacking this view "from the other side of the hill", much of the English-language literature on campaigns against the Japanese covers their side of the story in less depth and with less authority.

One of the most spectacular campaigns conducted by the Imperial Japanese Army was the conquest of Malaya and Singapore from December 1941 to February 1942. Singapore had been developed between the wars by successive British governments into the pivotal position for defending the Empire in any war against Japan. The overstretched British Empire decided after the First World War it could not afford to maintain permanent armed forces large enough to provide sufficient protection to all its far flung regions simultaneously, and a "Singapore Strategy" was developed to protect the Empire in the Far East. By 1940 a major naval base at Sembawang, on the northern shore of the island, the large commercial harbour, and four airbases were all prepared to process large naval, air and ground forces which would be sent to reinforce the relatively small forces on hand if the Japanese made any move against the region. Unfortunately for the British Empire the fortunes of war in Europe went against it in 1940, leaving Britain unable to reinforce Singapore as intended. This created a window of opportunity for the Japanese.

Singapore was one of the most important military targets of the massive Japanese offensive against the Western Powers launched in December 1941, second only to the US Pacific Fleet at its base in Hawaii. Japan's war aim was to expel the Western Powers from Southeast Asia, to allow Japan to exploit the large reserves of strategic raw materials in the region, especially oil. So fortified, Japan hoped to generate enough power to accomplish its most important national goal: to establish a lasting hegemony over China, which in the long run would make Japan both the dominant power in East Asia and a self-sufficient Great Power no longer at the mercy of a world

economy dominated by the West. Singapore had to be seized to
prevent the British Empire from sending in forces strong enough to
block the Japanese march of conquest in the region. The 25th Army
was assigned three of the finest divisions in the Order of Battle,
entrusted to the highly-regarded Lt.-Gen. Yamashita Tomoyuki, and
given powerful air and naval support to accomplish its mission: take
Singapore within 100 days.

There are more than a dozen full-length studies of the Malayan
Campaign and the conquest of Singapore in English, plus numerous
accounts in diaries, memoirs, biographies, and broader studies. Only
a few authors were able to draw on any substantial sources from the
Japanese side and those who did so often relied on translated accounts
written after the war by Japanese officers who participated in the
campaign. Only one important Japanese memoir, *Singapore: The
Japanese Version*, written by the notorious Lt.-Col. Tsuji Masanobu,
who led the basic planning for the conquest of Malaya and served as
operations officer in the 25th Army, has been published in English.
Yamashita spoke to an English-language readership only through an
inadequate biography published shortly after the war by John Dean
Potter and extracts from his diary used in various works by the dean
of Japanese scholars of the war in Malaya, Yoji Akashi. There is
certainly room and need for more English-language accounts of the
Japanese side of this important campaign.

Henry Frei was just the man to fill this notable gap. Swiss by birth,
cosmopolitan by choice, Professor Frei taught for a time in Singapore,
and for many years in Japan, whose history he adopted as his chosen
field of study. Fluent in five languages, including Japanese and English,
thoroughly grounded in the literature of both languages, and pointed by
personal experience towards this most jarring interaction between old
friends turned enemies, Henry Frei worked for many years to produce
this volume and fill a clearly-defined need. The great majority of
the wartime records of both the Imperial Japanese Army and Navy
were destroyed by American bombing raids on Tokyo in the summer
of 1945. This prompted the writing of the post-war accounts noted
above. These accounts plus the multi-volume official history of the
war, whose first volume covered the Malayan campaign, provide as
deep a document-based history of the Japanese side of the campaign
as will ever be available. Henry Frei decided to fill a different gap:

to produce an account drawn from the memories of Japanese soldiers who participated in the campaign, the view "from the sharp end".

This book is drawn primarily from the written memoirs of six different Japanese who participated one way or another in the Malayan campaign and the conquest of Singapore, and from interviews Henry Frei conducted with these men in their old age. One was a junior officer in the military police. Another was a battle-tested young infantry sergeant in the 18th Division. The third was a young infantryman in the prestigious Imperial Guards Division, the fourth a junior officer in the experienced and powerful 5th Division. Another was a reluctant private soldier in that same formation, while the final subject was a civilian businessman working in the rubber trade in Singapore and Malaya before the war, who was interned when hostilities began. Their personalities, experiences, and outlooks were as varied as their situations. The young 5th Division private bitterly opposed the war and the cult of empire that gripped his country and forced him into its aggression. Complaining that "there is nothing more useless than the Japanese army", he felt absolutely powerless in the grip of a system he despised. The young guardsman on the other hand remembered joining the army as "the most exciting thing [he] had ever done", and even the brutality of basic training could not drive the patriotism out of him. The sergeant took the experience in stride and relished the opportunity army life gave to sow his wild oats all over Japan and China, treating the coming war almost as adventure. The military police officer took a far more serious approach, wearing his patriotism on his sleeve like a badge. And the businessman, like many good Japanese "salary men", worked so hard to protect his firm's interests that he sacrificed his own.

Through the written and oral memories of these six men, Henry Frei helps us understand how the Japanese on the ground saw and understood the historic upheaval that drove them on to victory in Singapore. The picture that emerges is of an army more rounded, and more human, than appears in depictions by those who fought against it. The mood in Japan as the war spread, the harshness of life in the Imperial Army, the dirty business of war in China, the increasingly unreal quality of life in Singapore as war loomed ever closer, the intensity of preparations for combat in Malaya — these experiences all spring vividly to life in this most intimate glance at "the other side of the hill".

Henry Frei wisely decided to allow his readers to confront the memories and attitudes of his six subjects as directly as possible, both those held at the time and those expressed many years after the fact. Some readers will be surprised to encounter such a variety of opinions and personalities in an army often seen only as a gang of criminal robots, questioning no order, displaying no individuality. But many will be provoked more strongly to read justifications or explanations for acts the rest of the world has long regarded as inexcusable barbarism. As remembered here, the intensity of the fighting on more than one occasion, including the final battle for Singapore, belies the impression that this campaign was for the Japanese an uncomplicated parade. This book corrects more than a few points of detail on which students of the war hitherto had to rely on incomplete British Empire accounts; in other instances it confirms with authority things we have only been able to suspect. It is one of the most intimate accounts of how the Imperial Japanese Army really operated on the battlefield ever likely to be written. There is no effort here to go over the familiar ground of national policy, high command and strategy. This is the story of the men who did the fighting or were caught up in it, and how they remember their experiences. Seeing the conflict through their eyes finally makes it possible for the English-language reader to understand in the round the character and personality, the inhumanity but also the humanity, of the army that inflicted on the British Empire its most humiliating military disaster. It is our loss that this is Henry Frei's final contribution to our knowledge of Japan — but our lasting gain that he wrote such an important study.

Brian Farrell
Department of History, National University of Singapore

Introduction

THE Malayan campaign is a well-known story. A bibliography on the fall and occupation of Singapore lists 168 books in English, 30 in Chinese, 15 in Malay, and 3 in Tamil.[1] The British have, of course, most to say about their biggest defeat in history; Australian authors still debate the correctness of Gen. Gordon Bennett's escape after the surrender;[2] the Chinese reminisce as the prime victims of Japanese reprisals and revenge;[3] and Malay and Tamil sources reflect fewer problems with the Japanese who sought to woo these peoples. Just about every nationality present in colonial Singapore later told in book form about the traumatic fall of the British Empire, including Fritz Arbenz, the Swiss consul, whose posthumously published diary details the "Singapore Saga"[4] of a collapsing age.

What strikes one as odd in this fascinating literature is the paucity of detail about the Japanese. They "advance by brigade groups", "outflank the defence", "sustain many casualties", and remain altogether a largely faceless mass bicycling their way down to Singapore. The reader wonders, have not the Japanese their own stock of books that could be exploited to balance the lop-sided Allied histories? One is curious to know how Japan has remembered the Malayan campaign. With equal emotion? In as many books?

Japan does have its own literature on the Malayan campaign. A Japanese bibliography published in the same year as the one mentioned above lists 62 books and 15 articles on Japan's involvement in Malaya during the Pacific War.[5] Scanning this literature over the past half century, we notice a progression in the Japanese historiography of the Malayan campaign, from recollections that once stressed only glory to memories also of shame. Where earlier Japanese histories remembered victories, recent reminiscences now talk about war guilt as well. Today the former general staff recalls mainly the famous victory, soldiers remember the fighting, intellectuals debate the killings, and scholars adopt an interdisciplinary approach to promote objectivity in the recording of Japan's Malayan past.

The General Staff Recalls

Just as had happened after the First World War, military leaders sat down in the aftermath to explain their victories or justify their losses in the Pacific theatre during the Second World War. In 1944 Gordon Bennett, the controversial Australian General who slipped out of Singapore just before the surrender, published his account of *Why Singapore Fell* (and why he escaped); the commanding general, A.E. Percival, detailed the military disaster four years later in *The War in Malaya*, and in 1951 Winston Churchill characterised Britain's loss of Singapore as "the worst military defeat in her history".[6]

"Wishing to reply to Mr. Churchill's memoirs, boldly ...," the architect of the fall of Singapore, former Col. Tsuji Masanobu, borrowed Churchill's subtitle in the following year for his own version *Shingaporu: Unmei no tenki* [Singapore: The Hinge of Fate].[7] While the book offers valuable insights into the stratagems of Japanese army planning and factional strife by the man best able to explain these matters, its author is a controversial figure, and he tells only part of the story. In particular, he omits the infamous purge of the Overseas Chinese, an operation intricately involved with the Malayan campaign. In Japanese war history circles, Tsuji, the Director of Military Operations for the 25th Army, has long been pinpointed as the man who planned the mass liquidations of Chinese in the wake of the British surrender of Singapore in February 1942.[8] His book stops neatly at the time of surrender on 15 February. In 1961, Tsuji Masanobu vanished dramatically into the jungles of Vietnam.

Twelve years after his disappearance, Shinozaki Mamoru referred to Tsuji in his memoirs as "the one who made the plan for the Chinese massacre".[9] Shinozaki had been an embassy official in pre-war Singapore. After the city fell, he became an advisor to headquarters in the renamed Syonan-to (Light of the Southern Islands). The antithesis of Tsuji, Shinozaki is today remembered favourably for having freely issued "Good Citizen" passes that saved thousands of Chinese lives at the time of the purge. He also played a key role in starting the Oversea Chinese Association as a shield behind which many found protection. Written with an objectivity nurtured by regret, his *Syonan — My Story: The Japanese Occupation of Singapore*[10] is unadorned, straightforward, and creditable.

One hard-liner with whom Shinozaki had to contend was Col. Watanabe Wataru, the chief military administrator from March 1942 to March 1943, who gained notoriety for his "government by bayonet" (*budan gunsei*). Watanabe's five-volume diary (December 1941 to March 1942) has now been published in Japanese. His shorter "Daitoa senso ni okeru Nanpo gunsei no kaiko" [Recollections of the military administration in the southern region during the Greater East Asia War] throws light on the rationale that guided Japanese high circles at that moment. It is a vague, and also an unbending, document. While he is aware that the Singapore massacre ranks third after Nanking and Manila in the list of Japanese atrocities, he apparently knew nothing about it at the time, confined as he was to his workplace.[11] He was not a man to brood. If the Chinese of his generation in Malaya still remember with pain the 50 million dollars levied from the Overseas Chinese communities in Malaya, Watanabe glosses over this affair as "a life saving device"[12] to compensate the Japanese military in Malaya. He ends his soliloquy: "'Necessity is the mother of invention.' When people meet with hardship, as in this war many did, their self-healing power is sharpened. Like weeds, they stretch to overcome any obstacle, waxing ever more luxuriant."[13]

Japan's official war history grew out of memories of this sort, drawing heavily on diaries, official and personal military papers, and general staff records deposited after the war. Much of the material was written by former officers of the Japanese armed forces specifically for the Historical Records Section of the First (Army) and Second (Navy) Demobilization Bureaus of the Japanese Government. The Military Intelligence Service Group attached to the Headquarters of the United States Army's Far East Command translated the accounts.[14] Several volumes deal with Japanese activities in Malaya, including: "Malaya Operations Record, Nov. 1941–March 1942"; "Outline of Administration in Occupied Areas, 1941–1945"; "Malaya Invasion Naval Operations; Southwest Area Operations Record, April 1944– August 1945"; "Malaya Operations Record: 29th Army, January 1944–August 1945".

This huge body of material, sifted and gathered into 104 volumes, provides the foundation for Japan's official history of the Pacific War, compiled by the National Self Defence College between 1966 and 1985. The first volume, *Maree shinko sakusen*[15] [The Malaya Campaign, 1966], records the timetable of the Malayan campaign and provides maps to trace troop movements. *Nanpo no gunsei* [The Military Administration in the Southern Region, 1985], the last volume to appear in the series, supplements this information with a large collection of policy utterances from Tokyo.[16] Both provide excellent guides to primary sources at the Japanese Defense Agency,[17] and complement superbly Maj.-Gen. S. Woodburn Kirby's official *War Against Japan: The Loss of Singapore*.

As with Britain's official war history, they are essentially "battle pieces" that endorse prevailing General Staff doctrine about the proper conduct of war. Like Tsuji, the compilers of the volume on the Malayan campaign stop when they reach the surrender of Singapore. How the Japanese army handled the Chinese population lies again conveniently outside the sphere of their first volume. However, *Nanpo no gunsei* and other relevant material illustrate how policies that seemed harmless at home led to brutal killings in the field. The Diet, for example, on 14 February 1942 called for strict control over Overseas Chinese in Malaya, on the eve of the fall of Singapore.[18] To soldiers in the field, this instruction meant rooting out possible opposition by meting out swift death to suspects.

Scholars working independently have used this official material to develop more penetrating insights into the background of the Malayan campaign. Long before the completion of the official history, Akashi Yoji pioneered careful studies in English using primary material supplemented by interviews with former general staff officers to produce a balanced view of Japan's uneasy Malayan years. His seminal "Japanese Policy Towards the Malayan Chinese, 1941–1945" explains how high-handed actions by men such as Watanabe Wataru reversed the initially positive policies towards the Malayan Chinese and caused permanent damage. His other work covers Imperial Japan's administrative, educational, and cultural policies towards its multicultural subjects in Malaya, and shows how research in Japanese archives can add to the Sino-European version of the Malayan campaign.[19]

The Singapore municipal administration worked closely with the general staff. In 1986, 60 veteran administrators put together their own recollections in *Shonan tokubetsu-shi shi — Senjichu no Shingaporu* [History of the Shonan municipality: Singapore during wartime].[20] Their book bristles with vignettes showing how 300 civilian officials, who were at loggerheads with the general staff, kept a city of 800,000 going until the bitter end. The former administrative clerks firmly distance themselves from the military, and speculate about how different things might have been had myopic army policy not sullied government with the stains of violence and extortion.

At the highest level, then, Japanese participants have remembered the Malayan campaign with both repentance and intransigence.[21] One important memoir is missing — that of the conqueror of Singapore, who was hanged in Manila in 1946. How would Lt.-Gen. Yamashita Tomoyuki have written the story Gen. Bennett and Gen. Percival did live to write? Lacking published testimony from the so-called "Tiger of Malaya", we move on to the recollections of the men who did the fighting in his brilliant and brutal campaign.

Ordinary Soldiers Remember

Just three weeks after the fall of Singapore, Tsukushi Jiro completed the first book-length account of the Malayan campaign, *Shingaporu koryaku ki* [History of the Conquest of Singapore]. The censor removed personal names, designations of units and strategic locations from his history, since at the time of writing assault troops were still in the field. Tsukushi's narrative is from the perspective of an infantry officer in the 5th Division, who has come straight down the peninsula.[22] The table of contents applauds everything the Japanese accomplished in the invasion: "Brilliant beginning of hostilities", "Landing Operation at Kota Bahru", "Flinging human bullets at the pillboxes", "Capturing the aerodrome of Kota Bahru", etc.[23] Japanese troops had been received with happiness everywhere, he exults, and 2,000 natives on one little offshore island even welcomed them as heavenly envoys.[24]

So fresh is this instant history that it often reads like a travelogue. Tsukushi describes the various delicacies the soldiers sampled en route down the peninsula such as coconut water, the squalls they experienced, and moon viewing, and he gazes into a large mirror in a sequestered house, musing about what his family would say if they could see father now. He rejoices in the news of success on all fronts — missions accomplished in Burma, Borneo, and the Philippines, the fall of Hong Kong on Christmas day — and he wonders how long it will be before they could rip down the Union Jack at the tip of the Malayan peninsula.[25]

Tsukushi's book was, of course, meant for home consumption, to tell folks how well the war had gone, how valiantly they had fought, and how they had treated the vanquished. If it is not objective history, it communicates accurately the soldiers' pride in their successful invasion, and their feeling of invincibility, blind as yet to any prospect of ultimate of defeat. A very similar book, and possibly the second oldest history on the subject, is *Malaya Campaign 1941–1942* by Yokoyama Ryuichi.

It is a long way from these warped epics to Tsuchikane Tominosuke's *Shingaporu e no michi: Aru Konoe hei no kiroku* [Road to Singapore: The record of an Imperial Guard] written in 1977.[26] His view from the ordinary soldier's foxhole looks back on the Malayan campaign with more detachment than the battle pieces described above. Human development is the theme of Tsuchikane's straightforward narrative. In his pages we see a boy grow into a man, a civilian into a warrior. His metamorphosis moves from scenes of his childhood to the day he is proudly conscripted into the elite Imperial Guards, saddening his mother and father; it progresses to his first taste of battle in China, where he asks his superiors why he must burn down the house of a Chinese woman fleeing with an infant in her arms; and his amazement at the French boulevards and large colonial houses in North Vietnam. He remembers savouring British rations —the so-called "Churchill supplies" left behind — the asparagus, cheese and biscuits, a tin of which he kept like a precious souvenir from a trip abroad all through his later captivity.[27] He tells of plundering in Alor Star and being reprimanded by the *kempeitai*. He also describes his first killing of a white soldier — in plainer language than William Manchester uses to describe his first Japanese victim in his autobiographical *Goodbye to Darkness*. He writes without sentimentality, just moving on, constantly providing pictures of events on the war path, focusing and filing, focusing and filing.

The actual battle of Singapore gets more detailed coverage in *Shingaporu senki* [Singapore: A war record] by Arai Mitsuo, a book he completed in 1983 at the age of 71. Born in the southern city of Fukuoka, in Kyushu, Arai joined the infantry and arrived with the 18th Division at Johor Bahru on 30 January. They were surprised to see American Fords and Chevrolets in this part of the world, and he remembers the communication problems they had, the scarce food, and how they looked forward to better fare in Singapore.[28]

Swiftly preparing for the assault, they felled trees in the jungle to use as launch pads for their Regiment's 70 pontoons that would ferry 1,200 infantrymen and their tanks across the straits between Johor and Singapore. At 4:30 in the morning on 8 February they saw the Straits for the first time: "At this point it was of no use to think about life or death. In battle only fate counted. The curtain had fallen on the first act of my Malayan campaign experience. The next act would be quite different. For a brief moment I saw our house in my home town."[29] After viewing the moon at eleven, they began their ferocious and successful assault on Australian-held positions on the island. Arai offers a rare glimpse of what it was like to take Hill 200 in the fiercest of battles surrounding Bukit Timah. The focal point there was a three-way junction where today there is a dazzling McDonald's. In four days they lost 200 men, but on 12 February they reached the position.[30] The fall of Singapore was only a matter of time.

Onishi Satoru offers a more soul-searching version of the Malayan campaign from the angle of the *kempeitai* (military police). His *Hiroku: Shonan Kakyo shukusei jiken* [Secret record: The Shonanto Purge Incident] squarely addresses the problem of the killing of a large number of mainly male non-combatants after the surrender of Commonwealth forces. It created a wound that never healed, and fuels the question of how to view the Malayan campaign. As a tool of that tragedy, the former *kempeitai* chief wants to set the record straight.

He describes the glory he felt riding into conquered Singapore as a *kempeitai* officer, the difficulties created by the order to screen the Chinese population in just three days, and their mortifying appearance as defendants during the war crimes trials held in Singapore in 1946. Remorse wafts through his pages as he discusses the "three big stains on the army in Shonan": the public display of severed heads, the purge incident, and the extortion of money.[31] His problem-oriented military history offers a unique reminiscence of a nightmarish past. Sobered by the passage of time, how do people remember dark deeds they once committed in the name of self-defence, or their country?

This is a different kind of military history that the Japanese are writing; the bitter recollection of what should have been a splendid and singular victory. It inhibits remembrance of the fall of Singapore in glorious terms — the way the British remember Trafalgar, the French the Napoleonic wars, or the Allies D-Day — even though

Japan's strategic victory substantially helped define the post-war order in Southeast Asia.

Although in the end Japan lost the war and England managed to hang on to Singapore for another generation, Great Britain had lost its colony. The Overseas Chinese in Singapore had experienced a loss they would not tolerate in the long run. One Singapore Chinese observer, Lee Kip Lin, recalls when seeing the British soldiers disembark at Tanjong Pagar docks on 5 September 1945: "There was a lot of cheering ... over these white faces pouring into the city in lorries.... But ... it annoyed me to see the arrogant faces of some of the British officers. It was the same old arrogance that you saw before the war."[32]

Oral testimony such as Lee's adds another dimension to the memory of the Malayan campaign. His observations originate from a Singapore project that between 1981 and 1986 recorded 178 eyewitness accounts of the occupation by local inhabitants and some Allied personnel. Fortunately, the Oral History Department of Singapore subsequently extended its project to include interviews with Japanese veterans, and the collection presently includes around ten Japanese accounts.

In his interview, Tsujimoto Sanosuke recalled the boredom he experienced as part of a group of poorly-compensated soldiers performing warehouse duties, and their anguish at the time of the Japan's surrender and their repatriation.[33] In another interview, Nagase Takashi talks about his experiences as an army interpreter attached to Headquarters at Raffles College. There he lived separately with 200 other interpreters, drawing higher allowances that were the envy of ordinary soldiers. On days off, they would wander off to visit the "comfort women" downtown. For a short period he was posted as Japanese language instructor to the harbour Island of Sentosa. Twelve Korean girls had been unloaded there and he remembers how the virgins were all reserved for the notorious commanding officer, Lt. Miki, "who first tasted each one by one". He tells of the girls' sorrow in their dismal language classes, and at the end of the interview he weeps, saying in a whisper: "I am very, very sorry for what we have done here during the war time."[34]

Intellectuals Debate

Nagase made his apology in Singapore at a time when various intellectuals in Japan were beginning to scrutinise the history of the

Malayan campaign. His remorse was the kind of response historian Ienaga Saburo had been trying to educe from his government ever since he rose to prominence in the mid-1960s as Japan's foremost war guilt writer with his widely-read book *The Pacific War*, which examined the darker side of Japanese expansion into the Asia-Pacific region 1941–45. In 1985 he followed this work with *Senso sekinin* [War guilt],[35] a meticulous catalogue of the brutalities that took place in each war theatre, country by country.

Ienaga's books stimulated critical investigations of Japanese activities in Nanking and Manila, and in Malaya during and immediately after the final phase of the campaign. But Ienaga's accusations also generated responses from people who took the view that wars are inherently cruel, and saw no reason why Japan should be taken to task for what happened in a major human catastrophe. In the unfolding debate, these various standpoints added complexity to the conventional ways of writing military history. Together they explain how the Malayan campaign can be remembered in terms of glory as well as shame.

A year after Ienaga's clarion call, two books detailed the Chinese killing fields at the end of the Malayan campaign. Kobayashi Masahiro, a primary school teacher attached to the Japanese School in Singapore from 1983 to 1986, published *Singaporu no Nihon gun* [The Japanese army in Singapore].[36] This book explains how Singaporeans learn at school about the purge and the harshness of the ensuing occupation, and argues that Japanese students have an obligation to know about those events as well. Four months later followed a similar book, *Nihon senryo jo no Shingaporu* [Singapore under the Japanese],[37] an abridged version of an encyclopedic work edited by Shu Yun-Ts'iao and Chua Ser-Koon and entitled *Xin Ma Hua Ren Kang Ri Shi Liao* [Malayan Chinese Resistance to Japan 1937–1945: Selected Source Materials].[38] The book introduces the Chinese view of the suffering inflicted on the Malayan Chinese. Like Ienaga's work, the book addresses the question of war guilt and accepts high estimates of the number of massacre victims.

One of Ienaga's students was Takashima Nobuyoshi, a high school geography teacher in Tokyo. After the textbook issue broke in 1982, Takashima intensified his research into the behaviour of Japanese soldiers in Southeast Asia, and specifically in Malaya. He began to investigate sites in Malaya where massacres had occurred following the purge in Singapore. Takashima travelled to various villages and established contact with the victims' families, and obtained from them a book describing widespread killings in the province of Negri Sembilan in March 1942. Published by the Negri Sembilan Chinese Assembly Hall in January 1988, the volume featured photographs showing bayonet wounds local residents had suffered as children; left for dead, they miraculously survived the massacres. Takashima had the book translated, and it was published the following year as *Maraya no Nihon gun: Neguri Sembiran shu ni okeru Kajin giakusatsu* [Japanese soldiers in Malaya: The Chinese massacres in Negri Sembilan province].[39]

Takashima began flying groups of 10 to 15 Japanese to Malaysia twice a year. Between Kuala Lumpur and Singapore Takashima he lectured his countrymen on their recent past in Southeast Asia as their bus took them to various memorial sites, where they visited the graves of the victims (*ohaka mairi*) and met with survivors or their relatives. Communication took place, and a glimmer of understanding sparked up as the Chinese Malaysians strained to overcome the past. They were willing to forgive, but not to forget.[40]

Takashima's book appeared in the same month that the Society to Engrave in our Hearts the Victims of War published *Nihon gun no Mareesia jumin gyakusatsu* [The Civilian Massacres of the Japanese Army in Malaya]. This well-researched work relates how in March 1942 Japanese soldiers killed more than 4,260 people in 27 places in the state of Negri Sembilan.[41] It was the Society's third volume in their *Ajia no koe* [Voice of Asia] series. These studies, together with those produced by the even more prolific Society of Asian Women — *Kyokasho kakarenakatta senso* [The War They Did Not Teach Us About] — castigate Japan for its wartime behaviour by inviting former victims to speak up about their experiences. Both series continued well into the 1990s, and provided brutally frank material for yet another genre of war publication, five unequivocal war histories in comic book form (*manga*) that address the young. These utterly non-comical books include *Kogane iro no kaze* [Golden Wind], the pictorial biography of a recruit forced to participate in the atrocities in Manchuria and Nanking, and *Jufa no sora* [Sky of Vermillion Flowers] which uses gory graphics to criticise the massacres in Malaya.[42]

These highly-critical works were countered by other books that glorified Japan's Malayan campaign. As if in response to Ienaga's accusations, *Shingaporu koryakusen: Shashin de miru Taiheiyo senso* [The Singapore Invasion: The Pacific War through Photographs] was entering its ninth printing when the textbook scandal broke in 1982. Written by Tominaga Kenko, a former navy officer, and Ito Shunichiro, an ex-army officer, this pictorial textbook for high school students focuses on three outstanding accomplishments during Japan's Malayan operations: first, the rapid advance of the army down the Malayan peninsula with tanks and bicycles; second, the sinking of the *Repulse* and the *Prince of Wales* off the east coast of Malaya; and third, the airborne invasion of Palembang to secure Sumatra's oil fields. Rich in technical detail on how the army overcame strategic and tactical obstacles in the jungle, the textbook says nothing about how they treated the Overseas Chinese.[43]

Another slanted work is *Nihonjin yo! Arigato: Mareesia wa koshite dokuritsu shita* [Thank You Japanese! This is How Malaysia Became Independent] by Habu Yoshiki, alias Haji Abu Hurairah Habu Abdullah, a Japanese Muslim who went on the Haj to Mecca in 1984. He bases his account of the way Malaya achieved independence on interviews with Raja Dato Nonchik, a Malay who sided with the Japanese during the invasion and later went to Japan as an exchange student. But his historical narrative of the Malayan campaign omits vital points, as when he states that the conquest of Penang was a bloodless and successful operation. While it is true that the Japanese army suffered no casualties, 2,000 civilians perished in the bombardment.[44]

Among the writers defending the Imperial Army, Nakajima Michi stands out. A journalist and commentator, she published successful works on issues such as cancer prevention. However, she was also the daughter-in-law of Gen. Matsui Takuro, commander of the 5th Division that spearheaded the Japanese campaign, and she condemned the research carried out by Takashima Nobuyuki and historian Hayashi Hirofumi in the late 1980s, which exposed purges carried out by the army and besmirched the honour of 5th Division soldiers from Hiroshima. Nakajima travelled to Malaya to seek information about the March purges of 1942. Retracing the moves of the 5th Division, she interviewed a survivor of the massacre and turned the fruit of her research into a book *Nitchu senso imada owarazu: Maree "gyakusatsu" no nazo* ["Massacre" Riddles in Malaya: The Sino-Japanese War Has Still Not Ended].[45] Nakajima disputes the massacre numbers, taking issue, for example, with reports that 990 were killed in two villages wiped out completely by the Japanese army on 18 March 1942. She argued that it was impossible for the death squads to have been in those places on the date mentioned.[46] Moreover, her research suggested that no more than 200 victims died, and she said that those killed were guerrillas and bad types, who had to be eliminated for the security of the Malayan campaign.

This effort to minimise Japanese actions prompted Hayashi to carry out further detailed research that has taken him many times back to Malaysia, as well as to the Japanese military history archives in Tokyo. In a book published ten months later, *Kakyo gyakusatsu: Nihongun shihaika no Maree hanto* [The Massacres of Overseas Chinese: The Malay Peninsula under the Japanese Military],[47] he provides painstaking documentation of the killings in Negri Sembilan. To support his account, he uses Imperial Army diaries unearthed at the Tokyo Military archives and published in 1988,[48] that confirm local accounts by Malayan Chinese survivors.

Hayashi examines in particular the 7th Squad of the 5th Division's 11th Infantry Regiment. While Nakajima claims those killed were guerrillas and other bad elements, the army diaries refer to the elimination of everyone: the elderly, the young, men, women, and children. Hayashi examines the massacres killing by killing, basing his research on testimony from survivors and on Imperial infantry accounts. In related video reportage, former infantryman Miyake Genjiro, 79, remembered with grief and repentance how he had to participate in the bayonetting of around 400 Chinese prisoners near Kuala Lumpur.[49]

The historiography of the Malayan campaign is caught up in polemics that have spilled over into newspapers and intellectual magazines like *Sekai*. Claims and counter-claims that could fill a book feed the question of how Japan should remember the Malayan campaign. Glory or shame? As part of the larger issue of how to put Japan's recent past into history textbooks, the question has impeded efforts to produce an objective evaluation of the Malayan campaign.

The frank recollections by ordinary Japanese soldiers' of their days in Malaya — the writings of Tsuchikane and Onishi, and the oral testimony of Nagase — show that many middle echelon participants continue to be bothered about the past. Their testimony is amplified by the bold revelations of other veterans invited to speak out at forums organized in Japan by various groups. At such peace rallies these rare old soldiers talk freely about their wartime experiences — not to sensationalise their past, but to show the young why Japan should never again show an inhuman face.

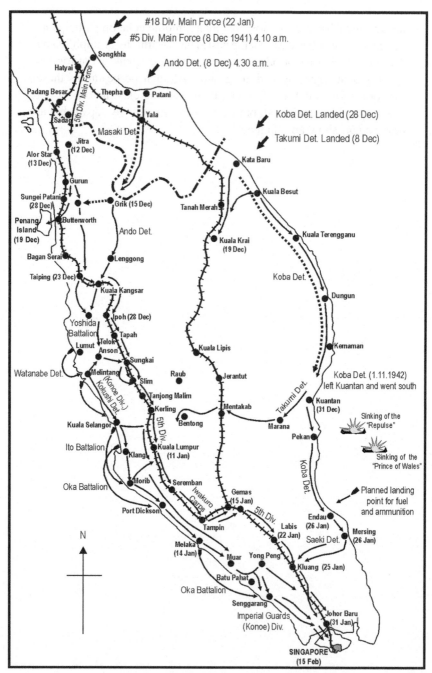

The Japanese Invasion of Malaya, 1941–42.

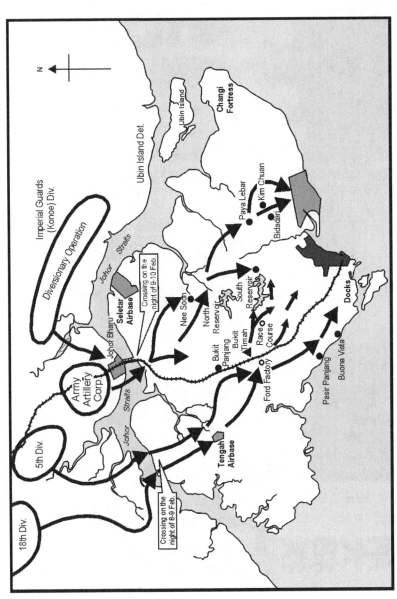

The Japanese Invasion of Singapore, February 1942.

Henry Frei with members of the Taiping-kai, an organisation for veterans of the Japanese 29th Army, taken during a reunion at the Yasukuni Shrine on 25 April 1998.

1

Day X

MILITARY policeman Onishi Satoru was in a building in Mukden, a garrison town in Manchukuo [Manchuria]. He stared down the corridor.

"Today our Empire has embarked on the successful invasion of Southeast Asia."

Impossible! His steps quickened towards the voice from the dormitory room at the end of the corridor. Inside, his men stood listening to Radio Tokyo. It was seven in the morning on 8 December 1941 and the weather was freezing, but already the police compound bustled with excited voices. Onishi's heart beat faster, now caught by the beat of the military tune that pulled him into the crowd.[1]

"At dawn today our Imperial Army and Navy entered into a state of war with the American and British forces in the Western Pacific," the voice said. Rousing march music and navy songs accompanied the news.

Unbelievable! It was great news received in icy Mukden, news that warmed and strengthened and reassured the soldiers, true men of Nippon that they were!

Three months ago they had arrived in Manchukuo from Osaka to prepare for a northern advance. As tiny cogs in a huge machine, they would soon help set in motion the massive wheel of the Great Kantoku Drill, a grand manoeuvre to fight the Soviet Union. Or so, at least, they had been told. Onishi's orders were to study Russian, to learn all about the country, and in the evenings to give seminars to his men on the Soviet Union. For three months they had been busying themselves with the Russian language and Soviet affairs.[2]

All the while, they had debated whether Japan should really go north, into the Russian far eastern territories. Would it not be better to go south, into the resource-rich European and American colonial territories? The West had stopped selling oil and was closing the noose

1

on Japan, now bogged down in a stalemated war in China and running out of resources. Diplomatic relations with England and America were at an all-time low. Even so, no one really imagined starting a war with either of those powers.

But now, in between cascading naval and army tunes, the voice from Tokyo informed them of daring raids on Hawaii and successful landings at Songkhla in Thailand and Kota Bahru on the Malayan coast.

As for themselves, they were soon told that war preparations were complete, that they were ready for battle and within days would be moved to forward positions. Only now were they told that all along their training had never really been for a thrust north, but south, to Malaya!

"Thank God we're going south," Onishi muttered to himself. Thirty-eight years old and the father of two young daughters, Military Police Lt. Onishi Satoru was a good leader, if sometimes tight with money. His clean-shaven features and round steel-rim glasses gave him both a bureaucratic appearance and the look of an intellectual.[3] He loathed the barbaric coldness of Manchukuo. It would have been no joy to invade the backward Soviet Union from the east. Far better to advance south. Malaya was part of Asia, part of them, with a proper ancient culture. It would be a real challenge, and an honour, to topple fortress Singapore, Britain's impregnable symbol of centuries-old Western domination.[4]

"We are about to give a respectful reading of the Imperial Rescript. Will every young man of Japan listen without fail," the voice announced at eleven in the morning.

"Guarding the throne since time immemorial, We hereby declare war on the United States and Great Britain. Our Empire's very existence now depends on self-defense. There is nothing left for us but to stand up resolutely and crush any obstacle in our way."[5]

None of the young policemen stirred. They stood in silence, as if bowing to the Imperial Rescript and renewing their resolve to serve their master, showing loyalty to a divine Emperor that gives in death its last full measure of allegiance. All Sunday they listened to the splendid voice announce one success after the other.

On 9 December, Tokyo's grand strategy incorporated their 2nd

Military Police Field Unit into the 25th Army under Lt.-Gen. Yamashita Tomoyuki. Their orders were to conquer Singapore.[6]

Five thousand kilometres to the south, garrisoning a tiny Chinese backwater in Japan's vast empire, ruddy-faced Arai Mitsuo felt uncomfortable. It was an annoying little envelope to receive. Short and stocky and 30 years old, his manner was no-nonsense and his rank sergeant. His 114th Regiment of the 18th Division was standing by at a village near Canton as the main reserve. It was Arai's fifth year of service. Along with everyone else he wondered where the next battle would be.[7]

"To hell with Canton. My service time is up. What's going on?" Arai had been called up in 1937, just at the time of the outbreak of the China incident. He'd seen the gates crash at Nanking, and had taken part in the ceremony celebrating the fall of the great city, but not in the ensuing orgy of rape and looting. Immediately afterward, on 17 December, his regiment had been transferred to South China.[8] After five years in the war zone, Arai longed to be back with his family and friends in Kyushu.

But rumours, and the envelope, informed him of a more formidable front forming. Only yesterday, soldiers below the rank of non-commissioned officers had received a small red envelope, pre-addressed "Military Mail", and ordered to "leave a sizable crop of hair and nails". The envelope would hold their last remains for loved ones back home, if they were unlucky. The fingernails and lock of hair would be sent with a letter of acknowledgment for duty well done. The envelopes were distributed with a personal message from Lt.-Gen. Mutaguchi Renya, the commander of the 18th Division: "In the coming war, do not expect your bodies to be collected and sent home for burial." Time would not allow for such civilities in the new war theatre.[9]

Ten days ago, their twin regiment, the 56th under Capt. Takumi, had left for Samah, on Hainan Island. Another detachment, under Lt. Kawaguchi, had sailed for Camranh Bay in Vietnam. Something very big was up, that was for sure.

Next they learned that the Takumi Detachment had landed at a place called Kota Bahru, in the face of stiff enemy resistance. Wherever that was and whoever the enemy might be, the heroic news was thrilling, as the 114th Regiment tried to comprehend the new situation.[10] But for Arai it was also bad news. Home eluded him even longer.

Some 3,000 thousand kilometres further south, Imperial Guard Tsuchikane Tominosuke was facing Day X close to Thailand. His division had driven from Vietnam across Cambodia, and soon the convoy would reach the Thai border. At 22, Tsuchikane was about to see battle.

Tsuchikane's mouth was dry, his stomach felt strange, his heart pounded. What would battle be like? Towards the evening they were told to check rifle, hand grenades, and bayonet. Uniforms, too, were inspected. Up on the truck they used thick string to attach to their backs green leafy branches they'd gathered at noon.[11]

"Commander, Sir, this means battle, doesn't it?" Tsuchikane asked his officer.

"I don't know yet. The order will soon be in."

The trucks stopped at a clearing in the jungle. All got off and gathered to hear the orders; the captain, too, was tense.

"In a couple of hours, tomorrow in the very early morning, we shall break through the Thai border. We expect a fair bit of battle. From here on you must stay alert. Even in sleep. All group and platoon leaders remain with me for further instructions."

The soldiers returned to their trucks.

"This is it," thought Tsuchikane. "The real thing." He was an Imperial Guard, but he felt jittery. Silently he did a rare thing, he prayed.

"For god's sake, what's taking this leader so long? Why isn't he returning to the truck? What are the instructions?"

The platoon leader walked back to the truck and explained that although it was *they* who were attacking, they must be very careful not to fire the first shots.[12]

That was even more unnerving. Why let themselves be shot to pieces first?

The trucks resumed the driving into war. Tsuchikane clasped his rifle, he wanted to stay awake, but he fell asleep.

"Off the trucks!"

Tsuchikane fell to the ground.

Fig. 1 Fording a river in the Malayan jungle.

"Third Detachment advance. Deploy to the right." The squad leader dashed ahead.

Tsuchikane plunged into the rice field, expecting immediate annihilation.

But all stayed quiet in the pre-dawn darkness.

"Advance!" He was wading through the mud in a wet paddy field. It was difficult to move in the water.

"Mount your bayonets!" — the final instruction before meeting the enemy. Tsuchikane had gone through the motions a thousand times in drill: "Yell! Stick! Turn! Retract!"

But there was nothing to stick. No shots broke the silence. They were told to hold their guns. It was quiet in the rice paddy. Tsuchikane had a sick feeling — when would the enemy shoot? All they heard was the slurping of their boots treading mud in the rice paddies.

"Stop!" All froze in their positions.

"Assemble!" One after the other, they left the rice paddy and climbed back up to the road. After the roll call, the commander announced: "We have now crossed the border into central Thailand

and we shall head for Bangkok. But watch out, the enemy may still attack. Be ready to fight at any moment."[13]

Again they were passengers on the road heading for war, a long convoy driving along in a blaze of sunlight as dawn broke over Thailand.

Three thousand kilometres further south, at the other end of Thailand, Japanese infantry opened the southern war front at Songkhla. The 14 transports had slipped in during the night and transferred the 5th Division onto landing barges that came jamming in to unload 14,000 men by the palm trees.

"Prepare for landing!"

"Jump!"

Second Lt. Ochi Harumi leaped into the surf of an empty, silent beach. The pearly sand crunched hard under his heel as he steadied himself after the high jump.

Soon the beachhead squirmed with Japanese soldiers running up and deploying on the white sand.

"Assemble under that big tree!"

Lt. Ochi fell in with his platoon and started the roll call. "One-two-three-four-five-six-seven-eight — complete!"

After two weeks on a boat, they could be professionals again. Crack trooper Ochi delighted in his métier. All had gone well. They did not meet the enemy. Songkhla slept on, with no one in sight. Far away one could make out the first dwellings, and hear the bark of a dog. The success of 5th Division's surprise landing was complete.[14]

At least one 5th Division soldier faced the busy morning with little enthusiasm. On that palm-frayed beach of Songkhla, Pte. Miyake Genjiro heard the declaration of war against America and England for the first time. That beautiful white beach, which was filling quickly with Japanese soldiers, row upon row, gathering in tight formations.

"We're doing such a useless thing," Miyake thought. "There is nothing more useless than the Japanese army."[15]

At the other end of all the upheaval from Manchukuo to Malaya, lay Singapore. And as reluctant Pte. Miyake was pondering the deceit of the Japanese army, a thud jolted businessman Omori Kichijiro from his sleep in his Singapore home. He dashed to the window.

"Kuso! War has broken out," Omori tried to read his watch. It was 4:45 a.m. and pitch black, but the heat was already sweltering. "Our planes from Indochina must be bombing Singapore. What daring!" that much he admitted, "— our men attacking the British impregnable fortress — but what about us? How the hell are we Japanese expatriates now supposed to get out of here?"[16]

When Britain's guns responded, Omori stepped out onto the verandah, fascinated by the tracers shooting light into the night. What should they do?

Omori was the sole remaining executive of Senda & Co.'s Renggam Rubber Estate. Overcoming the morose vacillations of his senior executive, Mr. Shinya, who had returned to Japan in 1941, Omori had asked the adjoining rubber estate, Anglo-Thai Corporation, to look after Renggam Estate until the world crisis blew over. For the past days, he and his five remaining staff members had been standing by in his mansion, waiting for a sea passage out of British territory and into the Japanese empire. Yesterday, four of them had boarded a regular steamer for Bangkok, only to be escorted off the ship a few hours later by order of the Governor. A diplomatic outrage it had been. Against all etiquette of international law. They had done nothing wrong. Japan intended England no harm. Forced back to their boss's house, they would try to leave Singapore with Omori and his assistant on the Tuesday boat bound for Saigon.[17]

The five came hurrying to his room. The worst had happened, and a rap on the door confirmed their doom.

"Come along at once!" said a tall Sikh constable in the doorway. He only wanted Omori. "You are allowed one small suitcase."

Omori tried to think. Should he take his jackets, and how much underwear, how many shirts? His executive sea trunk for Saigon had to be pared down and re-packed from scratch. The packing gave him a moment to gather his colleagues in the upper bedroom, where in front of the house shrine he improvised a farewell party with small cups of whisky.[18]

"Hurry up!" Impatiently, the bearded giant marched Omori out of the door to Orchard Road Police Station, where several Japanese stood gathered already with sacks and bags. Towards noon, their motley group having grown with other Japanese rounded up from the island, they were moved to a warehouse and kept at Keppel Harbour all afternoon. When they reached 150, they were crowded into a launch boat. Someone managed to get hold of a copy of *The Straits Times*. "Japanese Army Lands in Northern Malaya, Navy Attacks Hawaii", screamed the headlines. Incredibly, Japan had taken on not only Great Britain, but the United States, too! So ended their day, a long-dreaded scenario playing itself out, quite matter-of-factly. Omori cursed himself for having left things too late. "Where are they taking us?" he wondered, as their barge sailed north and night fell quickly on their once blissful life in the doomed town.[19]

2

Conscription and Mobilisation

AFTER the Imperial Guards broke through the undefended Thai border, Tsuchikane's convoy pushed on deep into central Thailand.

"Amazing," Tsuchikane thought, "negotiations did the fighting. Crossing into Thailand was like landing at Cap St Jacques in southern French Indochina." His buddies were all on about it as they journeyed on to Bangkok. "We didn't have to fire a single shot. Again diplomats settled everything."

Not a bad war, he thought. Up on the truck in the breeze, Tsuchikane felt like a traveller in the fragrant countryside, as they passed a strange mixture of exotic coconut groves; the rice paddies reminded him of home, and the crude jolts of the vehicle kept him awake all the way to the capital.[1]

The long ride gave Tsuchikane time to think. What had put him on this wild and wondrous road south? There'd never been

Fig. 2 Pulling vehicles across a waterway near Penang.

9

time to think about it. He yearned to piece together, one after the other, the tremendous events of his young past that were quickly making him old.

"Tsuchikane — qualified class A soldier!!"
The drill sergeant's voice still echoed in his ears. The phrase was one he was made to shout over and over again as he travelled on the road to war. On that fragrant day in April 1940, he had been very happy. The cherry blossoms flush in bloom, he had stepped out of the examination hall, into the spring of adult life, a proud and confident young man.

Back home, his parents had been less glad.
"I see," father had mumbled.
"Well, that's what I thought," mother said. "It couldn't be helped with your strong body." Illness had taken their eldest son five years earlier. Now they would probably lose their second son, too.

But young Tsuchikane would not let their mood dampen his joy. He called his friends and went out in the evening to celebrate his success in a downtown pub. They had a good time until two plainclothesmen came round to their table. A war was on and unconscripted youngsters were not allowed to drink or smoke. Yamazaki, puffing away, though older than Tsuchikane, but with a child's face, a beer before him, and with no identification papers, stood no chance. The two took him to the police station for questioning. Glumness had gotten the upper hand after all, and ruined the evening.[2]

The Japan-China war was then engulfing the mainland in 1939–40 and Tsuchikane's family was falling on hard times. Since graduating from the local commercial school, Tsuchikane had been helping in his parents' business. In his spare time, he played the clarinet in the band of the patriotic Young Men's Association. Each day they lined up at the West Station to send off local boys who had been called up.

"Soon it will be my turn," Tsuchikane knew.[3] His parents had already received the standard "Letter of Instruction from Military Authorities".

"Greetings to the Father," it read.

We have learned that your son will shortly experience the greatest joy and satisfaction possible to one of our nation by joining soon our company. We congratulate you.

When your son enters the barracks, the officers of the company will take your place in looking after his welfare. We will be to him as a stern father and a loving mother. We will always be concerned with his two-fold training, body and mind, so that in belonging to the Army he may become a good soldier and a loyal subject of the Emperor. We want to be able to teach him in such a way that he may be able to realize the highest hope of a member of our race [i.e., to die for the Emperor].

With the company and your home forming a complete circle we wish to co-operate with you to the fullest extent in order to administer his education and guidance along the most rational lines. In order to do this, we wish to learn as much as possible from you with reference to his personal history and character and the environment of his home. This information will be kept in confidence. If you have any misgivings, fear it will be difficult to learn your son's exact condition after his enlistment, or that he will not be able to advance in rank, or any other misunderstandings, rest assured we will be glad to discuss the matter with you. That our efforts to guide the young man will not be hindered, we beg you to fill out the enclosed form with the greatest care and return it to us as soon as possible.

The regiment, however, is not concerned entirely with the past life of your son, but in guiding his development — wishing unselfishly to emphasize his good points and strengthen his weak points — to develop all his powers to the end that he may become a good and faithful soldier, maintain a first-class record in the Army, and put his whole heart into fulfilling the mission of the Imperial Army.

On the day your son enters the barracks, we trust that you will accompany him in order that we may meet you and have an intimate talk with you.

Respectfully yours,
(Commanding Officer)
Imperial Japanese Army[4]

To join the army was the most exciting thing Tsuchikane had ever done, and he looked forward to it. He could not know how much he would have to unlearn of the goodness of a growing boy. Like Pinocchio side-tracked on his way to school, he marched with

the drums straight into the martial magic that was gripping the land.
"Let us regain Asia Pacific. Let us reclaim what Japan ceded to the
colonialists in the seventeenth century. Let glory be now restored!"

For that glory, Tsuchikane would lay down his life, gladly, like
the sudden petal of the wilting cherry blossom, shining, and then
dying quickly. It had been the ideal of the samurai for a thousand
years. And in 1940 Tsuchikane was a proud, willing little petal.
Nothing could deflate his excitement. Not his parents' resignation,
nor the nine golden rules older conscripts told him would ease life
in the barracks: "Always remember,

1. You are lowest in the army; always bow and salute everyone first!
2. When called, respond with a loud voice.
3. Never be later than your comrades.
4. Always carry mop and broom at daily cleaning sessions.
5. Always do the squad leader's laundry first.
6. Eat all meals within three minutes. Keep toilet visits short.
7. Keep your nails trimmed and your personal shelf tidy.
8. Always be quickest to fall in.
9. In case of insufficient members to line up, bring along one from
   another unit to make up the numbers."[5]

Tsuchikane memorised every rule in anticipation of the day he would
march into camp.

At last they came bobbing up outside his father's shop, welcoming
the new conscripts: country flags, army flags, and individual flags,
all congratulating "Conscript Tsuchikane Tominosuke". The beautiful
handwriting on the banners removed in him the last fear his parents
felt for him; though sleep came slowly that last night at home.[6]

The next morning Tsuchikane went to pray with his parents at
the downtown Enoki shrine. It was the point where the boys began
their walk to the station. The gathering crowd greeted everyone with
banzais: "For your country! For the Emperor!" before the warden
launched into a long speech.

After the ceremony, Tsuchikane was allowed to lead the crowd
and his family in a procession round the city, carrying the flag
proudly, and then down to the railway station which he knew so
well. Many times he'd assembled there with his brass band, only

today, it was his turn to line up in the large square. There were about 60 recruits. The Mayor of Kawagoe gave another farewell speech, followed by the resident military officer, the Women's Defense Society, and representatives from each section of the Young Men's Association.

"Banzai! Banzai!" The applause and cheers roared across the station square, as family and friends moved onto the platform. Where Tsuchikane had played his clarinet the day before, a junior now stood in his place at the first wagon. This tune was for him and his companions.

Family members were assigned a special place at the very front of the platform, where everyone stood clinging to the lively scenes of departure. When would he see his parents and brother and kid sister again? Leaning out of the window, Tsuchikane tried to catch a glimpse of their faces one last time as the locomotive reached the end of the platform.

Tremendous "Banzais!" filled the hall. Tsuchikane called out to his family. He couldn't understand what they were saying. Quickly their faces disappeared into the line of flag-waving people. Inside the wagon it grew quiet.[7]

Tsuchikane was headed for the barracks of the Imperial Guards north of Tokyo in Chiba prefecture. Two months earlier a notice had assigned him to the 4th Regiment. Their badge would be different from that of ordinary regiments. Infantrymen wore only a simple star, but the Imperial Guard's was big and gorgeous and embedded in the national flower, the *sakura*. Like the cherry blossom they would blossom strong and glorious, and, if fate so decreed, wilt quickly.

The ideal burned deep in their minds, and the selection committee had done its best to choose only high-grade material, strong young men from stable environments. Not only were candidates selected from all over the country, but their kin had been carefully screened along too. Honour thus befell not only the aspirant, but their families, as well.

The only obstacle before consummating that honour, was the final medical examination. Tsuchikane had piles, and if refused, he would never again be able to face those who had sent him off so splendidly. To save him from ignominy, his family doctor had given him a special injection for the moment he would have to bend over for the check.

"I feel very fine," Tsuchikane said in a voice almost too loud, "I have no piles!"

"O.K., O.K., you can go," said the regimental doctor. Relieved, Tsuchikane collected a uniform and passed inside the gate.[8]

He was put in the First Company, whose men were skilled in shooting and in rifle drill, and regarded as a particular asset to the Regiment. Tsuchikane soon found out that they were also an unruly and fierce company. He lived the first days like a zombie, obeying blindly the rules he'd memorised at home.

Each recruit had a bed and a shelf in the dormitory. At the call of the bugle they jumped out of bed, put the sheets in order, fell in for counting, and then exposed their bare upper bodies to the cold winter morning.

"Yoisho, yoisho!" Their shouts reverberated all the way to the temple grounds in the woods, as they spread their legs, and, making a fist, drew in the shoulders and lowered their waists. From that squatting position, they stretched both arms upward and then stood up and squatted, up and down, dozens of times, until their goose-fleshed bodies had a reddish tinge.

Every day they marched in full outfit with weapons, all the way from the barracks in Aoyama to the Yoyogi military grounds to crawl and run and steel themselves for lightning attacks in the coming battle fields of Southeast Asia.

Sometimes a recruit would lose his bayonet. A most unfortunate thing, it meant no supper that day. Everyone would have to search for the bayonet until late in the evening.[9]

Meals, too, were a drill. Tsuchikane learnt how to eat lunch and supper without chewing, swallowing for speed. The constant order to "Fall in!", endless weapon checks, elaborate examinations of eating utensils and uniforms — loose buttons were simply plucked off — steadily ground them into effective fodder for the army.

To these junior soldiers, second-year soldiers were men of authority; third-year soldiers they serviced like gods.

"First year soldier Tsuchikane is now going to do your laundry, with your kind permission, Mr Corporal, Sir!" They competed for this honour, sometimes to the extent of feigning a toilet visit when really they went out to do their senior's laundry in nasty weather.

A visit to the latrines was convenient for other things. To review lecture notes, out in the cold, in the moonshine, for next day's exams, or to eat in silence the food packets their families had sent the fledgling recruits.[10]

But no matter how hard they tried, recruits always ran into trouble, and an array of corporal punishments awaited the slightest misstep. Like the "round-trip" slap, the ordinary slap, or a simple boxing of the ears. On any day, the leader might snort: "Dirt bags, you're slipping!" and order them all in one line.

"Stretch both legs widely, now — wider than that! Now clench your teeth." Upon which his fists would come flying down on them, one after the other in utter abandon. Sometimes he would use a leather slipper. Those blows often caused cuts inside the mouth. "Fuck you, bastard," the recruits would think, "why this?" Angry inside, stoic on the outside, one had to endure. One knew not the reason for the mass punishment. It was part of the survival game. Everyone must be dependable, no one slacken.

The bruises were disillusioning. One would go to bed hurt, unable to sleep, watch the ceiling, and a tear steal down the cheek. Had they joined the great Imperial Army for this? Punishments to steel them for the front? It made no sense. Tsuchikane was a human. But the army needed, if not inhumans, at least efficient cogs for the military machine. The victories of the Japanese Army rested on the successful conversion of people like himself into consumer goods. You are "nothing but wretched one-cent men!" seniors shouted at them, quoting the price of the stamp on the conscription postcard.[11]

And yet, for all that, Tsuchikane was proud to be an Imperial Guard. Selected from the finest of the country, the class of 1940, it was their duty to protect the Emperor. And he was now one of them. After only half a year Tsuchikane found himself chosen for special guard duties. On the Emperor's birthday, he was allowed to present arms at a grand parade in Yoyogi staged for foreign dignitaries right next to His Majesty mounted on his white stallion. What ecstasy! A sublime feeling of devotion and sacrifice coursed through Tsuchikane's body and mind.[12]

When Japan's war in China expanded to the south, soldiers began to leave Japan in droves for the mainland where success was always reported as just around the corner. The news was intoxicating and the people got excited. But Tsuchikane hated the idea of fighting abroad. All he wanted was to protect his Emperor on Japanese soil and stand by him to the end in the capital.

Such wishful thinking faded away in April 1941, when a new sign outside the training grounds declared them the 7th Tokyo Company of the 4th Regiment of the Imperial Guards. A special bugle had everyone assemble on the large square outside the barracks, where from the rostrum an officer announced their imminent departure. Half of them would be dispatched to the war theatre in China, the other half retained to guard the throne.

All raced across to the huge board to check their name on the list. Tsuchikane's heart sank. He was slated for the mainland. All home leave was cancelled at once, though not visitors' day the next day. That would allow them to slip out messages via friends, to have them call their homes and tell their folks about their immediate departure for the front.[13]

That last morning in Japan, they all marched out of camp, chests swelling with pride, yet anxiously looking around to see if their message home had gotten through. Did anyone come to see them off? Over the year Tsuchikane had said good-bye so many times. This time it would be for good. Proudly they marched down Tokyo's Aoyama Boulevard towards the harbour, where a transport ship would take them either north or south — so little did they know.

The flags were out, and the marching band strutted, playing gleeful tunes to the onlookers' shouts of "Banzai! Long live the Emperor!" Happiness jolted Tsuchikane when he saw his father, brother, and sister, all rushing up to where he would pass. So his message had gotten through! The families joined their marching sons down to the docks, where at last they were able to talk.

But topics soon ran out. What was there to say? Silently Tsuchikane munched the rice cakes they had brought, and introduced his family to friends who had no one to see them off. Dad then greeted Tsuchikane's senior officers, and thanked them for their guidance and for continuing to look after his son well.

Once up on deck, it was difficult to make out family and friends down on the pier.

"There!"

"No, over there they are!" Tsuchikane waved frantically at his family, who had already seen him.

"Banzai! Banzai! Banzai!!" The ship left its moorings and steamed out of harbour as families and friends became tiny dots on the quay. For most it was their first ocean voyage, and the salty air promised a different world, as they slowly sailed south. Some clenched their teeth, and some shed tears, in the silence that engulfed their journey into the night.

Theirs was one of the last boisterous public farewells for mobilised soldiers. After mid-1941, all departures turned highly secret.[14]

The secrecy and chauvinistic mentality of the army bothered Pte. Miyake and he couldn't stand their arrogant attitude. Army haughtiness turned up everywhere, even where they were supposed to be having fun. At sports events, for example, the army interfered regularly with the games, propagating the virtues of military life in leaflets, and wanting to make the sport event look like a military event. It confused both participants and spectators — were they here for the game or for a bloody army exercise? Miyake hated the government's perfidious military manipulations.

Already primary school had fed him the ethics of filial piety and loyalty to the Emperor, a demi-god, the teachers told them, descended from sun goddess Amaterasu, founder of the Japanese isles. Mythology, in 1940, was taught as history.[15]

Despite the force-fed cock-and-bull stories, Miyake loved learning. When his parents no longer could afford his school, he continued to read books all through his apprenticeship. He read them feverishly and, at 17, had quite a library, until the day the police visited Miyake's home. People reading too many books were suspect. Young men had to be guarded from the possible contamination of "liberal thoughts". It threatened the position of the Emperor, upon which the Japanese State rested. They took away all young Miyake's books.[16]

When in August 1940 Miyake was conscripted into Hiroshima's 5th Division, the one-cent envelope delivered him into the 11th Regiment. A renowned crack unit with a tradition of having done well on all fronts, from the Sino-Japanese War, to the Russo-Japanese War, the Siberian Intervention, and now again in the China-Japan

Fig. 3   Ordinary Japanese soldiers (photograph taken in Johor).

War, it was the city's pride. But what to other youngsters, such as patriotic Tsuchikane, meant honour, to Miyake was a source of shame.

Inside the barracks, Miyake became even more disgusted with the system that subordinated everyone to the Emperor, and in which orders were absolute. Japan had turned into a gigantic militaristic pyramid during the 1930s, at the top of which sat the Emperor. Pte. Miyake, at the very bottom in a hierarchy he despised, felt absolutely powerless. It was no place for humans. And by the time the Emperor declared war, there was no hope for him to escape the system.[17]

Sgt. Ochi Harumi, in the same regiment, was quite different. Fond of weapons, capable, eager, manly, always amorous, aged 20, he had gladly reported to the local military authorities on 10 January 1939 (the anniversary of Emperor Meiji's conscription law). Above 150 centimetres, his chest more than half his height, and his weight over 100 pounds, Ochi met the basic physical standards of the Japanese infantryman.

He wanted to be a machine-gunner, but his character made the first three months in basic camp difficult. His father's rule: "You may fight older people, but never your juniors", got him into considerable trouble. His intransigence earned him a lot of blows from older soldiers [supposed to "be to him as a stern father and a loving mother—" , but was this the spirit of the conscription letter?]. Two or three rarely satisfied his seniors, 20 or 30 were better ["we want to be able to teach him..."], until blood dripped from his cheeks and mouth ["...in such a way that he may be able to realize the highest hope of a member of our race..."]; in his first 90 days Ochi counted more than 3,000 slaps from the flat of his corporal's hand ["... so that in belonging to the Army he may become a good soldier and a loyal subject of the Emperor"].[18]

But there were also pleasant sides to army life. A large factory near the barracks employed around a thousand girls, and there was nothing Ochi loved more than women. Some he knew by face, but he adored the whole bunch. And many factory girls did their best to respond to the men's fervour when pressed for dates. It was a time of ecstasy and tears, hello and good-bye, for love in the shadow of war was transient and uncertain, and eternity for the soldiers would not be in marriage, but more probably on the battlefield; at least for 75 per cent of them, according to statistics.[19]

Military police officer Onishi Satoru was then still stationed in the city of Tokushima, on Shikoku Island, in charge of internal security. It was a time of intensified propaganda. The people's confidence had to be won over for the cause of an impending large-scale war. Courage had to be revved up and righteousness dispensed, wherever necessary, by officers lecturing in temples, village halls, auditoriums, military clubs, barracks, schools, and industrial plants. They talked to brocaded priests, peasants, hero-worshipping school children, university students, kimonoed mothers, merchants, petty landowners, financiers, factory workers, and the cosmopolitan crowds of the cities. Together with Special Police Chief Yamada, Onishi travelled on

lecture tours all over the island of Shikoku. Yamada dwelt at length
and with enthusiasm on the importance of counter-intelligence, and
town mayors and managers supported him wherever he turned up
at school gatherings, factories and religious and patriotic meetings
in the province.

They made a fine pair, for Onishi's patriotism was no less
outstanding. It was a time when processions of men in black carrying
their fallen comrades in urns wrapped in white were a common
sight in the streets of Tokushima. When commuting round the city,
Onishi would have the bus driver stop the vehicle whenever they
came across the procession for a fallen soldier.

"Now, Mr. Conductor, please have everyone get off the bus and
pay their respects to the deceased." Such pious acts earned Onishi a
letter of commendation from Commander Sumitomo of the Tokushima
military affairs bureau.[20]

A phone call in late July 1941 ended Onishi's tour in Tokushima.

"Report to the 23rd Army in Osaka at 8 am on 2 August. And *no*
farewell parties," the caller said, "It's all top secret."

Onishi felt proud. As if personally selected by the Emperor for his
valour. He could be sent to any of the war theatres. But he was also
concerned about his wife, close to labour this hot summer with their
second child. He would have to arrange for his family's immediate
return to her hometown in Mie province.[21]

Onishi refused all farewell parties but one. He gladly had Yamada
take responsibility for a night no one wished to end.

The following evening, Onishi slipped out of Tokushima on a
night train, with one detail to look after his baggage as far as Osaka.
After a brief stop in Kawano to visit his parents and pay his respect
to the family grave, Onishi arrived in bustling Osaka, where first
he had a hefty lunch at a big department store. The rice was mixed
with udon noodles, and there was no second helping. But when he
asked the waitress for more, she didn't mind.

"Surely it is not enough for a soldier, Mr. Officer. Of course I'll
bring you some right away."

It troubled Onishi to find adulterated rice here in the big city.
In Tokushima he had experienced no such thing. The war situation
must be serious.[22]

When Onishi presented himself next morning, all were already lined up and about to relocate to Ooe Primary School. His new boss was Lt.-Col. Oishi Masayuki, an elite officer, assigned to them as an Imperial Gift from the Military Police Academy, so to speak. And if he had a boisterous side to him, he was also decisive and speedy in everything he tackled, and for that eminently suited to set up the new Second Field Unit of the Military Police.[23]

The primary school was quickly turned into a barrack. The men knocked down school doors to enlarge the rooms, spread straw mats on the school floors, and put up various signs all round the school. One said "no visitors", and the soldiers were not allowed out. Fear of counter-intelligence was omnipresent and secrecy began to shroud the school-turned-camp, as the new tenants evaded the public dissatisfaction that was usual wherever they set up their imperious quarters.[24]

3

Rubber Hub Singapore

WHILE Japan prepared for war, businessman Omori Kichijiro was learning the ropes as an employee of Senda & Co. in Calcutta. After graduating from Tokyo Commercial University in 1931, he had gone out to India to study the jute industry and gunny bags. Two years later he was transferred to Bangkok to combine his knowledge of jute sacks with one thing that went into them — rubber. Both jute and rubber fetched high prices in the world markets. After two years Senda moved Omori again, this time to Singapore, the hub of the rubber industry, to concentrate on the rubber business between Malaya and Japan.[1]

The Senda Company owned a rubber estate in Renggam in the Malay state of Johor across the Straits of Singapore. From headquarters in thriving Singapore, Omori commuted by train regularly to inspect the vast and increasingly profitable plantation.

A barely inhabited island on the eve of the arrival of Raffles in 1819, Singapore had developed into the most flourishing international port in the region. Cultivated since the 1840s as a prosperous financial centre, it lay at the crossroads of the Pacific and Indian Oceans and the South China Sea, with excellent connections to the Americas, Australia, Europe and to China.

Lacking any significant agricultural or industrial exports of its own, Singapore could only finance its consumption of imported goods by the profits made on its entrepôt trade.[2] Global in character, this trade showed tremendous growth as Singapore became an essential link between the industrial world of the West and the developing export economies of colonial Asia.[3]

Fortunately for Singapore, it sat at the southern tip of a treasure house. Malaya produced coal and iron ore, manganese and bauxite, but most of all tin. Mined for centuries on a small scale by Malays, tin became Malaya's major export in the 19th century with growing

Chinese investments. In the 20th century Malaya became the largest tin producer in the world, after it attracted European capital investment.

Trade and mining were the dominant economic activities until the early 20th century, when the advent of the automobile and bicycles brought an explosion of demand for rubber, and rubber cultivation became a major industry. During the 1930s rubber was the country's most important agricultural export. Two-thirds of the five million acres of cultivated land in the peninsula was planted with rubber, and Malaya accounted for more than 40 per cent of the rubber entering world markets.[4]

A transport network had developed along the west coast to carry tin from the mines in Perak and Selangor to processing and shipping centres in Penang and Singapore. This suited the needs of the rubber companies as well, and they opened land in areas that gave them access to these facilities.[5]

Singapore was the focal point for this vast, expanding trade. It was to this bustling port, 150 kilometres north of the equator, that the wagons rolled down the peninsula's railway, bearing their cargoes of crude rubber tapped by Tamils in lonely plantations to the north in the jungles of Malaya. The cargo train reached Singapore island — diamond shaped, measuring 42 kilometres across and 22 from north to south — via a causeway across the narrow Straits of Johor, and was unloaded at the docks on the southern side of the island.

The city was a place of extravagant contrasts. If there seemed to be no end to the colour and jumbled confusion of Chinese, Malay, and Indian houses, the government, business, and residential sections of the city were entirely different, with landscaped green spaces, white villas, and the orderliness of a typical colonial city. "White" Singapore was above all a beautiful green city.[6]

Singapore was the place to be, with plentiful food for every palate, and pleasure of all sorts, games galore, the clubs, and always parties. A young aide de camp detailed to Government House related the high-flying life he enjoyed as an ordinary police officer. Parties at Government House under Sir Shenton and Lady Thomas were always extremely enjoyable and well organised. And when Governor Sir Shenton Thomas was on an official visit up-country, very few of the attractive, young, unattached girls in Singapore would refuse the young officer's unofficial and illegal late night invitation to

Government House, with its swimming pool, and the prospect of skinny dipping late at night after a strenuous evening of dancing and drinking.[7]

Then again, Singapore had always been a city of pleasure. On a less exalted level, Singapore could look back on a significant history of brothel prostitution that had become one of the island's largest and most complex enterprises in the late 19th century.[8] So rampant was the *dolce vita* in Singapore in 1939, that the Governor engaged, at 500 Straits dollars per month, a Miss S.E. Nicoll from Liverpool (who had surveyed prostitution in Rangoon ten years before), on a two-year contract, to investigate the problem in Singapore, and a concomitant epidemic of venereal disease among British troops.[9]

That was hardly the danger the soldiers had been sent over to the East to face. But it squared with the propaganda of total security in British Malaya everyone was made to believe. When the war in Europe took a drastic turn for the worse in the spring of 1940, most Europeans living in Malaya were primarily concerned about their families in Europe. How fortunate to be living in Southeast Asia! War would not touch them here. There was an absolute conviction that nothing on earth could ever disturb the peace in the vast British Empire.[10]

It was a belief held throughout Malaya, not only by the 30,000 Europeans but also the Asians. A polyglot population, they included over two million Malays, about the same number of Chinese, 750,000 Indians, plus Armenians, Arabs, Javanese, and Burmese. To them war was not only unlikely, it was an event they did not even contemplate. There had never been a military governor or occupying army, and the law and order was maintained by a police force employing fewer than 200 British officers.[11]

And when the Sino-Japanese conflict disturbed the peace of East Asia, colonial administrators repeatedly assured the polyglot population that there would be no war with Japan.

Omori on his inspection trips across the Straits to Senda's Renggam estate was not so sure. The headlines of the Japanese dailies he read on his train ride to Renggam told a different story. He prayed that war would not break out; it did nothing for profits, and only benefited the politicians and the militarists. But it was clear from his reading that his country's military steamroller was firmly in place. And now that the war was going badly for the old colonial powers in Europe, Japan would surely do something about French Indochina.

Next, probably Thailand, and British Malaya — who could tell? And then, if all went well, surely also the Dutch East Indies with its oil.

It was a precarious situation if your business was rubber. Had he operated a trading company, Omori would long ago have closed the office and fled to another country; he didn't want to be arrested by the British. But with rubber you could not put out a closed sign and wait out the situation abroad. Arrangements had to be made well in advance. Otherwise, the plantation could be ruined within six months or a year. Omori racked his brain to find ways to help his company protect their business. Entrusting Senda's affairs to the neighbouring rubber estate run by a British planter might solve the problem. His superior, however, turned down the proposal, saying there was no precedent. Only when Mr Shinya returned to Japan could Omori write directly to President Senda, who was delighted with this solution.[12]

The neighbouring rubber estate was managed by the Anglo-Thai Corporation from offices in Singapore. Omori lost no time in seeing a British lawyer who negotiated a contract valid for one year. It could be nullified at one week's notice. Anglo-Thai would sell Omori's rubber on the world market and, after deducting operating costs, hand Senda & Co. the balance.

When other Japanese planters heard of this pioneering contract, they contacted Omori. "Look for a suitable estate to run your plantation economically," he advised them, as they copied down the details of the contract and the name of his lawyer, who was of course delighted about the sudden extra business from a potential foe already on the run.[13]

As expected, the headlines out of Washington on the ongoing Japanese-American talks got worse every day, and in late November Omori visited his neighbouring estate manager, Mr. Husband.

"Please take good care of our rubber."

"But all is peaceful. Why so early?" the manager asked, surprised.

Until 7 December 1941 it was difficult to realize that Singapore was a city on the brink of war. The place was steeped in the British-fostered myth of complete security, and even senior people believed their own propaganda. This included the Commander-in-Chief Far East, Air Chief Marshal Sir Robert Brooke-Popham. When the Japanese armada rounded the southern end of Vietnam on 6 December 1941, he preferred to believe that it was sailing to

Bangkok and not heading for a landing on the Malayan Peninsula. Brooke-Popham consequently failed in the last moment to launch Operation Matador, which was designed to preempt any Japanese invasion on the beaches of southern Thailand.[14]

In the end, even Omori left his departure too late. He had hardly paid off the remaining five Senda employees and booked passages for everyone out of Singapore when Japanese bombs fell on the city. When Omori and his loyal employees did sail, it was not up the east coast to Bangkok as planned, but up the west coast of Malaya. And they were not ordinary passengers, but part of Britain's first group of Japanese detainees. All through the night they travelled, going as far as Port Swettenham where in the morning they were placed in a squalid quarantine station designed for Tamil labourers. They were the first to experience life behind barbed wire. On the following days, Japanese men from lower peninsular Malaya joined them. The men had been separated from the women and children, who were kept on Blakang Mati and other islands, and they would not see them again until sometime later, when all the detainees were transferred to New Delhi in India.[15]

4

In China

JAPAN's impending sortie into Southeast Asia was modern history's best kept military secret, and they were all part of that plan: Lt. Onishi's 2nd Military Police Field Unit, Sgt. Arai's 18th Division, Pte. Miyake and Lt. Ochi's 5th Division, and Tsuchikane's Imperial Guards Division. They did not know the secret, but for all of them, the journey it occasioned began in China, where they were stationed in 1941 not long after conscription and mobilisation.

Shipped off with the Imperial Guards in June that year, Tsuchikane was one of thousands of boys in China unknowingly preparing to invade Southeast Asia. Twelve days after leaving his folks on the pier, Tsuchikane noticed the water turn yellow near land where rain washed treeless mountain soil into the sea. South China would be their destination, they were told. The next day they disembarked between Hong Kong and Macao, and immediately transferred inland to their garrison town of Sekki near Canton.[1]

Imperial Guards had arrived here one year earlier and established Sekki as their base camp for training purposes.[2] Known as Palace Detachment 3800, they had seen battle both at Canton and at Nankyo. Tsuchikane's regiment, which came to replace them as Palace Detachment 3803, was gradually integrated with these older soldiers.[3] Although the old boys treated them like kids, Tsuchikane and his colleagues had only admiration for the veterans: there was freedom in their sloppy beards, in their laundry hanging in confusion from various strings, and in the live ammunition piled up on open shelves. An extraordinary atmosphere of "letting go" pervaded this camp, an air that would have been wholly unthinkable in their pedantic barracks back home.[4]

After two months in camp, the boys were taken on their first combat mission. It was part of an exercise to subjugate guerrillas based on the "three all" principle: "Kill all, burn all, destroy all", a campaign that lasted throughout the spring and summer of 1941. It was Japan's answer to the "One Hundred Regiments Offensive" launched by the 8th Route Army in the provinces of Hopei and Shansi, and the method was to surround a given area and destroy everything there making it uninhabitable.[5]

Tsuchikane was accompanying his seniors to a hamlet several kilometres away, where guerrillas were said to have infiltrated, when they heard rifle fire. Tsuchikane's face began twitching, "Here we go, at last." He blinked at his elders who showed no emotion.

Deploying and advancing up to the hamlet, Tsuchikane saw several people scurrying off to the right in a vegetable field.

"Mount the bayonets!" screamed the squad commander. With saucer eyes, Tsuchikane watched his comrades on the left and right advance. No shots could be heard from the enemy side. "Advance on the double! Forward!!"

Everyone started to run. Tsuchikane followed his senior up to the farmhouse on the hill. It was empty. They darted to the next small thatched home. No one there either. Then Tsuchikane saw a woman with a child who had fallen behind run to the vegetable field, and from the roof of the other farmhouse fire leapt into the air. Tsuchikane saw soldiers setting fire to the thatched houses. Even the older soldiers in his platoon were putting fire to the houses.

Tsuchikane was perplexed. "Why, if there are no people, do we burn down their houses?" he asked his senior. "If we don't do this, they will all be back. Really, they should all be killed." Tsuchikane nodded. So this was the battlefield....

After the fire work, they caught the farmers' chicken and pigs and prepared a good meal. It was Tsuchikane's first lesson in larceny and theft. Somehow he had imagined it all quite differently. To suppress, curb, and quell the enemy, and then quench one's hunger ... what an operation. Back in barracks after the evening bugle, wrapped in his blanket, Tsuchikane pondered the pattern of their noon manoeuvre. Some kind of demi-gods, these older soldiers.... Tsuchikane sighed, reviewing each detail of the merciless scenes that kept him awake.[6]

All the while, officer selection continued at Sekki. Imperial Guards who learnt well could go on to officer training; the others would remain second-class soldiers and end up as non-commissioned officers. Around 30 members of Tsuchikane's battalion were recommended for selection by their commanders.

Tsuchikane was among them, having received lots of encouragement: "With your stamina and persistence you'll make a fine officer." Yes! And because he badly wanted to get ahead, he threw himself into the rigorous training with much determination.

Until one day, something in him snapped. It was down by the beach during the march drill in the sand. Tsuchikane simply could not get the drill pattern perfectly right. Time and again the leader forced him to repeat the turn of the right angle in the exercise. It began to exasperate Tsuchikane. "Leader, Sir, would you please show me how to do it?" There may have been just the slightest bit of reproach in the tone of his question, enough to anger his senior officer and seal his fate. From then on, Tsuchikane was no longer allowed to do his officer's laundry.[7]

South China was of course not the final destination of Palace Detachment 3803. In mid-July orders came to pack and crate everything for their next move. They wiped out every trace that might have betrayed their occupancy. Nothing was left behind, all utterly disposed of. As always, no one knew where they were going. Only on the open sea were they told that they would rendezvous with other ships off the island of Hainan for a move further south.[8]

In Samah, Hainan's huge assembly port and at the time Japan's southernmost naval base, every type of ship greeted Tsuchikane and his comrades as they climbed on deck. Capital ships on all sides; light and heavy cruisers, destroyers, torpedo boats, submarines, crowded troop transports, huge battleships... terrific... there had to be at least a hundred of them! "And to think that this fleet is only a small part of our Navy," Tsuchikane glowed, as dozens of naval planes droned above them. With such a splendid navy they would be invincible.

But to what shores would the powerful navy carry them? They were still in the dark when after a few days a well-armed contingent of the immense fleet swept them onward, beyond Japan's "inner" zone into the so-called "outer" area of the South Seas, or Southeast Asia.

Soon after departure, officer promotions were announced up on deck, and when to everyone's surprise Tsuchikane was the only candidate to fail, he did not understand. How could it be? Was it that obnoxious drill in Vietnam? He'd always seen himself as a glorious officer, now he would remain a second-class soldier with the rest. Trying to console him, the commander called Tsuchikane to his cabin: "These things happen, but whether you pass or fail is of little importance in this war. No matter what, give your country your best."

The results put Tsuchikane and those promoted literally into different boats. While the successful sailed back to the mainland for officer training (they would not see battle for some time), the remaining second-class soldiers stayed with the flotilla that now set course for South Indochina. It would be Tsuchikane's fate to experience the opening phase of the Greater East Asia war.

In 1936 the Japanese Government had already decided on a southern policy to secure resources,[9] and by August 1940, the Japanese Navy was pushing for the stationing of troops in French Indochina as a firm step forward in the southern advance to gain control over Thailand, Burma, and Malaya. Occupation of Vietnam was a crucial element in Japanese Navy strategy: "If ... Japan occupies all of French Indochina, there is a strong possibility that the United States will tighten its embargo. An American embargo on iron and oil would be a matter of life and death to the empire. In that event the empire will be obliged to attack the Dutch East Indies to secure oil."[10]

Since early in the summer of 1940 (after Germany had occupied Holland, France, and Belgium), Hitler and his Foreign Minister Ribbentrop had been prodding Japan to move into the European colonial territories and take Malaya and Singapore. Urgent action on Japan's part was certainly advised, lest Germany take control of French Indochina herself. In September that year, Japan occupied North Indochina.

Forward in the lead marched Ochi, playing his part in the occupation as cadet leader of a platoon of machine-gunners in the 5th Division. After one year of basic training in Hiroshima, he had been sent to China on 20 September 1940 (experiencing battle for the first time that day), and his platoon crossed the border of French Indochina two days later. After occupying North Vietnam, their battle-seasoned crack unit — the Ichikawa detachment of the 11th Regiment — rested at Lanson.

Ochi had already proven his mettle, doing well in China and in Vietnam, and when they were shipped back to Shanghai, he was made Second Lieutenant. It was a happy time for him. He loved Shanghai. There was something about the city, an over-ripeness, difficult to put in words, a certain culminating finesse, that Ochi had never found in his home country. With a battle tour usually lasting three months, followed by two months of rest, amorous Ochi, for the time being, could let himself go in the debonair quarters of the world city.[11]

In his still unattached days, Ochi frequented dubious places, one of them run by a Jewish madame. Girls from all over the world thronged the madame's night club. Ochi did not much fancy the Russian women, who were bold with little sex appeal. The Japanese girls were short and stocky, with short hips and their derrieres sticking out, and would not lift their legs properly. But their price was high class. The Chinese girls were cheap, and more beautiful with an above average constitution. Many shaved their pubic hair, and their bald deltas evoked thunderous applause when they appeared for a show. The Indian girls were good, but skinny. Sometimes their bones got in the way; it was rather difficult with them.[12]

In the spring of 1941, Ochi took part in major regional exercises preparatory to invading the south. The General Staff wanted to know how well the army and navy could cooperate. Ever since the Manchurian invasion in 1931 and the China Incident in 1937, large-scale manoeuvres had involved primarily the Army on the Asian mainland in anticipation of a possible confrontation with the Soviet Union. Now it was crucial to test the team spirit of the traditionally contentious Japanese Army and Navy for their degree of cooperation, because success in the coming war would involve vital amphibious landings on a large scale.

Decked out in tropical gear, Ochi's 5th Division played the invading army in mock assaults on southern Kyushu.[13] Landing on the Kagoshima coast, they captured Kurume and tried to guess where it would all lead. The coming battles would take place in the tropics, that much they were told: they would fight in swampy mangrove patches, traverse jungle, and be caught in thunderous squalls; there would be lots of rubber trees. Since the island of Kyushu resembled the Philippines, this was Ochi's guess, but he was mistaken.

After these manoeuvres they were put back on ships and returned
to the Chinese coast, their blank cartridges exchanged for real
ammunition. On landing they faced a real enemy at Ningpo, on
the opposite side of Shanghai Bay, which had been retaken by the
Chinese. Then they returned to Shanghai for more training.[14]

Under the new Prime Minister Tojo Hideki, an army man who was
an apostle of blitzkrieg tactics and a zealot for mechanised warfare,
the 5th Division underwent rapid mechanisation.[15] Giving up horses
for trucks and bicycles was a tremendous change. To graduate from
their mechanisation programme Ochi's unit had to carry out a long-
distance truck attack from Wuson to Kianwan. In the mock-attack,
Ochi sustained his only injury when, in the course of a breakthrough
to Kianwan airport, their truck failed to negotiate the final curve at
70 kms per hour. All of those on board needed medical treatment.[16]

In early October they were transferred back to Shanghai for a
massing of troops, and Ochi felt the day of departure fast approaching.
At a young age, he was already the senior leader of the first of the
four squads that made up their company of machine-gunners. The
other three squads were led by sub-lieutenants one year his junior,
all of whom had seen action in the landings on the China coast. All
were excellent front-line commanders, and hungry for more action.

Ochi did not attend his commander's final speech on the occasion
of their last manoeuvre; it would be the same old trite pep talk. If
only he could have had him answer squarely: were they sufficiently
prepared to beat their next opponent?

Three days before embarkation, Ochi and his men were told their
date of departure. Leave had already been cancelled, but someone
wanted to see Ochi badly, ... just one more time.

But what use was it? Even if he met Keiko again, it would only
make things more difficult. He was going into battle, probably soon
to be deified at Yasukuni Shrine, the final resting place for all fallen
soldiers, while she was chasing dreams with a future.

She was the daughter of an expatriate businessman, and they had
met in mid-November at the Shanghai Shrine built by local Japanese
near the Naval Brigade Building. The shrine was beautiful when the

flowers were out. But they rarely went there, preferring instead to spend time at the cinemas and in the coffee shops of Shanghai.[17]

Amorous Ochi had been in Shanghai for 200 days, and even learnt a bit of Shanghainese. "You only learn Chinese to buy girls," his girlfriend had chided him. Looking back, three days before their departure, he felt he'd led a foolish life. If only he could redo his life and come back, once more, for her ... but, no, he was sure he would not return a third time. And even if he did, he had no doubt that he would do it all over again and enjoy himself to the utmost.

She met him on their last day clutching a big box of candies, wearing a light blue kimono. It was the first time he had seen her in traditional dress. She was a great beauty and looked even better in Western clothes. Ochi would have loved to have taken her to the Jewish madame's night club. She would have compared favourably with any of the foreign girls there. Just once he would have liked to take her there. She probably had a great delta, too, with soft smooth skin. He would have loved to see those sights, at least once. But no, he had not even asked her to show him her beautiful private view. It was strange; he did not feel he could have touched her, because he loved her. How paradoxical humans were. It was the manner of a warrior, Ochi decided. Later, however, on the path of war, when often he would look back on those halcyon days, he never could figure out whether he had acted rightly or wrongly.

Her brother was in the 6th Company.

"Let's call him," Ochi said.

"No, don't," she said, "let's just be together, you and me."

But there was not much to say to each other. The short moment became eternity as they faced each other with vacant minds. One chocolate was still left when she disappeared into the evening sun. She never looked back.[18]

The next day more than 15,000 men of the 5th Division, complete with engineer corps, artillery and field hospital embarked at Kian Bay and sailed down the Yangtze River, where they boarded three 10,000 ton-transports. Ochi's 3rd battalion boarded the last one, the *Atsuta Maru*.

Late in the afternoon of 1 December 1941 they arrived at a wide inlet of what some said was Taiwan. All still believed they had been picked for an invasion of the Philippines.[19]

If Germany's earlier attack on Holland, France, and Belgium had given Japan the green light to push south into northern Indochina, Germany's lightning attack on the Soviet Union one year later, in June 1941, was a second green light to advance further south, unhindered. But having the Soviets pinned down in Europe also offered another strategic option. It presented Japan with the opportunity to knock out the Soviet northern threat in the Russian Far East once and for all.

It was for such a conceivable northern push that Onishi had been sent to Dairen with his military policemen from Osaka in August 1941. During their brief stay, the leader of the 2nd Military Police Field Unit, Colonel Oishi, offered to take the boys on a tour of Hill 203, overlooking Dairen. From that famous elevation their forefathers had wrested the northern gateway, below, from Czarist Russia in 1904/1905 at the cost of 58,000 dead and wounded. Again they had come to fight the Russians, this time to finish off the Soviet northern threat for good.[20]

From Dairen they entrained for Changchun, where they joined the Kanto Military Police training school on the outskirts of the city. Barrack life again had them rise and retire at the beck of the trumpet, with daily military drills, cramming, and riding — added after the delivery of 30 army horses, most of them small Manchurian ponies.

Only Sundays offered a relief from the monotony of military life. Then they were allowed to visit Changchun, the big city about five kilometres from their training grounds. The grand Army Building on Changchun's wide main street reflected the majestic appearance of the Japanese military, and the newly-completed Building of Justice displayed a degree of splendour unsurpassed even in their homeland. The area around the station resembled bustling Japanese streets, and the adjoining pleasure district of Yoshino was better even than similar areas at home. Department stores flourished and in the colourful streets one could find eating and drinking stalls and all sorts of entertainment. There was no better place to relax from the boredom of camp life and amuse themselves on a leisurely Sunday afternoon.

Nowhere outside Japan could one feel more proud of being a Japanese. In these grand buildings, power and prestige paired with a never-ending energy in the buoyant shopping streets full of Japanese.

But as soon as one set foot in the squalid suburbs of the Manchurians, the poverty was appalling. Japan's puppet state, Manchukuo, was still a long way from realising the North Asian slogan: "Harmony among the five families [Japan, China, Manchukuo, Taiwan, and Korea], the Kingly Way is paradise."[21]

Establishing this idyll under Japanese guidance was the task of Lt.-Gen. Yamashita Tomoyuki, commander of the Manchukuo Army Headquarters in Changchun. On 6 November a telegram rudely interrupted his work: "Come to Tokyo immediately, in a special plane."[22]

The next day the general traversed the long, dark, wooden corridors of the two-storeyed General Staff Building to enter the office of Chief-of-Staff, Gen. Sugiyama Gen, in the corner of the second floor nearest the front gates of the War Office Compound.[23] At this point Yamashita had no idea that on the previous day, the Imperial Liaison conference had decided to go to war with America, England, and Holland.

Inside Sugiyama's simply furnished office, the Navy C.-in-C. Adm. Yamamoto Isoroku, and Field Marshal Count Terauchi Hisaichi, overall Commander-in-Charge of Southern Command, were waiting for him. To his surprise, Yamashita was designated Commander-in-Chief of the 25th Army for the Malayan campaign and given control over all forces to take Singapore, the Gibraltar of the East.[24] Gen. Suzuki Sosaku would be his senior staff officer and Maj. Kunitake Teruto his Officer-in-Charge of Southward Operations at Imperial General Headquarters. Lt.-Col. Sugita Ichiji, who had studied in America, was his Intelligence Officer and, most importantly, Col. Tsuji Masanobu was the Officer-in-Charge of Operations, responsible for drafting the plans for military operations.[25]

One week later, Yamashita flew to Saigon to establish Southern Headquarters under the overall command of Terauchi. Gen. Yamashita would have as his three workhorses Ochi and Miyake's 5th Division (now standing by at Shanghai), Tsuchikane's Imperial Guards Division (now at Saigon), and Arai's 18th Division (at Canton). The three divisions would form the 25th Army and come under his direct command on 15 November at zero hours in the morning. From that time on, two ships would leave Shanghai every day with troops and materiel to assemble at Samah Harbour on the southern tip of Hainan, where they would remain on alert awaiting Yamashita's instructions for the invasion of Malaya.

On that Day X, both the 5th Division and the Imperial Guards Division would pound ahead in full division strength. But 18th Division at Canton was broken up into three detachments, each assigned a different task in three different war theatres. Only the Takumi Detachment would be immediately involved with the invasion, leaving Canton on 28 and 30 November to rendezvous with the 5th Division and the Imperial Guards Division at Samha, and it was given the difficult task of storming heavily-defended Kota Bahru in British Malaya; the Kawaguchi Detachment would steam out to Camranh Bay on 3 December, on its way to capture British Borneo; whilst Arai's 114th Regiment along with the headquarters of the 18th Division would continue to stand by in southern China.

It would be a long wait for Sgt. Arai and the remaining 4,000 men, most of whom were from Kokura in North Kyushu, many of them coal-mining types, sturdy and strong. No sooner had they and Arai completed their military training in 1937, then they were drafted into the army earmarked to quell the skirmishes around the Marco Polo Bridge in Peking in July that year. As disturbances spread south, Arai sailed with the 18th Division in November to land in the face of the enemy at Hokusa in Koshu Bay on the Chinese coast. After fighting ten days in rugged terrain and against many pillboxes, Arai's baptism by fire was over, and he was promoted from corporal to sergeant. Advancing via Shanghai, they continued on to Nanking where Arai's unit moved to the rear of the city, arriving just in time to attend a ceremony celebrating the fall of Nanking on 17 December. But they did not take part in the ensuing rape of the city; immediate orders for a gruelling 900-kilometre march brought them back to Koshu, where they had started.[26] They now had a reputation and called themselves "The Koshu Bay Gang". After spending much of 1938 in Koshu they captured Canton, where they stayed until the fateful end of summer 1941.[27]

5

To Malaya

IN July 1941, the Japanese military decided to push its next pawn south. With most of France in the hands of Axis-partner Germany, and the northern half of French Vietnam under Japanese control, the logical next step was to occupy southern Vietnam. This territory was indispensable, for Singapore would be within reach of Japan's Zero bombers flying from its southernmost airfields.

The occupation of North Vietnam had been spearheaded by the 5th Division. It was now the still untested Imperial Guards' turn to take South Vietnam in an even more flagrant breach of international law.

After leaving Samah on Hainan Island, the Imperial Guards Division soon learned that their flotilla was heading for French Indochina. Tsuchikane had no time to brood over failing the officer promotion exercise. The situation was serious and the weather fine, as he and the Guards rolled in on choppy waves at Cap St Jacques, around 40 kilometres south of Saigon, in fighting formation. Would the French resist? No. Relieved, the Guards heard on their landing crafts that a peaceful occupation had been negotiated at the last minute.[1]

The local Vietnamese people, near the French resort where they landed, watched them curiously as they scrambled up the beach, where lovely white French villas and wide avenues rarely seen in Japan greeted them. The soldiers proceeded to requisition the French barracks, a welcome luxury after their rough camp back in China. But they took pains to make their occupation a "peaceful stationing" by avoiding direct contact with both the French and the local people.[2]

Life had changed since their days in the Tokyo barracks, even since China. The juniors no longer did laundry for the seniors. And when Tsuchikane received his third star, it meant that even older soldiers had to greet him first ... in theory, at least.[3] A bout of diarrhoea landed him in hospital, and taught him otherwise, when he had to convalesce next to arrogant First Class Soldier Iwane.[4] Although one star lower in rank, Iwane was five years older than Tsuchikane.

"Hey, Tsuchikane! You slack bastard — you will never make a good non-commissioned officer in hospital!!"

"Yes," replied Tsuchikane.

"I can't hear you! Louder!!"

"Yes!" replied Tsuchikane with his little strength.

Iwane took special pleasure in ordering around Tsuchikane's younger colleague from the same unit, Pte. Date. Although of the same rank, Date obeyed meekly, doing errands for the saucy older soldier, even of the illegal kind, such as getting food and alcohol, which Iwane devoured sitting cross-legged on his bed.

They kept their weapons next to their bed, and Iwane had Date clean his rifle, then ordered: "Do also Tsuchikane's rifle!"

"No, that's not necessary," said Tsuchikane, "I'll do it myself."

"Then do it both together!" Iwane thundered. Iwane was really on fake leave. A shameless loafer, he drank rice wine every night, and foulmouthed even the young doctor.[5]

One day, a new patient with malaria joined their section in hospital. Tall and skinny, a complex thinker, and utterly at variance with having to become a soldier, Mori loathed the prospect of simply dying on the battle field. "I want to return to civilian life as soon as possible. That's all I ever think of."[6]

It puzzled Tsuchikane to meet a First Class Soldier who did not put duty to his country's mission first. But Mori was bright, a graduate student from a university in Tokyo, and Tsuchikane took pleasure in chatting with an intelligent person. There were so few of them in the field, and Tsuchikane was tickled that a First Class Soldier two years his senior would talk to him, a second ranking cadet. They had lots to discuss, though mostly they talked about their hometowns so far away.

Their friendly chats continued until one afternoon, during a rest period, the comforting shade of a tree lulled Mori into a mistaken familiarity; he began to talk to Tsuchikane as if he were one of his student friends back home.

"In the military we don't need brains," Mori said. "All we do is follow orders. Orders are absolute, and we must follow them like a herd of animals. Our final aim is to go to the battle field, where we either kill or get killed. We have no alternative." He had hated having to join the army.

How different from my own experience, Tsuchikane thought, as he politely continued to hear out Mori's criticism of the military organisation.

"At university many of us hated conscription. If we could wangle it, we would seek an exemption or an extension and join research institutes. But sooner or later we were called up. When I was conscripted, I began to have all sorts of ideas. As a graduate at least I would rise quickly. But nothing happened. I was forced into the military. I want to leave. But I have no alternative than to sit this damn war out."[7]

Tsuchikane was shocked to hear this sudden revelation made to him in all confidence. His own thought system had no room for Mori's reasoning. A healthy young man looked forward joyously to enter military service. After all, it was for his country that he went into battle. To fight was a natural thing. One shouldered the hard training gladly, dutifully, and with all one's power. There could be absolutely no thought of criticising the military.

Tsuchikane was now angry to know that soldiers such as Mori existed. He was absolutely against such so-called pacifist, treacherous elements. Their thinking was counter-productive and cunning at a time when one had to keep one's wits to fight for one's country. Had someone with a higher rank than Tsuchikane heard Mori's speech, it could have had terrible consequences. Anti-war elements were dealt with sternly. Court-martial could have ensued, possibly resulting in incarceration.

Tsuchikane saw himself on a personal mission. He was in Saigon because his country had big plans. The Emperor knew what he was doing and no petty talk by one of his unfaithful could bring down the grand design of *Hakko ichiu*, "the world under one roof", with His Majesty at the top. But Tsuchikane did not want to argue with this otherwise cheerful chap, and at the end of the one-sided conversation, he quickly disengaged from Mori and never spoke to him again.

Shameful Iwane hated Mori for a different reason. He could not stand students, especially not university graduates, and abused Mori on every occasion.

"Hey, you're strange! Can't you salute me? You dirty swine!"

"I'm sorry," said Mori. But Iwane's clenched fist already landed on Mori's left cheek and knocked him down.

Tsuchikane never saw Mori or Iwane again after leaving the hospital, when he returned to his unit and the higher mission that lay before him.[8]

Future war operations would require them to swim, and because the commander had seen how well Tsuchikane swam when they had disembarked in high waves at Cap St Jacques, he was ordered to give a special swimming class for the many who did not know how.

"Mr. Instructor, you cannot swim in the sea," warned local onlookers, "there are poisonous water snakes!" But an order was an order, his men had to learn how to swim, and fast, and he did not tell them about the snakes.[9]

It was a strange environment the troops found themselves here in French Indochina, in a hot climate, with different people, different languages surrounding them, tropical fruits, French beer, and exotic animals, and never knowing where they were going. Excruciating jungle training alternated with halcyon days by the sandy beach. Were they on a holiday?

The only steadying link in this weird experience was the mailbag. That magic bag with its wonderful contents telling them they were still loved, however little recognition they were getting at the moment. "Is there one for me?" every one would ask the NCO with his sack of correspondence, like children receiving a present. If lucky, one would take the precious envelope or postcard, seek out a quiet spot, read it over and over again, and then show it to friends. Tsuchikane received a great deal of mail, because he wrote a lot. But his sentences were often blacked out, and censorship allowed no place names, nor dates; but often Tsuchikane made a little drawing at the bottom of the letter, such as a group of palm trees from which the receiver could gather that he was not stationed in the northern tundra of Manchuria, but somewhere tropical, perhaps in Southeast Asia.

The gladdest thing was a letter from a female, as gleaned from the strokes on an envelope done in a delicate hand. That created a sensation and the letter would be passed around while the recipient's private life was subjected to excited cross-examinations. "What's your relationship with her? Are you going to marry her?"[10]

Comfort bags were as pleasing as the letters. These 30 by 35 centimetre packages usually came from complete strangers, and were channeled through ward offices back home, or from the Women's Defense Association, or from the Patriotic Women's Association, or from the Municipality. The soldiers would find in them drawings by the pupils of a patriotic primary school teacher, together with messages of encouragement; there were also mascots, or dolls of the province, temple charms, ornamental paper, photographs, usually some food, pressed flowers, anything folks at home thought would brighten up the spirits of their men at the front.

Replying made the soldier as happy as receiving the parcel. He would ask his comrades about the environment of such and such a mountain village, so that he could thank the friendly sender in a familiar way. If the comfort bag contained a letter from a girl, that was really fantastic. Then one imagined her face, her hair, her figure, her scent. One even dreamed of her, and nurtured hopes.

"Let *me* reply for you!" friends would beg the lucky soldier, hoping to relieve him of the delightful chore of writing back.[11]

Many comfort bags contained "Thousand Stitch Belts" — cloth belts 15 centimetres wide, decorated with 1,000 little red dots stitched in continuous lines by a thousand females. The splendid belts were supposed to ward off bullets and bring victory. In the homeland, girl-students would go around and ask passers by, girls and ladies, to take part in this patriotic action: "Could you kindly spare a moment for a stitch on a couple of my belts?" In Taiwan, too, girl-students regularly spent a couple of hours an afternoon getting together, each loaded with a heap of ten belts, and in groups of nine or ten go around town asking any women they met to do a couple of stitches on each of their belts.

Each stitch put as much gratitude in the heart of the soldier as it gave the girls pride in doing something positive for the success of Japan's Imperial soldiers. Tsuchikane had left Japan wearing one, and in the temperate climate of China his "Thousand Stitch Belt" had seemed comfortable enough. But the further south they went, the more the belt became a burden. It made washing difficult, and offered a splendid habitat to bugs travelling south with the soldiers.

In China the belts had given the boys spiritual support, but in the south they became both a physical and a mental torture. When Tsuchikane wished to throw his away, his conscience balked: "The belt has protected me until here. The bullets may hit me if I discard it. Not today — but tomorrow, for sure, I'll throw it away." Only after his first real battle was he able to break the spell and rid himself of the well-meant stitches.[12]

The Imperial troops in Indochina had still no idea where they were headed. Letters and comfort bags only made everything more eerie and uncertain. Something extraordinary was rushing at them, but they could not gauge time or place, or the magnitude of the approaching earthquake. When a call went out to courageous and patriotic soldiers who wished to volunteer for special missions — dangerous land or even paratroop operations[13] — Tsuchikane volunteered, too. Again this involved selection and elimination, and again Tsuchikane was not among those chosen. This time, however, he was given a reason: as the only precious son, whom his family depended on to take over the household, he must be spared. The Japanese army had its unexpected human side, too.[14]

The bugle that called them on 2 December 1941, was finally for real. Collecting a large quantity of live ammunition with a week's food ration, they put their bicycles on separate trucks and scrambled onto their own, ten soldiers to one truck, plus two drivers. It was very early in the morning when they departed, and the streets of Saigon were deserted except for a few curious onlookers. "But where to?" Imperial Guard Tsuchikane wondered along with thousands of fellow soldiers in the 5th and 18th Divisions. "What's the war aim?"[15]

Second Lt. Ochi Harumi asked himself the same question, time after time, and so did his comrades in the 5th Division as they, too, proceeded south in early December towards Hainan's assembly port of Samha.

"It can't be the Philippines. It must be Thailand."

"You bloody fool, in that case we would be sailing for Saigon and advancing overland which is much safer."

"We can't be going east, our Fleet is moving *south*. Are we going to Borneo?"

"What on earth for? To join the gorillas and the cannibals?"

"Idiot! There's oil there!"

"What? Oil in Borneo?"

"Yes, it must be Borneo."

"It certainly can't be the Philippines. The Americans are building it up as a stronghold."[16]

Ochi began to suspect that they were headed for Malaya. Felling Singapore — that would just be the right kind of challenge for the 5th and 18th Divisions, in Ochi's estimation the greatest fighting units, matchless twin stars fit to take Singapore![17]

Berthed at Samah, Ochi's suspicion was confirmed when the officer-in-charge of military operations, Col. Tsuji Masanobu, came on board to give them a pep talk about the coming campaign.

Tsuji stressed that after landing, their first major object after securing the airports in Malaya's north, would be to rush to the Perak River before the British could blow up the main bridge. To pass into Malaya with the least resistance, Tsuji had a plan, though one he frankly admitted had been given him in a dream: near the Thai-Malaya border, they would all disguise themselves in Thai uniforms and rush across into Malaya, shouting: "Japanese enemy — very terrible!" For credibility, and to make them look like Thai people, they would bring along a few Thai dancers.

As Tsuji covered each step of his mad plan, Ochi felt something missing, though he knew not what. Tsuji had admitted that the plan was based on a dream. Dreams could be good, but more often they were also an illusion.[18]

At Samah Harbour, Ochi's unit transhipped from the *Atsutasan Maru* to the *Kashii Maru*, a former luxury liner on the European and American routes.[19] They would sail right behind the *Ryujo Maru*, which carried Gen. Yamashita and 25th Army Headquarters in the first of the 20 ships that made up the invasion fleet.[20]

On board, they were briefed on chemical warfare. They must protect themselves, they were told, breathing in gas would kill them in three minutes. Ochi pondered the gas problem and Tsuji's dream plan as they began their approach toward the Thai and Malay coasts between 3 and 8 December.[21] A strange invasion it was going to be. So unlike their straight dashes into enemy fire on the China coast. Now they were expected to disguise themselves in Thai uniforms, wear gas masks, speak broken English, and learn Malay.[22]

That, at least, would come in handy. "Oi! 'Girl' in Malayan means 'Purunpan', and did you know what 'purun' means? — 'breast'!" amorous Ochi pointed out excitedly to his subaltern officer Morita.

"Yes? So what! What's the first thing you'll do when we land in Malaya?"

"Drink coconut milk."

"Liar! You're going after the girls."

"No. In this war operation we must forget about girls!"

"Well, at least just thinking of them should be O.K.," said Morita.[23]

Early on the morning of 8 December, Gen. Yamashita's 25th Army established two beachheads in Thailand, one at Songkhla, another smaller one at Patani. They were covered by a third assault on northeastern Malaya at Kota Bharu, where on Sabak and Badang beaches Maj.-Gen. Takumi Hiroshi's 23rd Brigade of the 18th Division lost a third of its initial assault forces to machine-gun fire from pillboxes manned by the 3/17 Dogra Regiment of the 8th Indian Brigade. Determined attacks by Hudson bombers flown from the nearby Gong Kedah airbase by No. 1 Squadron Royal Australian Air Force threw his second landing wave into confusion. These setbacks forced the transport vessels to retire out to sea, delaying the debarkation of the force of over 5,000 troops by a full day. But by midnight on 9 December Kota Bharu and its two airbases were in Japanese hands.

From Songkhla, the 5th Division occupied Haadyai, a major rail junction, and in a night attack on the border town of Sadao dispersed a screening force of mechanised troops from 11th Indian Division. The advance guard then routed the two battalions screening the Jitra Line, helping the main force smash through it by nightfall on 12 December. Alor Star, capital of the northern state of Kedah, and its important airbase fell the next day.[24]

When day broke after their unopposed landing at the coast town of Songkhla in South Thailand, the morning bulletin of 9 December 1941, brought Ochi and his men incredible news on the radio: "Yesterday, our Imperial Navy destroyed the United States Pacific Fleet at Pearl Harbor."

"Destroyed?" Pte. Yamate had doubts. "Is Pearl Harbor in Hawaii?" asked Cpl. Sanemori. Where did the news come from? They lost the radio station. First Class Pte. Honda fumbled with the machine until he found Radio Tokyo, between the Sydney and New Delhi radio bands.

The Japanese voice repeated the news solemnly. Ochi was dumbfounded — Pearl Harbor! that was America's mightiest naval fortress. How could one even get near it, much less attack it? The radio news must be fake stuff to boost morale.

But the voice went on steadily explaining all about Japan's successes as far as the Thai-Malayan border region. Well, that was true! Here they were indeed, successfully entrenched on the Thai coast. Perhaps the news was real?! Slowly the magnitude of their military successes began to sink in.

"If the Navy was able to destroy the Hawaiian base — we, the Army, will take Singapore!!" exulted the soldiers on their beachhead, still 1,000 kilometres from their war aim.[25]

Equally unopposed in central Thailand, the Imperial Guards Division heard the same news inside the arena of Bangkok's race course where, after crossing the Cambodian-Thai border, their long column of trucks had finally come to a halt. The American Fleet had been eliminated at Pearl Harbour, they were told, and everything between Bangkok and Kota Bahru on the East coast of Malaya was in Japanese hands.

Tsuchikane was stunned by the unexpected large scale gains in the new war theatre. The secrecy and training had all paid off, and the magnitude of the successful war front cast a spell on them. They were now more than ready to fight the British Army to the death! Japan had taken on the whole world by plunging into a large-scale war and all had gone well. When the first detailed news had sunk in, Tsuchikane and his men became serious and quiet, as they stood in the arena and comprehended that their time to die in battle had finally come.

A large number of Thai people had assembled at the race course. Many waved farewell as the troops remounted the trucks for the station to board the train for the Malayan border, where they would use bicycles to continue onward to Singapore.[26]

They pulled out of Bangkok station on wagons bursting with people and equipment, with Tsuchikane on top of a carriage, hanging on to the cargo by a strong rope. Thai hospitality greeted them everywhere, as they chugged through the paddy fields down South. Whenever they stopped at rural stations, local men, women, and children crowded round their wagons and offered the sweating soldiers coconuts to quench their thirst, bananas, papaya, mangoes, durian, and mangosteen. The tropical fare changed hands joyfully, and the soldiers viewed it as a sign of welcome. In return they gave them cigarettes. "Wakaranai." "Gomen nee!" "Sawardee krap!" None understood the other, but in the bustling heat hand signs and smiles did the job.[27]

When the cargo train disgorged them at the border town, they got out their bicycles from one of the wagons. It would have been difficult to cycle on Thailand's undeveloped road system all the way down to the Malayan border. But as soon as the soldiers crossed into British Malaya, a solid wide road welcomed them, like a red carpet, with rubber trees running down on both sides.[28]

The bicycles would facilitate hot pursuit and deny the enemy rest and reorganisation. Only the heat was a problem, causing the tyres to puncture frequently. A repair squad of two mechanics attached to every bicycle company would overcome that difficulty by each repairing an average of about 20 bicycles a day. Spare parts were easily available throughout Malaya since the cheapness of the Japanese bicycle had made them one of the country's chief exports to the whole of Southeast Asia.[29]

Tsuchikane's men quickly screwed the handles onto the frames, mounted their 40 kilograms of equipment and attached their weapons to the bicycles. Because their light machine guns and rifles glittered silvery in the sun, they were known as the "Silver Wheel Unit" in the Japanese press. Already in French Indochina, journalists had made much of their jungle training with bicycles. Tightening their chin straps, and waiting for the sign to depart, they were ready to make their mark as the "Malaya Silver Wheel Unit" and catch up with the 5th Division at the Perak River by 23 December.[30] From there the two divisions would march in tandem down the Malaya peninsula, the 5th following a central course, the Imperial Guards one along the West coast.

Rather than gratitude, it was jealousy that seized Ochi Harumi when he thought of their strong rear support. He had seen the photographs of the Imperial Guard's "Silver Wheel Unit" and read about them parading smartly about Saigon. Big deal, these "Imperial"

Fig. 4   Haircut in an oil palm plantation in Malaya.

bicyclists. They may have formed the first bicycle units, posing vainly on their bicycles for the Japanese press reporters, deluding the boys and girls back home into thinking they were the greatest looking "Silver Wheel Battalion" in the Imperial Army. And their stripes and extra stars and cherry blossom greenery adorning their uniforms were very smart. But how foolish to want to look smart on the battlefield! Ochi seethed. The Imperial Guards had absolutely no military achievements to their credit. Nothing like his 5th Division, which had occupied French Indochina first. They, too, had their bicycle battalions and they would show the Imperial Guards what fighting was all about.[31]

After breakfast his 11th Regiment left Songkhla for the next larger town of Haadyai, where Ochi envied the spacious homes, as they pulled up for a rest. These were not the squalid narrow buildings of Chinese towns on the mainland. The houses looked more as if inhabited by Indians or Eurasians or Whites.[32]

Suddenly he caught sight of a little girl across the street. He gave her a wink and tried to be friendly to her. But the seven-year-old was afraid and did not wink back. Her mother appeared and picked her up.

She didn't look like a Thai, and Ochi began trying to converse with her in broken English. The woman explained that her husband had malaria and was sick with fever, and wouldn't he come and visit them at home. Ochi followed them to their home. But he hesitated to enter. They might fear his wearing a uniform.

"Come on in," said the woman. She wanted to give him something. "What's your name?" she asked.

"My name is Ochi."

"Ochi? That sounds like 'watch'!"

Ochi smiled. He found the woman, whose name was Asuta, irresistibly beautiful, and laughed at her joke.

"Japanese don't like durians because they smell. But try it." Ochi's stomach turned at the stench, but it tasted good. She wrapped some of it in a handkerchief of hers.

"Will the Japanese soldiers kill a lot of English people?" she asked with concern.

"Don't talk nonsense," Ochi said. Asuta told him seriously that she thought nothing was more foolish than war. Just then, his unit was beginning to move on. He had to get back on his truck.

"Farewell Ochi!" Asuta saw him off.

"Forever Beautiful Asuta!" he shouted back, clinging to his precious souvenir, and the trusting welcome he would carry with him down the warpath.[33]

Three days later the Saeki Detachment, a battlegroup of less than 1,000 men, spearheaded a breakthrough that in 15 hours shattered the Jitra Line. Japanese staff officers took the position seriously, knowing it was built to be held for three months and manned by the entire 11th Indian Division. But this inexperienced formation, which consisted of only two rather than the customary three brigades, was poorly deployed and then caught off guard by the speed of the Japanese attack.[34] Ochi contemplated the night sky. They had suffered many casualties, but the gods had spared him, so far. Or was it Asuta's handkerchief that had protected him during the battle? He'd kept it in his left breast pocket all the time. Ochi's thoughts languished for a while on his brief encounter with Asuta in Haadyai. The beautiful Eurasian girl had given him a durian and her handkerchief. He would rather have had a kiss from her. He'd fallen instantly in love with her black eyes. All the mysteries of the East shone from them. Her handkerchief now wrapped in ecstasy his dreams. Who knows, it could soon be wrapping the urn of his own remains....

"God am I tired," muttered Ochi, "for heaven's sake, can't I have more delightful fantasies?! How I crave to undress my lovely Asuta...."[35]

After storming the Jitra position that protected the strategic airdrome of Alor Star, taking the city was easy. By eleven in the morning of 13 December the town was already mopped up and the 5th could continue their chase south.

News of the successful battle was immediately relayed back to the Imperial Guards following on the 5th Division's heels down from Thailand to catch up at the Perak River. It put strength into the "Silver Wheels" strokes, and the many repaired bridges they pedalled across told Cpl. Tsuchikane something of the speed with which 5th Division in front of them was pursuing the enemy. The weary cyclists in their dusty shirts, and their hats with backflaps to protect them from sunstroke, were already approaching the outskirts of Alor Star, which 5th Division had secured only two days ago.[36]

Fig. 5 Indians greet a Japanese soldier in Kuala Lumpur.

Strangely there were no ruins. The town must have been abandoned
in a hurry. It was encouraging to see people welcoming the long
rows of dust-covered cyclists. Many wore turbans. Those must be
Indians, Tsuchikane thought, as he pedalled along the dusty road
feeling weaker and weaker. What was the matter? Suddenly he lost
consciousness and fell by the roadside.[37]

"A bad case of diarrhoea," was the doctor's diagnosis, when
Tsuchikane regained consciousness. He had developed a 40-degree
fever pedalling into town, and after falling, had been picked up
by a local car. "Better diarrhoea than malaria," sighed Tsuchikane
relieved, as he lay in hospital, for the second time, waiting for his
fever to come down.

But the war could not wait for Cpl. Tsuchikane. His battalion moved
on without him to rendezvous with 5th Division. His commander
came to see him. "Cpl. Tsuchikane, I now have twelve men in sick
bay with malaria, diarrhoea, etc., like you. Presently none of you
can move before you get any better. I am placing you in charge of
these 12. As soon as you are fit to move, see to it that all come to
the front by the quickest way to re-join your unit."[38] It would be
their job to look after items not immediately needed in battle, such
as reserve clothes, blankets, and weapons.

Looking after the 12 junior and senior soldiers was troublesome. As soon as some felt better, Tsuchikane had them do bayonet practice, but the old roughnecks did not take his orders gladly. It wasn't long before they started to go out and loot and plunder. And this right under the nose of the military police already in town. Tsuchikane repeated the strict order: "Do not enter people's houses. If you need anything, tell me."[39]

All through their bayonet drills and guard duties, a 13-year-old youngster had been watching them in admiration. The Indian boy was curious about everything they did, and the men called him Taro. Tsuchikane took a liking to this fearless and good-hearted little fellow, and sometimes would give him some food. Taro didn't eat it, but always took it home. Tsuchikane found it difficult to converse with him in broken English, but one day, Taro invited the corporal to come and visit his home. Tsuchikane hesitated. He'd given strict orders not to enter the civilian houses. Now he was to break his own rule, even as a comrade warned him how dangerous it was to enter private homes.

But Tsuchikane trusted the boy so much, that he gave in to Taro's urgings and went over to his family's house. After asking him in, the father and mother were a bit confused and shy about what to say to this fellow Asian in uniform. Taro's five-year-old sister watched them all intently. Curiously she touched Tsuchikane's knee, then she nodded gleefully. It broke the ice. The mood changed quickly, with everyone nodding in approval, and Tsuchikane thereafter visited them daily.[40]

They had been in Alor Star just about a week, when the Military Police caught two of Tsuchikane's men breaking into a home. Then two more soldiers were marched off to the Military Police Station. Tsuchikane was immediately summoned to the Kempeitai officer-in-charge.

"What the hell do you think you're doing? Are you soldiers of the Great Imperial Army?" the Military Police corporal took delight in cutting an elitist Imperial Guard corporal such as Tsuchikane down to size. "As long as we have louts such as you, how do you think we can keep law and order in the cities? What are you bastards here for? I will lock every one of you up!"

Tsuchikane knew he stood no chance. Military Police were a special breed. They got extra military education and they, too, were selected from the finest. Even a non-commissioned Kempeitai corporal could roast any officer up to the rank of lieutenant with impunity. Tsuchikane knew he would not be let off with a simple apology. Best not argue with this military policeman. Tsuchikane straightened up, stood at attention, and answered in a clear and loud voice: "Yes, Sir!"

He was very pale and thought frantically. Here they were backstage, a tiny unit detached from their troops at the front, apprehended as criminals. If they were sent to the rear and shown off as unpatriotic elements, it would bring dishonour on the Imperial Guards and the disgrace would reach all the way to their villages back home. What a despicable situation! Even more unthinkable would be their shame if the news reached the front. What would his superiors and comrades think? "While *they* were fighting a life-and-death struggle, Cpl. Tsuchikane was relaxing behind in hospital and having himself a good time looting civilian homes with his band of soldiers...."[41]

Not once did Tsuchikane try to excuse himself or his men. Instead, he made a desperate appeal to his fellow corporal in the military police: "Please forgive me. Please let us do our best for our country and redeem and prove ourselves. Please let us return to our troops at the front as quickly as possible. Please accept my deepest apologies!"

Tsuchikane bowed very deeply, aware that his Imperial stripes and epaulettes and cherry blossom stars only made the Kempeitai only more irate. He knew there was not the slightest latitude for mercy. Nothing could be expected from this cold man in front of him.

"Go home," the policeman said. "Today I shall lock up only the four. Explain the crime to the rest of your men and bring them here tomorrow."

When Tsuchikane told his men about the arrests, everyone listened with drooping heads. Taro stood there, too, trying to understand what was going on. He didn't understand a word, but instinctively felt his friends were in a tight spot. Each one he asked: "What's the matter?"

Next morning, they all went to the Military Police Station, resigned to being locked up with the rest. When the police corporal called in only Tsuchikane, for some reason his words were much gentler. Tsuchikane asked to see the other men apprehended the day before.

Assembled in the next room, the looters admitted that they were guilty of having been taken by a sudden impulse of greed in the new war situation without realizing the severity of the crime that they were committing. The repentant four apologised profoundly to Tsuchikane, and pleaded to have their case reconsidered.[42]

When Tsuchikane returned to the Military Police officer's room, he saw to his surprise Taro, the Indian boy and his father, both decked out in ceremonial dress standing next to the Kempeitai officer. Taro threw Tsuchikane a happy smile.

"Corporal Tsuchikane," the Kempeitai addressed him solemnly, "for this one time only I will close an eye and let you go. It is your duty to return to your troops on the front without a moment to lose. There you will give your best. Do you understand me? Promise!"

The whole affair had taken an unexpected turn for the better only because Taro had persuaded his father to immediately go and plead with him the innocence of Tsuchikane and his men. Taro had told the Military Police officer that Tsuchikane had done absolutely no looting; he had been in daily contact with him and his men, and knew that they were not bad men. As a result, the four culprits were merely made to write an apology, while the others were given a strict reprimand and then allowed to go.

Tsuchikane and his men were immensely grateful to the little Indian boy and his father who had saved their reputation. The men became more docile and no longer absconded into town. Taro was happy, and worked all the more joyfully along side Tsuchikane's detachment, unaware that the happy situation would soon end.[43]

It was time to move on. While his men prepared everything for immediate departure, he began a frantic search for onward transportation. A liaison officer knew of a truck convoy about to head south, and Tsuchikane rushed over to negotiate with the artillery officer a ride to the front.

"It will be difficult to put all thirteen of you on one truck," the officer said, "but if you ride in twos on each truck I guess we'll manage. We won't be able to deliver you to your exact unit, but we shall drop you off close to the front."

Tsuchikane returned to inform his men. "Should we become separated on the way, it is your duty to make it back to your troops on the front on your own." He also tried to explain to Taro that they would be leaving for the front. The boy could not understand why his friends should suddenly depart and began to cry. Tsuchikane tried to explain the matter to the boy's father, as the Indian family looked on forlorn. Bundling everything carefully, Tsuchikane gave anything superfluous to Taro and his family.

Just when the convoy was about to depart, Taro came running to Tsuchikane with a gift for him. It was a beautiful silver bracelet. Tsuchikane was overwhelmed. It was as if a god were passing him the holy grail and a message saying, "Go forth and do your best in the name of the various peoples in Malaya." He thanked Taro and his family with deep bows, as the convoy set itself in motion, with the Indian family standing and waving until they were out of sight.

It had been a deeply emotional experience for Tsuchikane. Here in enemy territory he had made a friendship he would not forget for the rest of his life. How weird it was that he and his men had had to be set free by inhabitants of the very country they had come to occupy. Taro's silver amulet took on a deeper meaning. Tsuchikane discarded the "Thousand Stitch Belt", but Taro's silver bracelet he wore at all times proudly and with deep gratitude.[44]

They were approximately two weeks apart from their 4th Regiment fighting on the southern front. Where exactly were they? And how would they locate their units? Tsuchikane pondered these questions on their ride south down the West Coast, in the direction of Port Swettenham, where businessman Omori was then being held in the POW camp, about 500 kilometres away from his countrymen fighting their way southward.

Omori had never lived behind barbed wire or on two poor meals a day, consisting mostly of rice porridge. His only hope lay in the Japanese planes that he saw high up in the sky in increasing numbers. Omori wished with all his heart that the Japanese army would come and rescue them.

Because from the air their barracks would have looked like any other military camp, the inmates asked permission to make a Japanese flag from sheets to inform the Japanese planes that Japanese were interned here and must not be bombed. But the camp commander refused.

At Christmas they were moved because the Japanese advance on Kuala Lumpur was bringing the invading force near to the camp. Under cover of night, Omori and his compatriots were put on a ship that took them to Singapore Harbour. From there they were whisked off to Changi Prison by bus.[45]

The Japanese bombers they'd watched high above their camp at Port Swettenham gave the Japanese civilian prisoners confidence in Japan's grand strategy. Japanese equipment and troops, finely honed, were turning the Malaya Operation into a huge typhoon, the eye of which was Singapore. The spinning turbulence had been stealthily collecting troops from the farthest reaches of the Imperial realm, even from northern Manchuria where military policeman Onishi Satoru had been stationed. With growing speed, the winds rushed the elite troops toward the South China Sea, jettisoning them onto the Thai coast, where they all merged for a grand chase down the Malay Peninsula in an operation of unprecedented scale.

Ahead marched Ochi Harumi's machine-gunners, trying to keep up with 5th Division's crack Saeki Detachment, forging ahead with terrific speed at the very front. They were followed by the Imperial Guards, newly arrived from French Indochina and as yet unseasoned, but eager to show their mettle to the battle-trained 5th Division, and fight alongside them as frontline troops from central Malaya onward. All the while, Master Sgt. Arai Mitsuo's 18th Division Headquarters was standing by at Canton, ready to be picked up and whirled into the maelstrom.

On the very day that businessman Omori Kichijiro was moved from Port Swettenham back to Singapore, Military Police Lt. Onishi arrived at Hainan's Samah Harbour and received the glad news that Hong Kong had fallen on Christmas Day.

He had been stationed far away in the northernmost sector of the Japanese Empire. His Second Military Police Field Unit began the long journey south on 14 December 1941, travelling by truck and train to the port of Dairen, where they embarked on a 6,000-ton transporter.[46]

On New Year's Day at sunrise, as they entered the South China Sea, they gathered on deck to celebrate the first day of the 2,602nd year since the accession of their legendary first Emperor Jimmu. They washed their faces with precious water, and prayed for the victory of their Imperial soldiers and toasted the New Year with a little cold rice wine. Then they lined up on deck to salute commander Oishi with raised sabers and extend to him hearty New Year's greetings. Facing east, they prayed in the direction of the Imperial Palace, and ended by shouting three "Banzai!" — Long Live The Emperor![47]

After 11 days, they anchored off Songkhla. Land again! Onishi took the field-glasses and the shore leapt nearer. He saw the woods and the breaking surf, and brown roofs peeping through the palm trees. He feasted his eyes on the tropical vegetation along the coast, with row upon row of coconut trees. The land breeze blew in his face and smelt strongly of the minute coconut palms ashore and of frangipani, and the chill of it set him sneezing. He could not wait to go on land.

The landing craft carried the soldiers to a small jetty. A well-paved road led into Songkhla, where they assembled on a large square in the southern part of the city. The horses, too, were landed, and that night all camped out on the wide town square. The next day, leaving some of the horses behind in reserve, they headed in jeeps for Haadyai, arriving there in the evening.[48] The Thai city looked like any Overseas Chinese town and appeared to have been evacuated. No one was in the streets. Soldiers were billeted in the deserted market place, while officers quartered in empty Chinese rural hostels. The two-storeyed buildings had a cistern outside where rainwater collected, and they used it as a bathtub. After one month on board with little water, Onishi was happy to wash off the tropical sweat and grime. As he soaked and gazed into the star-studded southern skies, he never felt more grateful for water. And how good it was to sleep in a hotel bed. He looked around for a cushion and discovered the so-called Dutch wife of the South Seas and, making it his good friend, used the sausage-shaped bolster as a pillow.[49]

At the other end of the steadily narrowing theatre of war, Omori Kichijiro slept on a concrete slab in the middle of his narrow cell at Changi Prison in Singapore. The stony elevation served as a bed at night and a table during the day, and he had to take turns with his two fellow compatriots sleeping on the floor on either side of the concrete elevation. Food was hygienic, but meagre, and their only luxuries were a simple toilet in each room and shower facilities outside. But where on earth were their wives and daughters?

Japanese bombers broke the prison tedium almost every evening on their punctual run over Singapore. Then Omori and his friends would climb on each other's shoulders to catch a glimpse through the bars as the Japanese planes unloaded their bombs on the city.

When the situation got worse, British authorities decided to move the Japanese prisoners elsewhere. Unlike the trapped and desperate citizens who found it impossible to get a passage out of the doomed city, Omori and his group departed in mid-January on a British-paid voyage to India.[50]

As Omori steamed west out into the Indian Ocean, Master Sgt. Arai Mitsuo and his 18th Division approached the east coast of the Malay Peninsula. Standing by in China for one long month, they had been dying to get out of Canton and go to the front to share with their Takumi Detachment (that had landed successfully at Kota Bahru) the glory of taking part in the fight of the century.[51]

On 16 December, rumours flew about that they were to leave for the front on 20 December. Instead they received a standing order "to be ready for embarkation at any time". On 23 December they were told to be ready to sail on 25 December. This sounded definite; surely they would be at sea when the New Year arrived, and they threw themselves a big pre-New Year's party on the eve of their departure with all the bottles they'd accumulated. Only to be told the next day: "Stay on continuous stand-by!"

The wait became unbearable. In the market a non-commissioned officer overturned one fruit stall after the other, and with a great howl chased the shopkeepers down the road.[52]

Their long wait was due to operational uncertainties. The big question at 25th Army Headquarters was how to use the core of 18th Division standing by at Canton most effectively in the Malayan campaign. The initial plan had been for them to land at Endau, two-thirds of the way down the Malayan east coast towards Singapore, where a major battle was in the making. It would be fought against Australian battalions determined to stop the rout of Commonwealth troops along a defense line drawn straight across Malaya, from Muar on the west coast through Gemas in the centre to Endau on the east coast. While the Imperial Guards Division and 5th Division would take care of Muar and Gemas, Gen. Yamashita at first believed he would need the battle-seasoned 18th Division to cover his eastern flank at

Endau. It was for that pivotal battle that Gen. Yamashita had been
keeping Arai's regimental troops on continuous stand-by at Canton.

However, Japanese infiltration tactics, always managing to get in
behind enemy lines, proved enormously successful and caused the
Muar-Gemas-Endau line to collapse. It became clear that the decisive
battle was not going to develop in central Malaya, but would be fought
at Singapore. It was wasteful to risk the 18th Division in a dangerous
landing in the face of the enemy at heavily-fortified Endau. Instead,
it was decided to have the 18th Divisional Headquarters Regiment
sail on 7 January from Canton to Songkhla, where they would be
transferred to trucks and carried at top speed all the way down the
peninsula to be fresh for the battle of Singapore.[53]

High waves greeted Arai and the 18th Division when they waded
ashore at Songkhla on 23 January 1942. Settling in for his first night,
with his bayonet close at hand, Arai stared at the star-studded sky
of this strange new land. How much longer did he have left to live?

The sun was already high in the sky when they consumed a hefty
breakfast of rice and sour plum. During the meal, they noticed on
the main road a procession of people moving past them northwards.
Arai and his colleagues went over to watch the steady, silent stream
of men, women, and children escaping from the southern war zone.
According to Arai, the natives were naked up from the waist, men,
boys, but also the women and the girls, and the Imperial Guards
completely forgot about their breakfast as they stood and gawked
at the topless procession in their beautiful sarongs.[54]

Meanwhile, Omori and his 500 fellow prisoners reached India,
after a ten-day voyage. They berthed at Calcutta, and stayed there
for three days. At Changi Prison they had been divided into two
batches, and half of the original group from Port Swettenham had
not appeared. Nor had they seen their wives and daughters.

After a 70-hour train ride, they were unloaded in the middle
of nowhere and marched two hours with their bags to the bulwark
of an old fort. They filed through a huge entrance on which was
written "Pranakila". Inside, on a large patch of lawn, tents were lined
up in rows to which they were assigned, six persons to one tent.

One week later their missing families arrived, around 500 women and children, whom British authorities had held in separate camps on Blakang Mati (now renamed Sentosa) and other islands off Singapore.

Life at the Pranakila camp near New Delhi, on an Indian diet of curries, lots of beans and gallons of tea, was not uncomfortable. The women had their own quarters with partitions in between and their beds were lined up under the thick stone ramp which acted as insulation against heat and coldness. The men were treated according to the standards of Indian soldiers; they slept in hammocks, and when it got cold they were given hay in addition to a blanket. Slowly their numbers grew to around 3,000 as they awaited the day when they would return home.[55]

6

Fighting Down the Peninsula

ALL of them — Ochi and Miyake of the 5th Division, Lt. Onishi and his Military Police, Imperial Guard Tsuchikane, and Sgt. Arai of the 18th Division — would follow the same route, starting out from the small Thai fishing village of Songkhla to the rail junction town of Haadyai, past the bombed village of Sadao, and across the border, through the Jitra line into Alor Star.

It was in that Malayan town that machine-gunner Ochi Harumi and his men first tasted champagne. They had just entered Alor Star and were billeted in a wine merchants' house, where Ochi had taken a room on the second floor with a large double bed and the sheets arranged in a fluffy way. Smelling the sheets, the amorous Ochi immediately felt tormented by the fragrance of a ripe woman. Adding to his euphoria was the news of the sinking of the capital ships *Prince of Wales* and the *Repulse*. It called for a celebration! Ochi went downstairs to the bar.

"Here's something that looks like beer," Cpl. Sanemori said.

"That's not beer, it's champagne, an elitist drink that Westerners savour at Christmas," Ochi lectured him. They all had a taste and, from the larder, helped themselves to juicy tomatoes, sweet pineapples, branded whisky, biscuits, and chocolates.[1]

When Imperial Guard Tsuchikane came bicycling into Alor Star a few days later, the area was no longer a front-line city. Many buildings were off limits and secured by the military police. After their close brush with the military police, and the prospect of imprisonment and eternal shame, Tsuchikane and his men had been lucky to receive help from a 5th Division artillery officer who brought them to the front on his trucks. Passing Ipoh, about 200 kilometres south of Alor Star, they heard that the Imperial Guards had been fighting here not long ago. Moving on, they passed through Kampar and Tapah,

Fig. 6 Officer of the 5th Division, taken near Kuala Lumpur.

where Japanese infiltration tactics had wrought havoc on enemy lines all the way down to the Slim River, leading to a great debacle for the British. Motoring past the week-old battlefields, the air became malodorous and debris began to litter the road.[2]

Everywhere they found life-supporting "Churchill supplies" left by the retreating enemy, and later heard from frontline soldiers' stories of hot stoves, with lukewarm pots, ladles at the ready, and forks and knives still in place on dining tables. There was food galore, fresher the further south and the closer to the battlefront they got. Wherever they settled for the night, all was laid out. The brandy, the chocolates, even chewing gum — and cheese! Tsuchikane, who had never tasted cheese or tinned asparagus before, packed some of both to bring home to his parents. He would manage to hold on to his battlefield *omiyage* gifts for six years.[3]

The appearance of the Slim River area was bad. The British had lost 3,200 troops, mostly Indians, into captivity, along with 23 heavy artillery pieces, and 50 armoured vehicles at this last stand before Kuala Lumpur. It contrasted with the intact, whitewashed houses of Kuala Lumpur, abandoned as an Open City.[4]

Soon after Kuala Lumpur, driving fast, they saw the dust of other army vehicles ahead. Many Japanese troops crowded the road and there were ambulances, so the front could not be far. They would reach it tomorrow, Tsuchikane was told. Australian troops had mounted a strong resistance down the road at Gemas.

All day their truck had been like an oven. How many days had they been riding this furnace?[5] They got off for a last peaceful night. What would the battles be like? Tsuchikane turned over his perennial question as he fondled his bayonet, which the Japanese nicknamed *gobo*, because it was shaped like a burdock. Taking good care of it was rule number one; polish it in odd moments, like now, because a sparkling knife cut better. "'To be or not to be,' kill or be killed, the moment of truth is here." Tsuchikane gently tapped his sheath two or three times, "Gobo, guard me well."[6]

Roaring engines jolted him into being a warrior again, as they sped off into the early morning towards the pounding of cannon in the far distance. Approaching the front now meant business for the artillery soldiers who had been sharing their cramped trucks with Tsuchikane's men. "We're not gunners. How can we help?" thought Tsuchikane.

The artillery officer sensed their predicament. "How about staying on some more with our unit and give us a hand?" he asked during a stop.

"Thank you, Sir. Please tell us what to do."

They were near Gemas, where the Australian 2/30th was meeting the onslaught by Japan's 5th Division head on. The artillerymen deployed and set up their cannons and mortars. Tsuchikane and his men were told to unload the ammunition and carry the cases from the trucks to the artillery positions. Setting to, hoisting heavy loads, slowly they got the knack of balancing the explosives from the trucks to the guns. Some cases were marked with a red stripe but otherwise looked just the same, so they hauled those red-striped boxes up to the gun encampments, too.

"Put them back!" cried the first artillery man immediately upon glancing them.

"Back at once!" bellowed the captain.

Tsuchikane's men quickly returned the red-striped boxes. They had brought poisonous gas to the front. Chemical weapons were illegal since the World War I agreements. Tsuchikane got more worried. Utterly worn out, they all longed to be back with their own troops.[7]

When after five days of resistance the enemy finally retreated south, Tsuchikane and his companions drove past five of their own tanks, destroyed by ferocious resistance from Australian anti-tank gunners using 2-pounder anti-tank guns, backed up by infantry armed with Boyes anti-tank rifles. Gemas was a heap of rubble.[8]

Onward they rode on the hot truck, in mid-January, dirty and without a bath for days. Flies pestered their itchy skin, with all along the smell of death. Sometimes the burst from a machine gun caught their flagging attention. They had to be quite close to the front, with a battle on in full swing further up the road, as indicated by dead bodies strewn by the way side.

The convoy leader approached Tsuchikane.

"Corporal, your Imperial Guard Regiment is to the right. Malacca has already fallen. Your units must be fighting at Muar and Batu Pahat further down the coast. Our 5th Division artillery, however, is taking the central route and will go straight on to Segamat and Labis. You had better get off here and start looking for your own troops. You can requisition bicycles in this area. We pray for you." The two men bowed to each other in the jungle, Tsuchikane much deeper and longer, and they parted.[9]

Tsuchikane immediately ordered his 12 companions to commandeer bicycles, starting with two that were leaning against a nearby house. But the 28-inch saddles (two inches higher than the Japanese standard bicycles) forced them to adopt an exhausting half-standing, half-sitting posture that greatly slowed their progress.

At the next kampong a Malay family offered them bananas and coconut milk, and explained that many soldiers had been passing through and on to nearby Batu Pahat.

It was another two days before they finally ran into the 3rd Battalion of their 4th Regiment. "Your First Battalion is fighting more to the right," they were told.[10]

"Thank you!" Tsuchikane redirected his men off the road and into the rubber trees towards their unit. They had to push and carry their bicycles over the stumps, and felt very much like abandoning them, now that they were close to their battalion. But what if their original units were all advancing on bicycles?

"Lie down!" Tsuchikane yelled, when he heard voices ahead. With two of his men he crawled into the jungle to reconnoiter the situation. The words they heard were Japanese, no mistake. Quickly they got up and ran forward, shouting "Oooi. oooi!"

"Well, well, if it isn't Tsuchikane!" three or four of his old buddies cried out with delight. "Where do you come from?" "What happened?" "We thought you would never make it back."

The happy welcome lifted a tremendous burden from Tsuchikane's shoulders. He dismissed his group of 12 men who returned to their own companies, each treating their Alor Star arrests for looting as a close secret never to be revealed. The lost men were feted as heroes and gladly welcomed back into ranks that had been thinning. Many of their comrades had been killed, and a good third of their platoons lost to malaria and battle wounds.[11] Fortunately they had found their unit near a British depot, where they were able to exchange their filthy jungle clothing for fresh British uniforms.

The muffled sound of guns in the distance prodded the 1st Battalion on south, up and down the hills, on foot through rugged rubber tree terrain, when Tsuchikane's 2nd Squad saw dozens of

Fig. 7 Bicycle unit near Labis in Johor.

people dashing out of a compound ahead. The command came immediately:

"Front right — enemy! Distance 150 meters. Attack!!"

All rifles and machine guns spattered bullets. Some of the figures fell. The others fled left and right. Catching up with the fallen bodies, they noticed that this was not the white enemy. But the heat was on and the attack continued. They were pursuing a running target, and eventually got most of them.

Action completed, they collected the dead and checked them more carefully. It was as Tsuchikane had thought. All were natives. Seeing the Japanese approach, they had been frightened and tried to flee.

"We killed civilians. Why did we have to kill them?" Tsuchikane asked his senior corporal. It was the same question he had asked in China, when he could not understand why they had had to burn down the houses of Chinese peasants near Canton. Now this.

"How can we know they're non-combatants? You still don't understand anything!!"

"But of course."

Many of the fleeing group were heavily wounded and suffering. They were quickly disposed of with a bullet. Tsuchikane noticed that among the dead were also women and children. The battlefield was a tragic place. Had these people not left the safety of their shelters and trenches and tried to run away, they might have lived. There was no time to dig trenches for the bodies, and the corpses were left to rot in the sun. They moved on until they came to some empty houses, where they billeted for the night.[12]

Moving on through hostile territory the next day, they made contact with the real enemy. This was it. Here we go. Tsuchikane heard the leader shout: "Advance to the first three rows of rubber trees!" Another already cried: "Medics! Medics!!"

"Mount your bayonets!"

Tsuchikane was now a warrior, one of those whom another lowly soldier, fighting in the vicinity on the other side, Australian Gunner Russell Braddon, characterised as "squat, compact figures with coarse puttees, canvas, rubber-soled, web-toed boots, smooth brown hands, heavy black eyebrows across broad foreheads, and ugly battle helmets. Each man wore two belts — one to keep his pants up and one to hold his grenades, his identity disc and his religious charm — and when they removed their helmets, they wore caps, and when they took off their caps, their heads had been shaved until only a harsh black stubble remained. They handled their weapons as if they had been born with them. They were the complete fighting animal."[13]

Tsuchikane advanced. To be or not to be, live or die. An Australian soldier appeared out of nowhere; they engaged with naked bayonets, but Tsuchikane was quicker. The Aussie gurgled strangely, then fell to his knees. Tsuchikane pulled out his bayonet. It was smeared with blood. Anguish assailed Tsuchikane as he gazed at his red *gobo*. He had gone through the motions as if in a dream. He still couldn't quite grasp "killing the enemy". But the act was done. There was no going back. He must go on. He'd grown up. Suddenly he felt like a brave man all at once. That was what he had been trained to do for the past two years, and he had passed the test, had found the culminating purpose of war.[14]

In a similar way, Gunner Braddon had realized uneasily that there was a Japanese soldier just three rubber trees away. Terrified because of his ineffectiveness with the bayonet, Braddon moved to the tree in front of him and, as the Japanese ran crouching towards it, stepped out and thrust at the Japanese with a firmly-held rifle and bayonet. At the moment of impact, Braddon found himself thinking, "Just like a stop-volley at tennis." He spent the next hour musing, confusedly, over the unpleasantness of the situation. Daylight came. The victim of his stop-volley lay with his mouth wide open, showing good teeth. Braddon wished that he would shut it. And like Tsuchikane, Braddon realized now that he could survive the killing of many more men.[15]

After the battle, Tsuchikane's unit prepared to move on with speed. There was no time for elaborate burials. The infantrymen chopped off the hands of their dead at the wrist and put them in mess tins. These were easy to carry, body parts would be tagged and placed in urns, and eventually receive a proper burial. The corpses were buried on the spot.

Tsuchikane watched his comrades go through the pockets of the fallen Australian soldiers, greedily appropriating their wristwatches, like petty thieves. No one censured them. Why couldn't they just leave the dead in peace with their few possessions? "Does one become a pilferer on the battle ground?" wondered Tsuchikane.[16] He observed much degrading behaviour in these early days of his baptism under fire, as the soldiers combed each battle zone as though they were searching for lice. Mopping-up actions. Atrocities. Brutality. And always the random bursts of gunfire into trenches.[17]

Their fights in and around Batu Pahat (where Gen. Heath had hoped to pin down the Japanese forces on 21 January 1942, an Australian "Tobruk")[18] led to the fateful collapse of the final British-Australian line of defense in Malaya. The ruined village offered a gruesome spectacle. Tsuchikane noticed lots of Australian corpses, identifiable by their adventurous ranger hats, and also many villagers killed alongside the enemy.[19] Those who remained alive were in a state of terrified confusion.[20]

Tsuchikane's squad had penetrated deep into enemy positions, and he felt a tremendous insecurity as they stumbled along, sleeping even as they moved towards the narrow waterway that lay between Johor and Singapore.[21]

For the Japanese infantry, the early stage of the Malayan campaign was one big game of catch-up, a race over 1,200 kilometres of jungle following the narrow road linking Songkhla to Johor Bahru. Up front was the 5th Division, followed by the Imperial Guards Division. And just as Tsuchikane had been rushing to rejoin his Imperial Guards regiment on the front, Military Police Lt. Onishi Satoru and his 50 men were trying to catch up with Tsuchikane's Imperial Guards unit, to whom they were attached until reaching Singapore.

Their temporary dissolution as a unit had taken place in Songkhla, shortly after they arrived on the Thai coast in mid-January. To reach the front in the quickest way, Military Police commander Oishi had established six independent detachments with the following orders:

1. Let us not press the military too hard in their chase of the enemy to Kuala Lumpur.

2. Part of the Higashigawa unit (under Captain Higashigawa Yoshin) will remain here at Singora [Songkhla] and at Haadyai. The other part will be stationed in strategic positions north of Penang for the protection of military secrets, to intercept secret agents, and for other military police duties.

3. The Goshi unit (under Lieutenant Goshi Kosuke) will be attached to the 5th Division (under Lieutenant-General Matsui Takuro). The Onishi unit (under Lieutenant Onishi Satoru) to the Imperial Guard Division (under Lieutenant-General Nishimura Takuma).

4. Look for suitable transportation, press on with the main forces, and await further orders.[22]

With everyone scrambling south, Onishi had difficulty finding transportation. When trains started moving between Haadyai and Sungei Patani, he applied for boarding, only to be told that military police were not front line forces. He had to insist in several rounds of negotiations that they were indeed front line military police attached to the Imperial Guards before they were finally granted seats and arrived at Sungei Patani in the evening of 16 January.

At around nine o'clock that evening, several enemy planes bombed the airfield, and from the safety of their encampment they had an exciting bathing experience, soaking in oil drums while taking in the excitement of the battle.[23]

Fig. 8   Japanese troops in Kuala Lumpur.

Leaving Sungei Patani again posed a problem. Luckily a battalion of field artillery of the Imperial Guards Division was departing for the front. Onishi approached the commander: "I'm attached to the Imperial Guards and was ordered to move immediately up front. Could you please give us a lift even if we have to split up one to a car?" The commander agreed and they left Sungei Patani.

When they reached the 300-metre wide Perak River, the huge bridge was damaged, but engineers had already done a fine repair job. Vehicles were able to pass, even if passengers had to get off and walk as their cars moved slowly across the structure.[24]

By sunset they were in Kuala Lumpur. During an aerial attack that night, a shell sprayed sand on Onishi without hurting him. Japanese anti-aircraft guns fired back, but the enemy dropped flare bombs that lit up the town streets, so they had difficulty hitting the planes.

It was not long before they received the order from military headquarters: "Overseas Chinese are suspected of flashing signals to guide the enemy's airplanes. Go and investigate the situation!" Captain Oishi immediately dispatched a team to check on alleged "torch spies". Lt. Onishi doubted that the Overseas Chinese had the technical ability to guide airplanes by flashing torchlight signals; but he kept his thoughts to himself.[25]

The next morning, Cpt. Oishi supplied Onishi with two trucks and four drivers. With their own transportation at last, they passed bombed out Malacca at noon and headed for Muar, a large town situated on the south bank of the Muar River. But already on the north bank, where three roads merged, a congestion of trucks and soldiers brought them to a stop. The column started again and they went a little further, then stopped again. The stalled column extended as far as the Muar River.

They didn't make it into Muar that evening, and had to camp out on the north bank of the river because nothing was moving. During the night, a British destroyer directed a ferocious artillery barrage at the mouth of the river, and the shells exploded near their point of crossing. Nevertheless, Muar was soon occupied, and Onishi's party managed to cross the huge river the next day. It had a width of about 500 metres and a rapid flow of water. In the middle of the crossing, the superstructure of a 5,000-ton ferry protruded from the water, probably sunk by the enemy while retreating.[26]

After crossing to the south bank, Onishi drove straight to Imperial Guards Division Headquarters located in the rubber plantation. There Lt.-Gen. Nishimura Takuma and his Chief of Staff Officer, Imai Kamejiro, welcomed him warmly. Leaving them three of his men as bodyguards, Onishi began his job as the Kempeitai chief attached to the Imperial Guards Division.

First of all, he had to sort out the language problem. The Russian they'd learnt in Manchuria was of no use here. Onishi needed someone who could speak both Japanese and the local languages. Two Japanese women married to native Malays showed up. Originally from Kyushu, they were former *karayuki-san*, ex-prostitutes, and could speak both Japanese and Malay. With an additional Overseas Chinese from Taiwan who spoke some Japanese, Onishi's unit launched into their main job, which was arresting stragglers and spies.

But they were good at finding many other things as well: a large quantity of clearly-printed coloured maps in the government buildings and schools; two warehouses full of rice on the outskirts of Muar; 600 drums of gasoline in a rubber plantation, abandoned caches of arms and ammunition, and vehicles, all of which caused them to be swamped with urgent demands from officers of every unit. The Chief of Staff was very pleased and instructed them to go on searching.[27]

The military police also supported the special "F-Kikan" intelligence in its effort to reform British Indian soldiers into Japan-friendly Freedom Fighters for an independent India. The F-Kikan had set up an office in Muar, in front of which Indian soldiers were queuing to disarm and surrender.[28]

Keeping discipline among the troops was a more difficult task. On the coast near Senggarang, three soldiers had been supervising provisions for the next war operation. When a woman living nearby approached, not knowing her intentions, they took turns raping her, alleging later that she neither raised her voice, nor resisted. When the Kempeitai investigated the incident based on the deposition of her husband, it transpired that she had been so terrified of the Japanese soldiers that, when she chanced upon them and was told to stop, she was slow to respond. Without thinking further, the soldiers raped her one after the other. When the Kempeitai summoned the victim and her husband, the couple showed no inclination to proceed with litigation, and the case was dropped, with only a severe warning given to the soldiers. Crimes of this magnitude at the height of the campaign were decided on a suitable basis according to the situation in the field, and often resulted in no more than a stern warning.[29]

On 31 January, Onishi and his men approached the Straits for the first time. An indescribable feeling seized their hearts when they laid eyes on Singapore, a short distance away, the island for which they had come all the way from Manchuria. Some soldiers caught a young pig and made a delicious soup. After supper, they moved forward to Masai at the tip of the peninsula facing the Straits, where the Imperial Guards Division was preparing for the attack.

Headquarters needed above all intelligence on the enemy. Onishi and his men searched for people who had left Singapore and could tell them about troop numbers and the British and Australian positions on the island. Every day they worked until midnight, but the statements only exasperated Headquarters since they tended to grossly underestimate the troop numbers of the enemy.[30]

While Onishi was preparing soft intelligence reports for the coming battle of Singapore, Master Sgt. Arai Mitsuo and the main forces of the 18th Division were still at Songkhla, facing everyone's problem of how to proceed south. Fifth and Imperial Guards Divisions were reluctant to spare them any of their trucks for transportation down to Johor Bahru. This so incensed Campaign Manager Tsuji Masanobu that he personally phoned the logistics people in charge at each division: "If you have none to spare, that's too bad. Then Lt.-Gen. Mutaguchi Renya will be in an awkward position to get his men down for the battle of Singapore and you will have to go it alone."

At once, the two divisions dispatched 150 trucks each. Relieved and grateful, Gen. Mutaguchi ordered that they would leave on 24 January: "We will depart tomorrow for the front, in 50-truck convoys, each leaving at hourly intervals from 10 a.m. sharp."[31]

Arai, attached to Regiment Headquarters and part of the first group to leave, went to check out a suitable vehicle for Headquarters personnel. A wide variety of American brands greeted him at the truck pool: splendid Fords, Chevrolets, and Dodges, but for the battalion and regimental commanders, he chose a heavy British Austin.[32]

On the seventh day of their thousand-kilometre journey, covered in six legs of 180 kilometres a day, they came to a halt in the Sultanate of Johor, around 15 kilometres west of Kluang, where Gen. Yamashita had located his 25th Army Headquarters.

Kluang was the meeting point for all three divisions. The 5th and Imperial Guards Divisions had already passed through, leaving liaison officers behind as their main forces continued on to the very tip of the Peninsula. Gen. Yamashita was very happy to see Lt.-Gen. Mutaguchi with all his soldiers intact, not a single one lost in a mindless landing previously planned for Mersing. He could now line up the entire army of three divisions and throw these first class veterans from China against western forces across the Straits of Singapore.[33]

The Takumi and Koba Detachments, both belonging to the 18th Division, also arrived at the Kluang Headquarters, exhausted but right on time for the coming finale. Slowly the 114th Regiment was able to form a picture of what had happened to their crack troops who had born the brunt of the invasion at Kota Bahru. Five minutes after landing commenced at 2:15 a.m. around eight kilometres north of Kota Bahru, the sinking of their troop transporter *Awagisan Maru* had preceded the destruction of the *Arizona* at Pearl Harbour by 70 minutes, making it the first vessel destroyed in the Pacific War. Owing to the weather, their attack on Kota Bahru had been advanced by one hour because of high waves. It was the only adjustment in the overture to the Pacific War and resulted in an earlier attack and earlier losses than Pearl Harbour, usually considered the first action of the Pacific War.[34]

From Kota Bahru, the Takumi Detachment had hurried south to the train station of Kuala Krai, setting in motion a great escape by rail of the entire British North-Eastern defence force. Twenty-two days later, half-way down the east coast of the Malay Peninsula, Takumi stormed Kuantan on New Year's Eve, rounding out a stupendous year for the Japanese forces. From Kuantan, Takumi swung west, moving inland towards Kuala Lumpur while the Koba Detachment continued on down the east coast to capture Endau and the strong Mersing fortifications.[35] Mutaguchi was overjoyed to see both Koba and Takumi alive. He was once more in control of his entire 18th Division — with the exception of the Kawaguchi Detachment, which was in Borneo, and doing splendidly.[36]

Arai's 114th Regiment, whose task was to protect and move 18th Division Headquarters, was told to establish a billet 20 kilometres south of Kluang, at Shimpan Renggam, in one of the many rubber plantations. Renggam was the rubber-rich region businessman Omori Kichijiro had been forced to leave behind, when he had handed over his Senda Renggam Estate to Mr. Husband of the Anglo-Thai corporation two months earlier. And even as Yamashita's troops were clomping all over the entrusted rubber estates, Husband, now in Singapore, was keeping the accounts dutifully under the most adverse circumstances during heavy bombing of the island. The Senda Renggam Estate accounts handled by the Anglo-Thai Corporation were kept up to date until the entries stopped on 14 February.[37]

7

Crossing the Straits in the Face of the Enemy

For some time we were at a loss to know how the Japanese had conveyed their landing-craft to the Johore Straits, as it did not seem possible that they could have been brought round by sea without our knowledge.... It must be admitted that the Japanese feat in mounting this attack in the space of about a week was a very fine military performance... completion and implementation in that short time would have done credit to the staff of any first-class military power....

Lt.-Gen. A.E. Percival,
The War in Malaya

OCHI Harumi's 5th Division marched in the front lines, on to the Straits at the tip of Johor.

It was an unusually quiet afternoon.

"Johor Bahru — berry far?" Ochi asked the Malayan boy standing in the road watching the battalion pass.

"No, not far," he laughed with shining black eyes and white teeth, completely unafraid of the soldiers.

"Are British soldiers still around?"

"No."

"Seen any Japanese soldiers?"

"No, but yesterday all British fled into Singapore and blew up the causeway."[1]

After three o'clock, Ochi and his men reached a ridge that allowed a sudden view of the Sultan's palace with its white tower. Before them sprawled Johor Bahru, and beyond it the island of Singapore, the prize they had come to collect.

"Who's that there?" shouted a soldier.

"That must be the Okabe regiment's Kobayashi battalion," Ochi said. They'd stolen a march on them. Already the Japanese flag flew from the Sultan's palace. The conquest of the Malay Peninsula was complete.[2]

"It will take you eighteen months and five divisions to take Singapore," Field Marshal Goering had lectured Gen. Yamashita in Germany. Well, they had reached Singapore in two months with only three divisions. Just 35,000 Japanese soldiers had defeated 80,000 British, Indian, and Australian troops.[3] The Japanese had lost 1,793 men, the Commonwealth troops 25,000. The Japanese counted 2,772 wounded, whilst the British number was not known. In 55 days they had covered 1,100 kilometres. Every day they had advanced an average of 20 kilometres, fought two battles, and repaired four or five bridges.[4]

No, they were not a militaristic country, mused Ochi. But they would gladly sacrifice their lives to capture the island that symbolised Anglo-Saxon world domination and now lay silently waiting beyond the Johor Straits. He could not say why they would die for it. No, it certainly wasn't militarism. Perhaps it was simply the price to pay for their rise in history, and, who knew, perhaps their fall one day thereafter. But now they were on the rise. They must swoop down on the fortress island across that glistening stretch of water, even if they incurred heaven's heaviest retribution.

Their Ichikawa Detachment had been constantly on the go, except for a three-day break at Kuala Lumpur. In those 50 days of jungle fighting the soldiers had lost on average ten kilograms. At Shanghai, Ochi had weighed 72 kilos. After the Malaya battles, his weight had come down to 55 kilos, a loss of 17 kilos, or 340 grams each day.[5]

Regimental Headquarters had already arrived several days earlier at Johor Bahru. This was their last stop before the final assault, and a few days of calm and rest in the jungle would do them good. The unit was ensconced under the sheltering leaves of rubber trees in the Skudai delta near a creek deep in the jungle, a cooling pool in the stream relaxed their bodies at the end of the day, when they gathered there to wash themselves, do laundry, swim, or take a stroll. It was bliss down by the murmuring brook. Only an occasional shell broke the silence. Noise from the real world. They knew not where it landed, only that it came out of Singapore.[6] They might know more if they climbed the hill, but it was out of bounds.

When Ochi decided to climb the forbidden hill, he took with him James, an artillery lieutenant, with whom he had struck up an acquaintance. The British prisoner of war might be useful in pointing out a few things about the impregnable fortress. James was tall and an odd bird, who had protested being sent back into custody of the rear troops.

"Do you intend to cross the Straits?" James asked gratuitously as they walked up the hill.

"Isn't that what we have covered a thousand kilometres to come down here for?"

"Please take me across with you," James said suddenly.

"Don't be foolish! Do you think we can launch our offensive by taking along prisoners of war? There would never be an inch of space on the assault crafts."

"Try to hide me on one of the landing craft!" James persisted.

"What rot — you don't want to die in a hail of bullets from your own men!"

James looked at Ochi for a long time. "Sub-Lieutenant Ochi, do you take me for a fool? Do you think I'm crazy? I want to witness the heroic Japanese onslaught at first hand."

"I see," Ochi said.

"Sub-Lieutenant, I would not ask anyone else for such a favour." Artillery Lt. James now spoke to Ochi almost in the tone of a superior. "But I thought by asking you this favour, you would grant it."

"Why?"

"Because you are a true man of the East."

"Of course I am. But we all are from the East."

"No, that's not true. Not all have the quality of inscrutability."

"We all are inscrutable. We do not show our feelings like you Westerners do."

"You in particular are a striking example of Asian inscrutability. But look, I'm not trying to discourse on this subject. All I would like is for you to take me across the Straits in your first line of assault."

"You will only die. Do you want to die at the hands of your own people?"

"No, I don't want to die. But if I do, that's OK. All I want is to observe the battle as a military officer."

"You're a very strange fish, you know," Ochi replied.

James had been with them for five days, and he was on speaking terms with Ochi's colleague, Yamaguchi, too, and from him downwards on greeting terms with everyone in Ochi's platoon.[7] James knew a lot about Japanese soldiers. He was keenly interested in the Japanese and their psyche, and why they were all so marvellously confident that they would conquer Singapore.

From their elevation, Ochi and James looked across to Singapore. Belching smoke rose like big black pillars from the burning tanks. The causeway had been blown away in the middle, clearly separating Singapore Island from Johor Bahru.

A single airplane came trundling in. "It's a Hurricane!" James exclaimed.

"Once we were discovered by one of those planes," Ochi smiled wryly.

"You were swept by its fire," James said.

"Well, it seemed to have trouble firing. Instead, we fired," said Ochi.

"What — with that machine gun?"

"Yes, we have anti-aircraft devices. That day only one aircraft approached. So we only brought down that one single plane."[8]

James scanned Singapore with the mien of a poet.

"There is Tengah airfield!" Ochi said.

"You do know Singapore's geography well," James marvelled.

"Well, let's see ...," Ochi showed off some more, "we cannot see Bukit Timah from here, but over there, that must be the hills of Mandai, with three oil tanks burning. And down by the coast one can still see some cruisers around."

"Of course. At least more than ten," said James.

"Then we shall have to line up four heavy 50mm guns to destroy Seletar Harbour. Otherwise the crossing will be difficult, won't it?"

"Do all of you have this strategic knowledge down to Second Lieutenant?" asked James. "It's unthinkable in Britain. And when the commander dies in battle, it causes much confusion."[9]

Ochi said nothing.

"The Japanese die for their Emperor, don't they," James probed deeper.

"It's a very difficult question," Ochi said.

"But isn't it so? We learned it that way."

"Where? In the Army?"

"No, at school."

"What did you learn?"

"OK. Well, the Japanese believe the emperor is descended from the gods. They have to obey his orders absolutely."

"Well, that's more or less true," said Ochi.

"It means you, too, believe so."

"Well, in England, how do you think of His Majesty the King?" asked Ochi in return.

"We think that from early times, he is the descendant of a family line of monarchs who have exerted themselves most for England. Today they are still the most beloved and respected family in England," said James.

"I see. But isn't there more to the Royal family? Even though, today, you have a Parliament in which you all gather under a prime minister, where on earth is the real foundation of your country? Don't you British have the same feeling of divine duty to be loyal to the Royal family? If the King were any ordinary human being, would it be natural to bestow upon his descendants the same respect and privileges only because he is a child of the monarch?" paried Ochi.

"All this is not logical, Second Lieutenant. It has to do with the feeling of love among the British. It's not so much divine loyalty and duty."

"Isn't it? It's exactly the same with the Japanese. But whether you call it a people's devotion, duty, or love, we shall never come to an understanding in the little time we have here."

"Quite."

Ochi looked into the blue transparent eyes and laughed.

"Maybe I *will* take you along into the battle for Singapore," Ochi said. "Do you know how much artillery is on the island?"

"Who knows," said James, "there must be four to five thousand pieces."

"More or less," Ochi said, "there are about one thousand, you understand."

"Soon the attack will be on."

"About your coming along, you must of course keep it a secret from the other soldiers," Ochi said.

When all of a sudden cannons started firing in their direction, the two ran down the slope, catching their breath only in the ravine when they turned to look back. Substantial fire had been trained on them. Perhaps the enemy had seen their silhouettes on the top of the hill.[10]

In camp, orderlies were preparing a hot bath in drum cans from which steam was rising.

"Where did you get those drums from?"

"We exchanged our pineapple cans against the transport soldiers' large empty drums." Ochi's unit had found superb pineapple juice in a pineapple factory nearby. Transport soldiers had gladly parted with their large empty drum cans for pineapple juice in return, with some pie thrown into the deal. Now they could make *ofuro* [hot baths], and when the water was piping hot, Ochi jumped into the drum.

But his body seemed to get stuck to the bottom of the drum can.

"Hey, Adjutant! What's that?"

"It's pineapple juice!"

Shots. Nervously Ochi tried to extricate himself from the drum, which started rolling down the soft slope toward the river pool. Should he stick his head out or keep it in? The drum rolled down for about 20 metres until it hit the cool water with a splash. When the water reached his neck he tried to swim away.

Cpl. Sanemori, Aoyama, Ito, Yamanote, Morita, all ran down to the pool to see what was happening. Sanemori jumped into the pool to help his boss, and even James jumped in. Splashing about, James in his excitement let out a raucous laugh. Suddenly Corporal Sanemori silenced James with a strong blow to the head, putting him in place: "Arsehole! What's so funny?"

Holding his head, James quickly sought out Ochi's side. It was so funny that Ochi now himself let out a loud laugh and everyone joined in the brouhaha.

"Idiots!" shouted Yamaguchi, "lift out the drum!"[11]

The drum episode that evening in Ochi's room, was the main topic, when at ten Lt. Shimada appeared at the door.

"We're all same level officers in here, you, too, Shimada, don't be shy, come on in."

"I'm sorry, but you're all weaklings. Not used to drink!" he said as he sat down opposite Ochi.

"Wrong! We're just being polite. Holding back. Waiting for you." Soon the evening had heated up sufficiently for Shimada to let the cat out of the bag: "The main forces of Eighteenth Division have just arrived." That was impressive news.

"They are stronger than the Imperial Guards Division," Aoyama rattled on; "it's great that they came all the way through the jungle, past the tigers and elephants!"

"It's about time," another threw in, "our unit lent them forty trucks to get their asses from Songkhla down here."

Fresh ammunition had arrived with them, which was even better news. Boxes with thousands of rounds for each mountain gun. They came in ten-box units, each containing 10,000 rounds to be distributed among the 500 small and large artillery pieces assembled at Johor Bahru.

Their talk drifted to the position of their C.-in-C., Gen. Yamashita, over there, entrenched on the fifth floor of the Sultan's palace, a grand eagle's nest from which to oversee the invasion of Singapore island.

"What, from that glasshouse?"

"Yes," nodded Ochi.

The day to cross the Straits was fast approaching.

"What shall we do with James?" asked Sanemori.

"Well, let's not hit him too much," Ochi side-stepped the issue cleverly by returning to the night's topic of the drum adventure, and soon had them all roaring with laughter again.[12]

Singapore — Asia Dominatrix. For a hundred years the tiny island had been at the heart of European domination from Malacca, to Djakarta, Manila, and Shanghai. It was one of the world's four big strategic harbours (next to Gibraltar, Pearl Harbour, and Malta), home to the world's second largest floating drydock, protected by an array of coastal artillery that included five 15" guns, the heaviest such guns so deployed in the British empire, and defended by aerodromes at Tengah, Kalang, Selangor, and Sembawang. Three were on the island, but the other was were up-country and already in Japanese hands.

In early 1942 Singapore lay prostrate, and utterly at the mercy of Japanese troops who had come in through the back door. The colours of the high-flying Union Jack were fading fast, as the Japanese army prepared the final attack by first of all evicting to the north all residents living within 20 kilometres of the Johor Straits. The railway troops and sappers cut roads, laid track and built bridges in the Johor Bahru region. Engineers cleared the jungle and prepared launch sites in the Skudai estuary from where the main assault would take off down Skudai River into the Straits. Transport soldiers wheeled ammunition boxes and small motorised folding boats to relay stations and ammunition dumps organised near the embarkation points. Crocodiles waddling into the water became calories for the sappers, and within a few days, the creatures disappeared completely from the vicinity.

Screened by the jungle, the immense operation largely evaded British and Australian intelligence. Hidden deep in the foliage, artillery units built gun emplacements, carried box after box of ammunition to their positions, and endlessly calculated angles and ranges to enemy positions based on their poor surveys. To prevent the enemy from releasing oil into the Straits and setting it on fire, Gen. Yamashita ordered every oil tank in sight pounded and set ablaze.[13]

The huge preparatory operation to cross the Straits was supposed to be completed by noon 7 February. This would give the troops four days to capture Singapore by Kigensetsu, 11 February, the birthday of legendary first Emperor Jimmu and a national holiday.

However, on the seventh only Army artillery was able to confirm "preparations completed". All other divisional staff officers longed for one more day of preparation, 8 February.

The General Staff Office was angry. Nothing was impossible. Military directions were cast in stone. Orders were absolute — that's all they knew.

At this point, Gen. Yamashita stepped in decisively to extend battle preparations by one more day. This unusual generosity earned him tremendous admiration from every divisional commander down the line. Everyone pledged in his heart to honour their leader by doing their very best in the coming battle.[14]

The Imperial Guards Division had massed to the east of the blown up causeway, their task to feign an impending attack on Britain's huge Sembawang naval base directly across the straits. By spreading their

36 field cannons, 12 regimental cannons, and four heavy cannons on a wide arc, their bombardment from early in the morning on 8 February was meant to trick the defenders into believing that the main attack was developing in this sector, as the British expected.[15]

In reality the main assault by the 25th Army would take place west of the causeway. The 5th and 18th Divisions lay there in wait to land after midnight in Singapore's Kranji and Choa Chu Kang mangrove swamps and make their way to Tengah airfield early in the morning of 9 February. After taking the airfield they would advance to the Jurong highlands, and on the following day capture Singapore's highest point, Bukit Timah. From there they would secure the reservoir area and, if the enemy had not yet surrendered, they would launch a full attack on the city of Singapore.

At this point the Imperial Guards Division dissented, and on 7 February they requested 20 to 30 collapsible launches.

"What for?"

"Tonight we're landing on Ubin Island."

"What?" Col. Tsuji Masanobu felt his campaign management challenged, if not ridiculed, and immediately set out for Imperial Guards Division Headquarters. Ubin Island was an uninviting place of rocks and bauxite. But the east side offered high elevations from which Britain's Changi and Seletar fortifications spread below only a couple of hundred metres away. Pulau Ubin in Japanese hands offered a strategic advantage, and reinforce the idea that the assault would come from this direction.

"OK." Tsuji decided to go along with this addition to his plan. "Let's take it!"[16]

Only a couple of 4th Norfolk patrols were on Ubin Island, and they quickly escaped back across the Straits to Changi. The strategy worked. British forces began to re-deploy reserves from their main forces positioned in the causeway area to Changi's eastern front where now they expected a further attack to materialise.

Lt.-Gen. Nishimura wanted one more change in the initial battle plan. It galled him that his Imperial Guards were relegated to a diversionary role by having to stay behind the 5th Division in a secondary line of attack. After all, they were frontline troops. Elite soldiers; the best. Nishimura wanted to open a new front, immediately

Fig. 9　Defensive works along the Straits between Johor and Singapore.

west of the causeway on the left side of 5th Division; this would give his division their own front and allow them to advance shoulder to shoulder with 5th and 18th Divisions in one continuous front line.

Although battle plans, once issued, were rarely changed, Gen. Yamashita could easily reject form and opt for substance if the situation warranted it; plans could be rewritten, and he did not lose face thereby. In a way, Yamashita admired the new plan to attack together *en masse*, even though it would leave the main attacking force without reserves. And so he let Nishimura have his way.[17]

All the while, 5th and 18th Divisions were standing by quietly on the western front in the Skudai river estuary. Once or twice they lobbed a shell across to test the enemy, but their fire was not returned.

More miraculous still, on their side, the Sultan's looming tower escaped bombing completely.[18] Perhaps the British did not want to damage the Sultan's precious possession, or did not anticipate that the Japanese would set up headquarters in such a lofty place.[19] But holed up in the five-storey observation tower Gen. Yamashita had chosen the glass-enclosed top room as his observation post. From this perch overlooking the Straits, Gen. Yamashita sent a telegram to each division: "Am watching you all from the Sultan's Tower above." The brief sentence inspired his soldiers down in the field: "We will conquer Singapore!"[20]

The 5th Division had quietly been selecting their landing points all afternoon. They would come ashore in the mangroves and swamps in the Lim Chu Kang area held by the 2/20th Battalion of the 22nd Australian Brigade under Brigadier Taylor, some 1,500 metres away.

Ochi fixed in his mind one peculiar tree on the other side to the left of which he would land his unit. A strong tide would carry toward the enemy line, which appeared to be held with a thin group of machine-gun trenches.[21] The next 30 metres he imagined to be swampy grassland, with slight elevations beyond, held probably by one large machine-gun. Ochi quickly sketched the topography of their landing scene and the enemy positions and handed it to his subordinate, Second Class Soldier Honda who looked at his crude attempt at a map and asked: "Are those machine-gun positions arranged in a three-storey house?" drawing laughter.

"It may look like a house on paper, but the real situation has depth, is more dispersed over a wide distance," replied Ochi, trying to keep a straight face.[22]

In the evening Ochi's machine-gun company assembled in the rubber plantation, squatting in the dark, and James looked on fascinated as the company commander gave a pep talk. "The enemy across is around 70,000 soldiers and trying for a last stand of Singapore. Our forces depart Johor Bahru at midnight to deliver the coup de grace and to conquer and occupy the island of Singapore!" Capt. Itami's voice thundered in the jungle.

Tonight I'll get it, mused Ochi, as he stepped down through the rubber trees to his embarkation point. It was dark and to their left in the distance they could hear the rumbling of the Imperial Guards guns, a violent non-stop "Pa-pa-pa-pa!" Sappers had cut paths in the jungle, each leading to prepared secret harbours along the Skudai River. White arrows showed Ochi the way down to his embarkation point. He began to walk in muddy water. The mud got deeper, seeping into his clothes and shoes, and reaching his thighs. Worried about the boats running aground, engineers had fixed the embarkation points far from the shore. Unfortunately they had made their calculations only from the surface of the mud to the surface of the water. For the infantry, however, the real depth reached all the way from the bottom of the mud, where they were now stuck.

Engineers furthermore had miscalculated the timings of the tide. They knew about the Straits two metre-tidal difference over 24 hours, but had not taken into account the finer three hour-difference, from actual boarding time to departure time, between nine in the evening and midnight. The soldiers cursed the idiotic mess as they squiggled towards their too far out collapsible launches like 4,000 muddy rats, trying frantically to scale the sides of the boats, losing several of them during the ordeal.

All the while, sappers were shouting out the boat numbers for the various platoons, waving their hands, calling the artillery and assigning them reserved gun emplacements on the folding boats. Overseeing the chaos, the eerie silhouettes of the engineers on the boats called out in low, leaden voices, looking very chic in their managerial positions.[23]

"So you're taking him along," whispered Yamaguchi.

"Shut up! Not a word." Under cover of night, Ochi had secretly managed to put one more charge on board. Without a word, James was gallantly following Ochi to his boat. Such a man was James. He would really come along. Those had not been empty words up on that hill. James was excited, but acted with composure. Skilfully he negotiated the side and lay on the bottom of the boat, where thanks to Sgt. Yamaguchi's broad shoulders, he remained concealed.[24]

Ochi's first machine-gunner platoon was attached to 12th Company, crossing the Straits on the left side of the front battalion. His immediate boss, Lt. Oue (replacing the 12th Company commander who had been injured), sailed along with Ochi's platoon. Oue placed himself to the left at the front of the vessel and Ochi to the right. Two engineers sat at the motor behind with the captain. Each captain had a schedule that he had to follow. The tide was ebbing, making the river narrower, causing ships to bang against each other. It was time to leave.

A signalman at the tail of the ship communicated with the other ships by flags, moving his arms up and down. Ochi's boat left its moorings and picked up speed down Skudai River into the Johor Straits — 150 boats roaring all at once. The wolf pack quickly reached the Skudai's wide mouth by the Straits, where they spread out, making way for the ships pouring into the Straits behind them. Owing to the uneven coastline, the enemy did not spot the vast number of boats spitting out of Skudai River to hug the coast in the shelter of its raggedy inlets. The launches drifted sideways close to the Malayan coast to await the massed crossing at midnight sharp.

The Southern Cross shone left above them. It was almost time. Ochi moistened his lips, which immediately felt dry again. He peered into the darkness, trying to see the tree that during the day had risen conspicuously out of the water at their intended landing point on the opposite side. Whenever he glanced into the boat, 20 men stared right back at him.[25]

"Look! The Southern Cross." Ochi unscrewed his water bottle and held it up. They uncorked their bottles, too.

"Kii, kii" went the corks, followed by two or three gulps. All was quiet. Ochi watched his men drink slowly. He was proud of them. In this situation they were unusually relaxed. How far into the Straits would they make it before being spotted and destroyed?

"All are more relaxed than me," he thought, as he watched James hold his helmet in both hands. "Was he afraid after all?" But this was not the time to speak in English. Ochi glanced at his watch. It was one minute to midnight.

"It's midnight," Ochi turned to Lt. Oue.

"Well, then, Captain, shall we slowly get a move out into the sea?" the lieutenant said in an unconcerned voice, but loud and clear. To their right, a flurry of boats dashed into the open Straits. They could make out five to six launches, and as many on their left.

"Rev up the engines to nine hundred!" shouted the captain, as the coastline fell behind.[26] Like the massive start of a grand marathon, the 300 boats sped into the middle of the Straits.

The short journey across seemed like an eternity. The opposite coast gradually came closer upon them, with the small tree they were aiming for becoming a huge towering image.

They were half way across — another 500 metres, 400....

Something flashed and bathed their landing point in a red glare. This was followed by bursts of fire from the dark three-tiered defence line. As shots whistled around them, their boat nosed left, seeking out a darker spot to land, although that meant sailing into dense mangrove.

"Captain, steer left!" Ochi barked. The ship was knocked about by the shots and the captain's desperate manoeuvres to evade them. "Here, Captain! Return and align to the left!" Again the ship sought out the dark. "Straight ahead to that other tall tree!" yelled Ochi.

Artillery fire began. A swish, then a thud, and an explosion. The sounds followed each other all at once: swish-thud! front, back, right, left — explosions. They were familiar sounds, but on land they could run. Here they were sitting ducks.[27]

They still had another 200 metres to the coast.

"Captain! What are you doing, zigzagging along?!" Lt. Oue meant it as a joke. But no one laughed. Ochi found their nonchalant lieutenant a refreshingly new and reliable commander.

Their huge landing tree began to appear on their right in the midst of the firing. But if they did not land there, the firing right and left would confuse the platoon still more.

"Shit, we've got a hole!" Wada said.

"Shut up, you fool, put a finger in!" Ochi said. "Captain! You're on the right side again – too much to the right!" A pillar of water rose on their left.

"Were you hit?" Yamaguchi asked.

Enemy fire struck the boat to their immediate left. A direct hit. The boat sank.

Another hundred metres![28]

Another boat was burning to their left. In the glare of the fire, Ochi saw three other boats aligned with them. One was jiggling along without its rudder.

The captain looked desperately ahead.

"Waaah! I got it in the thigh!" the soldier who was stopping the machine-gun hole in the ship cried out.

Enemy shells came flying amid crackling rifle fire raking down the mangrove leaves and ricocheting off the branches.[29]

Tsuchikane clung to the roots, watching the chaotic situation, trying to sort things out. On the right side, fire lit up the sky brightly, while his immediate surroundings were still dark. To the left, many Japanese soldiers were bustling about. Tsuchikane was walking toward their end of the beachhead when enemy fire opened wildly, with an explosion nearby.

"It's over!"

"It hurts, it hurts!" Painful screams flew around.

"Hey, what company is this?" Tsuchikane screamed moving towards seven soldiers who were shielding a wounded soldier.

"It's only a light wound, keep it up, boy!"

"At it, boy!" Risking their lives in the face of enemy fire they encouraged their mate.

"What company is this?" Tsuchikane once more yelled in desperation. The answer was that of a completely different unit.

Tsuchikane had stumbled into another company's position. Quickly he began to move back in the direction he'd come from. Another shell exploded near the soldiers he had just left.

"Mother! Mother!"

"Don't die! Don't die — you must not!"

"Tenno heika banzai — Long live the Emperor!" Tsuchikane pulled himself together, moving cautiously to find his unit.

Close to him, fire lashed out over the mangrove set on fire. It spread quickly, feeding on oil poured into the Straits, gushing onto the surface, and then shining on the water.[30]

"Mother! Mother!" the moaning voice could still be heard. It was a picture of hell — Abikyokan — Buddhism's worst of all hells.

Tsuchikane's gun felt slippery in his hands as he stumbled along the edge of the beach. Fire in all directions threatened to engulf him. Where to go? It seemed impossible to advance or retreat. Then he stumbled across Cpl. Nemoto!

"We'll burn to death just standing here — let's attack!" he yelled to Tsuchikane.

"If we're going to die, better in an attack," agreed Tsuchikane. Shouting out their battalion and platoon names, they advanced, hoping to be recognised. "Corporal Nemoto, Corporal Tsuchikane!" One, then two comrades joined them. Soon they were five black figures, looking all alike, with only the white of their eyes glinting in the darkness. They were all covered with the heavy black oil retreating forces had released along the front to set the mangroves ablaze.

"Advance!" Nemoto shouted. Yelling at the top of their voices the five forged ahead like war furies.[31]

Inland they could hear motor engines. Was it lorries in retreat? Behind them, the mangroves burnt ferociously. Tsuchikane worried that many Japanese soldiers were still caught in the mangroves.

Cpl. Nemoto motioned all to advance left towards a storehouse on the embankment, inside which to their relief they found several Japanese soldiers.

Out of a corner in the bare concrete room sounded a faint voice: "It hurts. It hurts." The soldier was badly injured. To his side, an officer also lay wounded; and across the room another one, but he seemed already dead. A pool of blood was drying on the floor where the officer lay on his side.

"Treat the soldier first!" the officer told the doctor. But his leg wound with fragments, if left too long, could quickly cost his life. There was not a moment to lose, and yet, the officer said: treat the other first! With the help of two medics, the doctor put the officer on the table and pulled off his torn bloody pants. Then he took out an amputation saw. Holding it in his right hand, he set the blade at the root of the officer's leg and, without saying anything, quickly began to saw off the leg.[32]

Tsuchikane and his men quickly left the place.

"My god," sighed Nemoto. Silently they walked back to the spot where they had come ashore. Several of their troops were assembling there, waving their hands, happy about their safe landing, and checking their men. Tsuchikane's 2nd Platoon had only lightly wounded. But 1st and 3rd Platoons had many dead or unaccounted for. While the medics looked after the wounded, the fit pulled out weeds and grass and frantically wiped off the slick oil crust, before they went to collect their weapons. The light machine guns senior soldier Ueda had brought over were covered in oil and mud from muzzle to ammunition.

Three members of Tsuchikane's company were reported missing, but several days later they returned to the company. Engulfed by fire during the landing, and thinking it was the end, they had decided to swim all the way back to Johor Bahru. Since an Imperial Guard was supposed to move forward, the three were not welcomed back warmly.[33]

Before leaving Johor Bahru, Tsuchikane had been designated platoon messenger by his captain, and since his platoon had suffered least casualties, the company commander ordered them to send out scouts and reconnoitre the place.

As platoon messenger, Tsuchikane was designated to do this job. A scout was usually an excellent soldier, or a long time corporal. Young and energetic, Tsuchikane didn't mind, but he would have to include four others in his party.

Were there any volunteers? Most soldiers sitting in the grass, or sprawling in repose, looked away from the officer's searching eyes. Older soldiers unashamedly waved him off; they at least had a case; men with wives and children should be exempted as far as possible.

"Tsuchikane, have you got your scouts?"

"Yes. I shall go myself!" Tsuchikane said promptly.

"Fool! I'm telling you to choose your members! What are you waiting for?" The company commander briefly talked to the platoon leader, who came over to Tsuchikane, and then announced:

"OK. Corporal Tsuchikane. Go out with four scouts of your own choice!"

Tsuchikane acknowledged the order. Selecting four chaps was now his responsibility. That made it easier. He first chose Senior Soldier Yamamoto, who had put up his hand. A reliable man he'd known in Malaya, he was good to work with. Cheered by this man, Tsuchikane chose one more senior soldier. For the remaining two he settled on one superior and one ordinary soldier; with that combination, asking them to do something would be easier.

Tsuchikane collected his orders from the commander who gave him a map and lots of explanations. "Yes sir! Understood!" Remembering clearly only the direction in which they were to go, he set off with his four soldiers.

When they passed the hut where the wounded soldiers had been operated on, Tsuchikane thought it good to go inside and ask about their unit and find out more about the neighbouring situation. He opened the door. The doctor and medics were gone. On the concrete floor lay the lieutenant with one leg, flanked by the two other mortally wounded soldiers. Their hands were folded on their chests as they lay there peacefully on the hard floor. Tsuchikane told his buddies about the amputation. "It hurts, it hurts!" He remembered most how the lieutenant had insisted that his junior soldier's heavy wound be handled first. The comrades saluted the three soldiers in silence, praying for a better life in their next world, and hurried on their way.[34]

They walked up a small hill and into the rubber plantations torn by the Japanese shells that had softened up the beachhead and beyond. Advancing up and down elevations, it was increasingly difficult to tell if close by was friend or foe.

Ahead, at the end of the plantation, they could make out a single house, which they approached carefully. A baby started crying from out of a trench by the side. His finger on the trigger, Tsuchikane ordered everyone out of the ditch: "*Dete koi!*" One by one, the hapless group scrambled out: a young boy, his sister, the grandparents, petrified, all emerged shaking, the father, aunt and uncle, with the baby crying on the mother's breast.

"OK. Now go back in again."

Tsuchikane and his men entered the house. The first things they looked for were fresh clothes to replace their uniforms, which were soaked in heavy oil and unbearable to wear. Though the native clothing hardly fit the Japanese soldiers, Tsuchikane changed into a dark blue suit. His companions found all sorts of white, blue, and green, and yellow shirts. Only their rank insignia and military badges they cut from their uniforms, and attached to their fresh clothing with safety pins. One first-class soldier went to the trouble of dirtying his shiny white suit.[35]

After changing, they quickly advanced again, memorising the topography as they passed through.

They walked into an open field, Tsuchikane in the lead with two of his scouts, and he planned a dash to the next shelter, hundred metres ahead. The senior soldier proved a rotten apple, and constantly delayed the advance. This time the senior thought it a bad idea to dash across the open space; besides, he had to go and pee. It would slow down the manoeuvre, because the senior always took his time.

This is a difficult guy, Tsuchikane thought, sick and tired of him. "Take your finger out at once! What the hell are you doing there all the time?!" Upon which the soldier reappeared from behind and declared loudly: "You know, bullets whistle not only up front, we have to check the rear, too!" for all to hear.

What a fool to have among them as a comrade in arms, Tsuchikane thought. Only in rank was this guy a corporal. In the eyes of his juniors he was worthless. Ignoring him, Tsuchikane took the other junior soldier with him, and sauntered across the open field.

"Bullets not only whistle up front.... They come from behind, too, you know!" A real asshole! Tsuchikane had heard those words before from older soldiers discussing rotten cowardly comrades in Manchuria, and in the China incident. In one situation Tsuchikane had heard that a demanding officer who did not please one of his reticent soldiers was shot from behind when they went out as scouts. It was "enemy bullets from behind", the killer would declare, and even pretend to have tried to protect the officer, who got a hero's funeral, and the matter was hushed up.

Tsuchikane's party accomplished their mission, and the troops moved safely into the reconnoitred area.[36] They marched through a rubber forest on a hill that offered an excellent outlook on their surroundings. About 150 metres below ran a narrow road. To the left, opened a sugar plantation; to the right, spread a vegetable field. Beyond these open spaces there was more rubber, left and right. The distance from their rubber forest, across the sugar and vegetable plantations to the opposite rubber forest, was about 800 metres.

As the soldiers were taking a break among the rubber trees, the sentry yelled: "Enemy ahead!"

Up front could be seen the silhouettes of many men come marching straight out of the opposite rubber forest towards the vegetable field. The company commander watched them through his binoculars: "No doubt it's the enemy. They haven't seen us yet. We will let them come as close as possible. Hold your fire until we have them all in the open vegetable field."

On their highest position he ordered the two heavy machine guns placed. Crouched forward below, and spread out along their ridge, covered by the roots of the rubber trees, lay the sharp shooters in wait, whilst the rapid firing guns stood by in a lower firing position.

The enemy soldiers were drawing closer, careless and noisy.

Tsuchikane positioned himself next to one of the heavy machine guns and unclipped his safety trigger.

The several dozen troops kept chattering along into the open vegetable field. They wore khaki shirts and half-trousers, and the distinct flat tin helmet. Clasping small rapid-fire guns, they sauntered along with an occasional laugh, as if on a field trip. Utterly oblivious to any hostile activity, they walked into the middle of the vegetable field, exposing themselves to full view.

When their front man reached the narrow road that cut from the side 150 metres before them, the Imperial Guard commander shouted: "Fire!" All opened up at the same time.

Tsuchikane had locked into sight one particular man, pulled the trigger, felt the slight jolt, and watched the man fall flat on his face. Many of those around him likewise fell like ninepins. Shouting loudly, those who could fled into the sugar plantation to the left.[37]

The heavy machine guns opened fire into the chaos: "Bata, bata, bata!" Just then, Capt. Matsumoto, crouched next to Tsuchikane, screamed out: "Waa! I'm hit!"

"What happened Captain Matsumoto?" cried Tsuchikane.

"Medics, medics!" Suzuki appeared immediately.

"Medic, Captain Matsumoto was hit. Check him please!" Tsuchikane said, aiming again at the enemy.

The enemy, fleeing back into the opposite rubber forest, left many dead. "Stop shooting!" rang out the order.

Only Capt. Matsumoto had been hit badly. Shortly, the medic informed Tsuchikane of Matsumoto's death.

"Where was he hit?" Tsuchikane asked the medic who looked puzzled.

"Corporal Tsuchikane, Sir, it is very strange, the bullet entered from the back of his right shoulder and progressed to the left of his heart," the medic explained showing him the exposed back. He was very polite. It was unusual to say "Sir" in the field to a soldier of the same rank. It bestowed on Tsuchikane a superiority that he felt was misplaced. Tsuchikane examined where the bullet had entered, a wound without much blood. The bullet must have travelled from behind straight to the heart.

The platoon and the leader gathered round them. Tsuchikane took him aside and explained the path of the trajectory. It looked as if a bullet from one of their heavy machine guns behind them had hit the trunk or the branch of a rubber tree and ricocheted off, hitting Matsumoto from behind.

Without disclosing the true cause of Matsumoto's death, the platoon leader commended his valiant character and told his comrades he had died a glorious battler's death.[38]

The company commander ordered a rest and a meal, and with three other soldiers, Tsuchikane went to bury Capt. Matsumoto. The platoon leader ordered him to cut off Matsumoto's hand at the wrist and lent him his company sword to do the job.

Tsuchikane found a thick branch from a rubber tree and had his assistants lay Matsumoto's arm across the branch to expose the wrist. Then he swung the sword down on the wrist. It would not cut through the bone. The fresh cut gaped open widely, exposing white flesh. Swisssh again, but still the bone would not cut. No blood came out of the wound. Tsuchikane tried a little further down the wrist, without better results.

"I'm very sorry, Matsumoto. It must be hurting badly," Tsuchikane apologised to him in his heart.

"Put strength into it. Do it in one hard blow!" lectured the platoon leader.

Tsuchikane tried a third place, and finally the bone snapped. They dropped the severed hand into Matsumoto's mess tin and put it carefully away in the ordinance bag of Senior Soldier Otsuka, who hailed from the same province. When time allowed, the wrist would be burnt and made into ashes. For now, they buried Matsumoto and from a branch Tsuchikane plucked the leaves, peeled the bark, offered an inscription, and stuck it on the mound as a burial marker.[39]

Leaving their hill, and avoiding the open vegetable field, the soldiers detoured to the right, through the rubber forest. After a while they came across a water pipeline. "If we follow it along," explained the company commander, "it will take us straight into Singapore city." The rushing water inside was beckoning them into town. "Just a little farther," several shouted, "and we're there. Let's go!" "Singapore, here we come!"

The 20-metre strip of open grass on both sides of the pipeline made walking easy, but for safety reasons the company commander decided to advance inside the rubber trees.

Presently they came to a small river. Clean water flowed in it. Soaking their handkerchiefs, they first washed their faces. Then they drove the wet cloth from the neck down over their naked torso, circling under the armpits, getting rid of the sweat on their chests, circling sideways down the flanks of their waists. The glorious feeling brought them back to life. They felt like stripping off every shred of clothing in the sultry heat and enjoying themselves in the water.

"This is not a break!" the captain's bark brought them back to reality.[40]

After several hundred metres crisscrossing the stream in the rubber forest, they heard gunshots to their left. Obviously they'd been spotted and were coming under fire from an elevated enemy position inside the gently rising rubber forest.

The mortars that lashed their company still fell wide of the target, but were constantly being corrected. They quickly left the river and began advancing from rubber tree to rubber tree, using them as shields.

"Senior Soldier Kubota, advance to the second rubber tree ahead!" the platoon commander shouted.

"Light rifles, advance to the rock in front!"

Both sides got closer, showering shots at each other, until they could only advance to the next tree, and fling themselves at its roots.

A hand grenade exploded on Tsuchikane's right side against the root of a rubber tree. He could now clearly see the enemy moving in front and hear the Australian soldiers calling to each other. Only about 50 metres separated them.[41]

Tsuchikane took a hand grenade from his belt, pulled the safety pin, and drove his heel into the ground. Counting one, two, three, four, five, he hurled the grenade into the enemy. Way over their heads, it exploded harmlessly in the brush. A good baseball player at senior high school, Tsuchikane realized that he had used too much strength to pitch the grenade. He reached for another, pulled the pin, and this time felt the grenade firmly before throwing it over. This time the grenade exploded among the enemy, and he could make out the horror in their faces as they yelled out in anguish.

But just then an enemy grenade came rolling towards him, stopping a couple of metres away. Instinctively he dove down behind the root of the rubber tree, gripped his steel helmet firmly, and buried his face in the ground.

"Bang!" Earth and sand sprayed up and there was a pungent smell of sulphur. Tsuchikane lifted his head. He could not see for the white smoke and had to wait for it to disappear. Shifting his gun into his left hand, he drew himself up on his left leg.

"Mount your bayonets!" came the final order. "Forward attack!" With all his might Tsuchikane kicked the earth with his military boot and jumped up.

"Charge!!"

Amid the platoon's murderous yells Tsuchikane hurled himself forward, mixing into the melee straight into the enemy position. Many of the Australian 27th Brigade were already turning their backs to him. Tsuchikane closed in on one, ran after him, pulled him to the ground, and with his bayonet pierced his opponent from the back of his shoulder out through the front. The enemy expired with a deathly yell, as Tsuchikane pulled out the blade, splattering his jacket with a crimson red.

The enemy position stood on a slight precipice. By standing up, they had put the one and a half metres to good use by concentrating heavy flank fire from a standing position down on the approaching Japanese enemy. Many of the dead lay just beneath the precipice. Having lost their nerve, some soldiers were simply cowering in terror, squatting down and avoiding the hand-to-hand combat in a wait and see position. They, too, were bayoneted or shot without mercy.

Beyond the precipice, a field continued on towards the large open base of the enemy. Its right side had come under attack by another platoon.[42] The company seized a number of guns and also captured 18 prisoners of war, several of whom were British, including a red-bearded officer.

After disarming them, Senior Soldier Asakawa began his interrogation. A junior high school teacher in civilian life, he had been appointed by the company commander in the capacity of translator. But his skills proved useless.

The prisoners were dangerous baggage. Walking them into the next battle would greatly hamper tactics. They would require several guards at a time when they themselves suffered 60 dead and wounded and the battles for Singapore were just beginning. Fortunately, an artillery unit in the back was willing to receive the 18 prisoners, to the great relief of the Imperial Guard company.[43]

8

On To Bukit Timah

HAVING pushed back the Australian 22nd Brigade on Singapore's northwestern flank (between Sarimbun River and Berih River), 18th Division immediately fought on to reach Tengah Aerodrome. The airbase, the first objective of the assault plan, was occupied shortly before noon on 9 February, only a bit behind schedule. Later that day Yamashita moved his headquarters up to the base.[1]

It was while having breakfast there with Gen. Yamashita at dawn the next day that Campaign Manager Tsuji heard how the Imperial Guards' first wave across the Straits had run into a fiery inferno.[2] From the Johor side, they were informed, it looked as if the entire Kobayashi Regiment had been wiped out by fire, an impression reinforced by those who, unable to land, had swum back to tell the story. "The Regiment burnt to death. General Kobayashi's fate, too, is unknown." Adding insult to injury, Imperial Guards Divisional Headquarters blamed 25th Army Headquarters for recklessly forcing a passage with inadequate preparations; they now wanted to change orders and follow behind the 5th Division's first line.[3]

"Ah! Another change!" Gen. Yamashita was upset, but when an Imperial Guards staff officer told them at breakfast about the destruction of the entire regiment and how one engineer had returned to tell about it, Campaign Manager Tsuji exploded: "You fools! Who changed the original plan in the first place and said that the Imperial Division should be in the first line?! At this stage there is no need for battle plan change. Fifth and 18th Divisions can go it alone. Return and tell your general that he can do as he likes!"[4]

These words, uttered in an hour of high tension, Tsuji would deeply regret in the next days.

After Tengah airfield, the next strategic object was "Bukit Timah". The 177-metre "Tin Hill" sheltered reservoirs and provision dumps, and inspired the saying "Who controls Bukit Timah, controls Singapore." Its tactical value consisted of a forked road that would allow development of a pincer movement, with one division driving straight down Bukit Timah Road into Singapore town, while the other division branched off right down to Reformatory Road to penetrate the British western flank and then move across Kent Ridge down to Pasir Panjang and into Keppel Harbour to the south of the city. So important was the island's highest elevation that Japanese Headquarters believed the battle would effectively be over once it was in their possession.

Like the 18th Division on the western flank, the 5th Division, too, had successfully reduced the Australian eastern flank (2/18th and 2/20th Battalion defence positions) in the Ama Keng and Kranji River area. Moving on to Bukit Timah, Ochi's company came across some of their own men.

"Ooooi!"

"Who are you?"

"We're the 12th."

"We're the 11th machine gunners." They talked to each other about their losses. Ochi said nothing. Just smoked silently. The cigarette left a bitter taste in his mouth. Yasuda, whose platoon alternated with Ochi's in the front line, appeared.

"How many did you lose on the crossing?"

"Two."

Eighteenth Division was already at Tengah aerodrome, Yasuda had heard. On to Bukit Timah! Let's not fall behind them.[5]

Fifth Division's plan was to "break through west of the causeway in full force on to Bukit Timah and from there take all enemy positions". To Division Gen. Matsui it looked deceptively simple as he issued orders from Namazi Estate to attack British positions at Bukit Panjang, around four kilometres northwest of Bukit Timah. That was where he expected to encounter the British main force. And once they'd finished with the British at Bukit Panjang, they could race at top speed into Singapore. His optimism reflected a gross underestimation of the enemy, while overestimating the capacities of his own forces, a trait common to the Japanese military forces, and one that Campaign Manager Tsuji did his best to exploit.[6]

When in the late afternoon of 10 February, Bukit Panjang fell without much resistance, and 18th Division had already battled to a point southeast of Bukit Timah, the machiavellian Tsuji showed up at the 18th divisional headquarters, where he told Gen. Mutaguchi: "You know, Fifth Division just overran Bukit Panjang."

"What? Then we shall overrun Bukit Timah tonight with me at the very front!" Mutaguchi said.

"You will be successful," Tsuji said, "the enemy is ill-prepared. Best of luck!" Immediately he sauntered over to the fifth divisional headquarters to tell them of Mutaguchi's decision.

"What?!" shouted Gen. Matsui. "Then we, too, can do the same as well!"

"Yes," agreed Tsuji, "since your forces are located right east near Bukit Timah!"

"We'll encircle the enemy from the left and finish him off," the general completed the sentence. It was vintage Tsuji, for Gen. Matsui ordered an immediate break-through on Bukit Timah without waiting for nightfall.[7]

To the west, Lt.-Gen. Mutaguchi was giving his troops a rare pep talk. Tomorrow would be Kigensetsu, the anniversary of the founding of the Japanese Empire 2,602 years ago by legendary Emperor Jimmu. They must win: "Tonight we carry out our final attack on Bukit Timah. Soldiers, I pray for your battle success." Short words, but his longest speech in memory. For the first time in five years of warfare, the general had encouraged them in person; they were moved; all pledged: "I will do my very best."[8]

The 25th Army Headquarters' original order had been to attack Bukit Timah from the north and the south. But during the battle, the two-pronged attack was abruptly changed to an attack from all sides. This caused confusion. Eighteenth Division's 55th Regiment, actually on standby as a reserve force, got carried away, and advanced to the southern three-way crossing. It wanted to dash down the 5th Division's main trunk route, but was rebuked for intruding into another division's battle area. Eighteenth Division soldiers were surprised to be stopped in their successful engagement when 5th Division had not yet even reached the location! It was all very competitive; everyone wanted to be first into Singapore. Why hand the finest morsel, the Grande Finale, to the 5th Division? It made no sense from a military strategic point of view. If they dashed ahead, Singapore was theirs for Kigensetsu.[9]

On the Commonwealth side, the counterattack to retake Bukit Panjang was never executed, while a Tomforce effort to retake Bukit Timah was repelled. There was a strong fear that if the Japanese continued their advance at this speed, they could split the British defences and occupy the city during the morning of 11 February.[10] Gen. Percival, who had been planning for a three months' siege, recognised the danger and decided to create a close defensive perimeter around the town (from Kallang airfield to Paya Lebar airstrip, Woodleigh crossroads, Thomson Village, Adam Road, Farrer Road, Tanglin Halt, and thence to the sea west of Buona Vista village), a tactical move that involved the withdrawal of all beach defences. Percival also went to see Governor Shenton Thomas to explain the dangerous situation on the Bukit Timah Road axis, causing the governor to order the destruction of the Singapore Broadcasting Station and most of the currency notes held by the Treasury.[11]

The Japanese belief that they would meet no resistance in the southern Bukit Timah area was a miscalculation. During the night of 10 February, as the Japanese 18th Division waited for the advance of the 5th Division, the Australian 22nd Brigade and the Indian 44th regrouped. Joined by British troops, they began to form a strong defensive line south of Bukit Timah.

Only Col. Tsuji Masanobu from Headquarters came to the front to check on the situation, and the strong British resistance at Bukit Timah dismayed him. If only the Imperial Guards Division could come to their aid from their eastern position in the Mandai ranges! How irresponsible of him to have said they could take Bukit Timah without them. The Imperial Guards could have relieved the severe fighting with a push from the east. Many times Headquarters had asked for fire support that didn't come. It wasn't even offered, since Tsuji had told them: "Do as you like!"[12]

Bukit Timah was taken as intended on Kigensetsu, but Percival's army nevertheless fought on. All Gen. Yamashita could do was drop leaflets over Singapore saying: "Surrender now. Have a high officer come along Bukit Timah Road with a white and a British flag."[13]

The surrender note, however, made the British more aware of the 5th and 18th Divisions' positions at Bukit Timah, and only strengthened British resolve. General Percival at Fort Canning Headquarters would not gratify his opponent by sending peace envoys on the birthday of the first Emperor. Instead, he sent reinforcements from the east, and ordered a heavy bombardment from Fort Siloso of the southern three-way crossing at Bukit Timah to cut off and isolate the Japanese forces there.[14]

At nightfall on 10 February, Japanese troops secured the west side of the race course along Bukit Timah Road, and Gen. Matsui issued fresh orders to break through British lines at 8 p.m.[15] His 5th Division overwhelmed the 12th Indian Brigade after dark, and by midnight tanks and infantry arrived at Bukit Timah where, fortunately for the British defence, they paused. Meanwhile, at the southern fork road, the 22nd Australian and 44th Indian Brigades engaged the 18th Division, and at dawn, after a good deal of confused fighting, stopped its advance. Both Japanese divisions had reached their second objective, Bukit Timah, but from here on were slowed down by the difficulty of getting supplies and ammunition across the Johor Straits.

9

Victory

I then proceeded on a final tour of the front.... First, to inspect my troops for the last time — a sad business — and second, to reconnoitre my route of escape, for I had determined that I would not fall into Japanese hands.... I found the headquarters of the 2/20th Battalion in a beautifully furnished house where I had afternoon tea from unusually high quality dishes.... Officers and men were very upset at the state of affairs. One officer broke down completely, saying, "We can't surrender to the Japanese."

Lt.-Gen. H. Gordon Bennett, 15 February 1942,
Why Singapore Fell, pp. 193–4

AFTER the Commonwealth troops lost the Bukit Timah elevation and its water reservoirs, Singapore began to suffer water shortages, while food and gasoline were also scarce. At 2 p.m. on 13 February, Gen. Percival held a conference with all principal officers and formation commanders present. The general championed the possibility of a counter-attack to recapture Bukit Timah. But most doubted the wisdom of attempting to recover lost ground, citing exhaustion and poor morale of the troops. Lt.-Gen. Heath and Lt.-Gen. Gordon Bennett even advocated capitulation to save the city population from disaster, but Percival decided to continue resisting as ordered by the supreme commander, Wavell, in Java.[1]

The next day, Percival met his senior officers again to assess the battle situation. Continue or surrender? Percival wanted to hold out as instructed by Wavell, who had received an order from Churchill in London to fight to the last man. Again the District Commanders replied that it was impossible to mount a counter-attack. Still, Gen. Percival held that the situation was serious but not desperate, and ordered everyone present to continue fighting.

At the same time, Percival telegraphed Gen. Wavell that they were unable to resist for more than a day, and requested to be allowed to make a decision based on his own discretionary powers. Wavell responded that it was absolutely essential to continue fighting.[2]

On 14 February information came from the municipal water engineer and the Director-General of Civil Defence that a complete failure of the water supply was imminent, owing to breaks in the water mains and pipes caused by bombing and shelling. Wavell received a telegram from Churchill empowering him to decide whether to continue or surrender, and left the decision to Percival.

> So long as you are in a position to inflict losses and damage to the enemy and your troops are physically capable of doing so, you must fight on. When you are fully satisfied that this is no longer possible I give you discretion to cease resistance.... Whatever happens I thank you and all your troops for your gallant efforts of last few days.[3]

On 15 February, Percival called a final conference at Fort Canning at 9:30 a.m. They could either counter-attack to regain control of the reservoirs and the military food depots, or capitulate. He put these alternatives squarely to his commanders. The majority view was to capitulate.[4] At 11 o'clock in the morning, Percival called on the District Commanders and the Civil Defense Superintendent and announced his decision to surrender.

At two o'clock in the afternoon, British envoys drove up Bukit Timah Road and from the Adam Road junction began to walk up Bukit Timah Road toward the Japanese front line. They were Brig. T.H. Newbigging (the officer-in-charge of administration), Hugh Fraser (the Colonial Secretary), and Maj. Cyril Wild (the interpreter, a sharp young man who had been doing business in Kobe before the war). After proceeding for some 500 metres, they were stopped by a Japanese patrol of the 5th Division. They handed over a note reading: "By means of a cease-fire at six o'clock on the 15th, we wish to discuss cease-fire terms in Singapore."

The front line unit that received this information dispatched its staff officer for communications, Lt.-Col. Sugita Ichiji, to the Sugiura Unit Headquarters. When he returned, he handed Newbigging a list of demands. Sugita flatly refused a request by Percival that Yamashita come to Fort Canning to hold the surrender discussion, insisting that Percival come to Yamashita instead. It was a matter of controlling the meeting. He also wished to have the Japanese flag, hung from the tallest building in Singapore, the Cathay Building, for ten minutes in the afternoon, as a sign of good faith.[5]

At around seven o'clock in the evening, a five-man team consisting of Brig. Newbigging, Maj. Wild, Chief-of-Staff Brig. Torrance, the Commander-in-Chief of the British forces, and Lt.-Gen. Percival, led by Staff Officer Sugita, arrived at the damaged Ford automobile factory at Milestone 9 on the Bukit Timah Road. An intact office room had been fitted out for the surrender talks with a heavy long oak table.

Presently the Army Commander-in-Chief, Gen. Yamashita was seated, and at a quarter-past five in the afternoon, the negotiations started. During the one hour discussion, Percival insisted on 1,000 men retaining their arms for the purpose of maintaining order. Believing the shaky British general was stalling for time, at one stage during their parley, Yamashita knocked the table:

"Is the British Army going to surrender or not? Yes or no?"

"Yes. But I would like the retention of 1,000 armed men sanctioned."

"Very well."[6]

Yamashita also forbade any Japanese troops to enter the city. The two generals rose, and shook hands. Yamashita looked at the thin body and pale face of the defeated British general. He could see Percival was under great strain, and as they were shaking hands he wanted to say one last word of sympathy to him, but could not find the appropriate English phrase; and the kind of thing he wished to say was not for the ears of an interpreter. So he said nothing.[7]

The Japanese newspapers reported at the time: "British Army Surrenders Unconditionally" and "General Yamashita Struck the Table Menacingly, Demanding an Answer". However, there was nothing in the "Surrender Summary" about unconditional surrender, nor were the words used at the time of the meeting. A clause allowed the British 1,000 armed troops to keep order. As for demanding a "yes or no answer", Gen. Yamashita believed that it was best to accept the surrender, and work out details later. The gaggle of reporters waiting for news outside exaggerated this moment and Gen. Yamashita's majestic appearance. The subject of a guarantee for the safety of the Overseas Chinese following surrender was never broached, though it was subsumed in the general terms of safety once hostilities ceased.

At 6:10 p.m. Gen. Percival signed his name to the document of surrender and at 8:30 p.m. the British Army ceased combat activities. Thus ended the 70-day campaign. The official figure given for the total men lost as battle casualties was 130,246.[8]

As soon as the surrender was communicated to all the Japanese forces, the Balloon Corps floated the victory balloon. Climbing high up into the sky, it was an unforgettable feeling for the troops to see the attached large Japanese flag glowing resplendently in the evening sunlight. No man who had not been there could ever completely understand the lordly feeling of victory and gratefulness that filled every Japanese soldier at that moment.[19]

* * *

Five days earlier, on the night of 10 February the 18th Division had moved west, away from the front, down Reformatory Road (today's Clementi Road), to the southwest coast of Singapore Island.[10]

The action initiated a giant pincer movement, but to Arai's sergeant-level understanding it seemed strange to divert the 18th Division away from the main assault line down Bukit Timah Road, handled now only by the 5th Division. This way they would never be able to deal the British a decisive blow. Separating the two divisions would only prolong the fall of Singapore.[11]

But it was not for him to have a strategic opinion. As he tramped along in the dark rubber forest behind his regiment commander, he could hardly see ahead but for the fireflies. On his heels followed the Adjutant, whom Arai repeatedly had to help up over the tree trunks. Many soldiers dozed even as they walked.[12] By daybreak on 12 February, they entered fresh fields, along which they proceeded on the eastern edge of a rubber forest.

A small hut appeared on their right side. Three young girls with short cut hair were working, seemingly oblivious to the war. The scene reminded Arai of the Chinese girls back in Canton. The soldiers were much attracted, but silently looking at the tantalising scene, they passed on.[13]

Presently they came under mortar attack, intensive 20-minute affairs, every 30 minutes. How could the enemy know their march route when they were covered by the rich green jungle foliage?

Singapore Island was becoming a small place for the 90,000 men fighting the Japanese in the vicinity.[14]

When the third attack ended, headquarters moved up with Gen. Mutaguchi enjoying the spectacle, and five tanks moved in. Opening their turrets, the operators were looking out carelessly when suddenly the attack resumed.

Now an order went out to catch the three girls they had passed earlier, "under suspicion of having betrayed our position". As Master Sgt. Arai looked on from his concealed position, the girls were brought forward and each was bound to a wooden pillar. They were about 20 years old, and stood there with lowered heads. Arai doubted that they were guilty of anything. Because it happened all the time. Tanks moved into the shooting zone and were attacked. It did not mean that anyone had betrayed them. Arai couldn't stand the sight of these poor girls and returned into his trench.

When the heavy attack continued, all soldiers and officers ducked back into their trenches.[15] But the three girls tied to the poles were left out in the open. When the shells began to fall, they went half crazy with fear. Shaking their dishevelled hair, they cried out loudly. When the attack was over, they were still alive. Regimental commander Okubo, who could not take it any longer, ordered a soldier: "Stab them!"

But there was no reason to kill them, Arai thought. To deflect the situation and keep the soldier from doing it, he yelled out to him: "Wait! Don't stab them there, you'll only mess up the place!" The soldier looked at Okubo, who said nothing and disappeared inside his trench. Relieved, the soldier left the girls alone and went away. With the gun attack turning away from them, everyone became busy, contacting their next troops and sorting out their next advance, and Arai forgot all about the girls.[16]

Arai's 114th Regiment had been the right wing up to here. From now on they would be the left wing. Only their side changed; they were always in the front, never in reserve. At 2 a.m. on the morning of 13 February, information reached them that Hill 200 was completely secured. Better catch a nap, or lack of sleep would hinder tomorrow's big operations.[17]

But Arai could not sleep. The three girls in their pitiful situation bound to the pole kept coming to his mind. He could not leave them like that. He must go and release them. He would tell the regiment

commander that he had killed them at another place. Arai approached
the three poles and could make out faintly in the dark the white of
their blouses, about 15 metres away. No one was around. Not even
a sentry stood there. The three girls kept their chins sunk on their
chests, motionless, their black hair dangling forward in the breeze.
Were they asleep?

Arai snapped his fingers to give them a sign. They did not stir.
He crept up from behind and shook the first girl from the side: "Oi!"

No reply. He loosened the rope round her body to set her free.
Something cold and wet dripped on his finger — was it blood?
Instinctively he withdrew his finger. Someone had cruelly stabbed
her below the breast. The two others must have suffered the same
fate, Arai thought. Inside of him he felt a fiendish inhuman devil had
come to attack them. One much worse than the enemy they were
presently facing. Arai went back into his trench with an unbearable
feeling. He closed his eyes, but was unable to get the three dead
girls out of his mind. If Japan became a war theatre, they would be
visited with exactly the same beastliness. Violence begetting violence,
a continuing sequence, one bad thing leading to something worse,
and sleep still would not come.[18]

"Wake up! We're pulling out in twenty minutes!"

It was 8:30! Arai quickly ate breakfast, which always consisted
of the other half of the leftover supper, dunked in soup made from
powdered bean paste. During their advance they had no time for
lunch. And no appetite during the roaring shell attacks. The British
biscuits and powdered milk from Tengah aerodrome helped them
through the afternoon, and Arai had a little condensed milk left. "On
to Singapore!" was food enough.[19]

Arai marched with commander Okubo and adjutant Kakuhira up
the gentle slope of Reformatory Road that broke from the southern
three-way crossroads east to Keppel Harbour. On their way to Hill
200 on the left they passed a makeshift hospital with about ten
wounded. Company commander Lt. Waseda was trying to lift his
upper body to salute the regimental commander.

"Don't rise!" ordered Kakuhira.

"Yes, thank you. Nishito and Waseda were wounded. Abe fell
in the second attack. The enemy was three to four times stronger."

"You did an excellent job. Hill 200 is very important for our next operations. All take good care!"

"Thank you."

"All the best!"

"Please win!" They were cases to be sent home and would not see the fruit of their efforts.[20]

When Arai and his commanders reached Hill 200, the dead were already buried and the wounded sent to the rear. The attacking 3rd Battalion had lost 33 dead and 43 wounded. Since crossing the Straits, the 114th Regiment had lost 200 men. Over a four-day period they had lost 50 soldiers per day. They had 300 wounded men. Put differently, each day one complete squadron was wiped out and two complete squads were wounded, reducing regimental strength by one-third.[21]

At 1 p.m. Gen. Mutaguchi issued the next orders: "Attack Hill 270. Advance along Buona Vista Road. Attack Pasir Panjang Heights. Then advance to Keppel Harbour."[22]

Without delay, they left Hill 200 in the direction of Ulu Pandan Road. Walking with commander Okubo about 20 metres ahead of their group, Arai watched his commander carefully. Always a man of few words, he now said even less and the serenity in his face was gone. Deputy commander Kakuhira was keeping a distance behind them. Terrible things had happened in the past few days. The 114th Regiment had suffered huge losses, especially the 3rd Battalion. Of its three company commanders, one had died, the other two were severely wounded.[23]

The scouts announced "mines at Buona Vista and strong enemy troop concentrations on Hill 225, but no special fortifications". In the evening, mortar and gunfire increased, but the shells high above were heading northeast to land four kilometres away, and were meant to stop the 5th Division's advance.[24]

That night, they took Hill 270. It had a formidable fortress, a square, independent fort, with concrete fortifications and lots of barbed wire.[25]

When day broke on 14 February, they saw right before them billowing into the sky the huge black plumes of the Pasir Panjang oil tanks. They had been burning since mid-January. As they passed in front of the fiery display, Arai took a moment to watch the burning monsters. Sgt. Katayama passed him and handed him some tomatoes.

"Have them all!" he said. Arai ate with delight, mesmerised by the huge burning containers. Why did our military bomb these tanks? Was it to deny them to the British? Or to put psychological pressure on the British? What a waste, he sighed.[26]

Their military objects were Hill 225 and the Tiger Beer brewery. But there were no enemies on Hill 225, nor on 226! And the few who shot back were not British, but Malays, the 1st Division, who since losing Hill 270 had been in retreat.

Since the road was mined, 114th Regiment advanced on its edge to the Pasir Panjang Heights. Arai took a last look back at the burning oil tanks.[27]

After lobbing a dozen shells way over them, the British guns focused again on the 55th reserve Regiment. They still seemed not to have noticed the advance of 114th Regiment. Night fell.

Tomorrow would be the decisive battle. They had gotten as close to the centre of the British fortress as possible. Arai thought of his loved ones at home, his family, and friends. He pondered his school days, recalled his school friends' faces. He remembered his adolescence and life as a young man. Then the battles came to mind since they had crossed the Straits, his dead comrades, and his heavily-wounded friends in hospital, his juniors, and seniors. In this campaign there had been little laughter, no frills, but lots of loss, one thing leading to another. And now they were here, near the terminal point.

Arai and his unit descended a wide asphalt road until barbed wire stopped them. Ducking under it, they entered the populous metropolitan area of Singapore.[28] They found a large compound with a deserted two-storey building. From it, Arai followed a side path down to the sea, and saw a sandy beach only five metres away. Even here there was barbed wire; the enemy must have thought of digging himself in seriously.

About one and a half kilometres away the island of Blakang Mati loomed in the darkness. Tomorrow they would occupy Keppel Harbour, and the British would either surrender or retreat to Blakang Mati. In which case the unenviable task of taking Blakang Mati with the world's heaviest fortifications at Fort Siloso would fall to the 114th Regiment, the unit closest to the islet.[29]

They rose to another splendid morning. Since their crossing, they had not once had rain. "You're pitch black!" they greeted each other.

It was the soot from the burning oil tanks. During the hot day it had stayed high in the air, but come down to settle in the cool of the night.

"Sergeant, we found a wash place. There's no water, but we've been able to wash ourselves with beer." The taps in the house had been cut off, but a soldier had found row upon row of beer upstairs and brought two bottles down for Arai. With the first bottle he wet a towel and wiped his hands and face. He looked in the mirror and gave a good rub, twice, three times.

It was the first time Arai had seen his face in a mirror since getting off the ship at Songkhla. A strange bearded face it was. In the previous big battles, such as Nanking, etc., he had always carried a shaving kit and soap, and he had been able to trim his moustache from time to time. But not during this campaign. The mirror showed him a burnt face, grimy, dirty, with caved in cheeks and eyes staring out of sockets. He muttered to his face: "Well, finally, this must be the last day, I'm sure."

His teeth, too, had not been brushed since getting off the trucks two weeks ago. With the remaining second bottle of beer he brushed his teeth. All this etiquette just for the finale. Better look good in the end. Like a dying samurai. Look fresh even in death. He still had half the bottle. Arai gargled several times, poured the rest into a towel, squeezed it, and disposed of the bottle. In combat they had no desire to drink beer. Battle instinct nullified any such lust.[30]

On 15 February, the fall of Singapore appeared to be only a matter of time. Their orders were to take Hills 130 and 136, and the Empire Docks. Hill 130 seemed only lightly defended at first. But then they got a strong response and several high-ranking officers fell to machine guns, including battalion commander Sako, stitched across the chest at 8:40 a.m., together with his aide-de-camp.

Several wounded called out: "Oi! Arai, give us some beer!"

"It's not good if you're wounded," and Arai gave them coconut milk instead.

He also gave some to his war buddy, Sgt. Shiroishi: "Well, the time has come. From now on we forge straight ahead. I probably won't be seeing you anymore. Take good care."

"Yes, thanks, you, too. Take it easy." Sgt. Shiroishi had often been dispatched to Headquarters from 2nd Battalion to get orders. The chap was always at ease, never lost his cool, a good comrade.

Arai turned once more to his commander on the stretcher. In death Sako had a peaceful, gentle face, and because his face was dark tanned, it retained all the freshness. With his balding forehead, his kind face and his open eyes, he seemed to be just about to say one more thing to Arai, calling to him, something about ... crossing the Johor Straits, or about their life and death battle on Bukit Timah the other day ... Arai saluted him a last time and went into the final battle, as Sako's duties passed to 3rd Company commander Onishi.[31]

The British had finally noticed that the 114th Regiment was advancing fast on Gilman Heights and Keppel Harbour. Coming under heavy fire, the 1st Battalion of the 114th Regiment moved forward at around 10 a.m. to attack Hill 130. To the right, the 3rd Battalion suffered many dead and wounded. Company commander Tanaka, severely wounded and heavily sedated, kept repeating: "The war is over, the war is over," with his eyes open wide.

British fire was intense as Arai moved forward into the shade of a tree, with the wall of a house as protection.[32] He remained in that position for two or three hours.

From 4 p.m. to 6 p.m. British artillery launched a strong attack. Many shells fell behind 114th regimental headquarters. Arai was about 50 metres ahead and tackling the one kilometre between Hill 130 to Hill 136. The path was sloping and then flat, with obstacles such as houses and roadside trees for shelter. Wriggling forward on his quivering belly, down the slope, he wormed towards Hill 136 in the shadows cast by rubber trees, amidst the never ending barrages.

The shells were aimed at the hills along the southern shore's entire length. They also came crashing down around Hill 130 and adjoining Hill 95, just to the south. The 7th Company was trying to secure that hill, but seven men died in the barrage. Arai heard sounds behind him. Sgt. Nakagawa and Sgt. Katayama came crawling up. "114th Headquarter's Ito and Matsumoto are dead," Katayama said. How close the two young soldiers had come to success.[33] Anger welled up in Arai as he cursed the British artillery. The British infantry appear on the verge of surrendering, yet their artillery keeps pounding us; they all should be shot.

Then at six, the guns fell silent. All firing stopped. Just nothing. On the entire front. Arai, Nakagawa, and Katayama looked at each other.

Singapore without shelling was a novel experience, extraordinarily out of place. An empty ringing persisted in the ears.

"Now is the time to run!" the three decided, jumping up. Four or five comrades nearby joined in their bolt. They ran like mad over the remaining hundred metres to the foot of Hill 136, then scaled the final 50 metres up the steep slope to where a large two-storey concrete barracks stood on top of the hill, with the walls painted black, and above the entrance a big Red Cross sign.

Was the sign camouflage to escape Japanese artillery bombing? But when they entered, they found to their surprise 60 pale faces staring at them out of pyjamas, from beds arranged tightly in a U-shape in the wide room. The barracks, indeed, had been turned into a hospital. Those who seemed asleep, with only their faces turned to the entrance were the severe casualties. Those who sat upright in their beds and those standing next to their beds all held their hands up high, indicating surrender. Only a moment ago Arai had entertained the idea of killing them all, even in surrender. But now looking into the ashen faces of these wounded soldiers, the thought quickly faded.

"Who is the man in charge?" Arai wanted to ask in English he'd learnt ten years back in junior high school. But nothing came out.[34] Good, well, he mumbled to himself and stepped outside, where he found the regimental commander and his adjutant just reach the top of Hill 136 with the expression on their face: "Aah! So that's what we'll find up here!" They seemed to be well aware of the existence of the barracks on Hill 136.

"Vice-Commander, inside the barracks are many wounded British soldiers, about fifty to sixty!" Arai said.

"*Aah, so desuka*, is that so!? Call Lieutenant Marumo!" He was the translator attached to their unit for the Malayan campaign. Kakuhira also ordered the supervisor of the hospital summoned. At once a British officer appeared; he was around 50, in beret and short trousers, with stockings and low shoes.

"Ask him about the British military dispositions," Vice Commander Kakuhira ordered Marumo.

The translator was not much of a military man. After graduating from university, Marumo had worked as an English teacher and had been drafted with the rank of lieutenant more for his English skills than his qualities as a soldier. Overly polite, he was the opposite of the British major, and the tone and expression of the officer, with his stiff upper lip, showed that the interrogation was going nowhere.

Irritated, the fretting vice-commander asked: "What is he saying?"

"Yes, Sir. This person says he is the sanitary troops Major in charge of this hospital. He respects international law. From that stance he takes a neutral view of the whole situation and knows nothing about military matters."

Like hell he does, Arai thought to himself, barely able to control his rush of adrenaline. He was standing to the immediate left of the major, with the regimental commanders and sergeants all waiting and gazing at Marumo, nauseated by the weak interrogator and the major's recalcitrant mien.

Arai could take no more. "Sit down!" he barked, hitting the calmly standing major with all his force on the left cheek. The slap sent the British officer reeling to the floor, where he sat himself down on his knee, took off his green beret, and turned to Arai with a look of reproach on his face.

Instantly, the act relieved all tension. All were surprised to see the usually mild-mannered Arai slap the senior officer. In all his army life, not once had he been seen to slap a soldier. Arai himself was astonished by his sudden action. Was it a reaction to all the shelling he'd endured over the past ten hours and the great loss of dead and wounded suffered in the past final hours?

It certainly was infectious. The blow put strength into Marumo's cross-examination, which now went smoothly. According to the major, this was Gilman Barracks and housed around 1,000 patients.

One party stayed behind to guard the wounded British, as the 114th Regiment occupied the adjoining Hills 312 and 345. Where on earth was the British infantry? It was unbelievable to simply leave behind 1,000 wounded soldiers to their fate, thought Arai. What kind of people was this? It was the same as letting the wounded die before one's eyes without helping. If they surrendered, they should have been frank about it and raised immediately a white flag. Abandoned by their own soldiers, the frightened eyes stirred neither pity nor sympathy in Arai.[35]

Later in the evening, Arai sensed a sudden commotion from the back moving up to their front. It seemed to be coming from the coast, through the valley, rising up the hills, like a growing tidal wave to engulf them. The sound was also heard on Hills 130 and 136, and on other elevations, ever more clearly. The roar grew closer and louder. The bearers of the tidings must be somewhere out there. One could not see their silhouettes, but the force of their voices was shattering.

"BANZAI! BANZAAI – BANZAAAI!!"

The soldiers all along the front were congratulating themselves on an astounding victory won at the last desperate minute. Mixed in with the banzais was also the breathless shout: "114th Regiment! The enemy has surrendered! Hold your attack!! Hold your attack!!! Stop the advance!!"

"So the enemy did surrender...?!" Often thought about, but hard to believe, it had become reality. So all had been worthwhile. No one had died in vain. They were here to stay.

At the same time, the announcement wafting from afar stirred some jealousy. "Fifth Division must have gotten into Singapore much before us...." "They stole a march on us...." "Being on the main trunk line straight into the city, it was only natural...." "It couldn't be helped...." It was a mixed set of emotions that assailed the members of the 18th Division, not quite satisfied with the perfect news, even if they should be glad about the victory, ... but the surrender had not come from their part of the city. They had wanted so badly to be first. After all, 114th Regiment had reached the furthest point of the campaign target, Keppel Harbour, in downtown Singapore. Surely the surrender should have originated from their section....

About a hundred metres from their elevated position, they saw Pvt. Kanda run up, shouting out the orders received from Divisional Headquarters. Arai called down: "Kanda we understand! We are up here!" He looked at his watch. It was 20 minutes past eight in the evening. The sun was already setting. In 20 minutes it would be dark.[36]

At 8:30 p.m., Vice Commander Kakuhira confirmed Kanda's message to "cease fire", and ordered each unit to secure their battle zone and wait for further orders. In the meantime they quickly had to take care of the wounded and bury the dead. Arai gave his rice portion to a wounded man.

At 10:30 p.m., commander Okubo issued Order No. 70 from Gilman Barracks. It was the final order of the campaign:

1. The enemy has surrendered. We extend condolences to the fallen British Commonwealth soldiers.
2. The Regiment will retain its present position throughout the night.
3. Each unit will gather its forces and disarm the enemy according to orders. One detachment will inspect the wounded enemy assembled in Gilman Hospital.
4. I remain on Hill 136.[37]

At midnight, commander Okubo mustered officers and soldiers for a minute of silent prayer for the deceased British soldiers, saluted the Regiment Flag with deep respect, bowed low in the direction of the Imperial Palace, addressed his thanks to the entire Regiment, and led three rounds of Banzais.

For the first time in combat, Arai did not try to hold back his tears. It had been a savage war. Too many older and younger companions had died. Slowly the soldiers settled down, each with his own memories, letting one scene pass after the other, with a heavy heart.[38]

* * *

Arai's jealousy had been misdirected. The 5th Division had neither surged into the city nor forced the surrender. Since Kigensetsu, on 11 February, it had been bogged down along the Bukit Timah Road.

After securing the adjoining Race Course, Ochi's unit looked for the Golf Course on their way to the MacRitchie Reservoir. Close-cropped luxuriant grassland spread before them. Was that a clubhouse? Soldiers could be seen carrying things into a building ... and coming out empty-handed. "Darn! it must be their provisions warehouse — let's take it!" A dangerous undertaking, across 800 metres of a golf course. Besides, the house was heavily guarded, with around 200 soldiers about, and some armoured vehicles.

Ochi's side opened the attack, creating total confusion. "Forward!" the commander shouted. Grimy with deep black soot, the Japanese whirlwind uttered its beastly war cry. The beautiful English lawn became a terrible killing field, with British and Australian soldiers fleeing in all directions, everyone for himself.

No, Ochi thought, the British and Australians were not inferior, but at the decisive moment, when faced with no option but to show spirit in the defence of Singapore, many tried to escape instead.

Ochi was amply rewarded. His objective turned out to be a provisions store that had deeply concerned Gen. Percival.[39] Percival himself was then close at hand at his Sime Road Headquarters. Disturbed by all the sounds of the machine-gun fire, Percival sent out his aide-de-camp to investigate the situation. When Stonor of the Argylls reported back that a battle was going on at the end of the golf course, about a mile from where they were, the general decided it was time to join rear headquarters at Fort Canning in the downtown area.[40]

During the night of 12 February, the British launched a full-scale counter-attack.[41] Spectacular night flares lit up the reservoir area, where a frightful scene developed, with lots of yells and moaning and crying. It was Ochi's first experience of an enemy attack at night — were the British trying to imitate them?

Ochi's men drew up their heavy machine guns. But would their ammunition last? "Give ammo!"

"None left!"

"Then prepare hand grenades!" the platoon commander ordered. "Quick go and get some!" Ochi dashed off into wild firing. Who was friend? Who foe? Everyone was killing each other with indiscriminate firing. With some extra ammunition Ochi ran back, to continue the fight until three in the morning, when they checked their wounded and buried the dead, going without sleep.[42]

On the morning of 13 February all was clear; there were no enemy soldiers in sight. With blackened sooty faces they ate rice cakes. Running low on ammunition made their advance more difficult. Contrary to the expectations of Army Headquarters, the British had not automatically raised their hands in surrender after the fall of Bukit Timah; fighting had only intensified. One wrong step, and the campaign could easily collapse and end in a general rout of the Japanese.[43]

Their heavy guns were still on the other side of the Johor Straits. Nor had ammunition reached the front. What an idiotic war plan. The staff officers should all have come forward to the front to see for themselves! While 18th Division was fighting a desperate battle at Keppel Harbour, and the Imperial Guards Division was battling hard on the eastern front (taking Kallang airport and severing the eastern suburbs of Singapore from Singapore city), their 5th Division was stalled on the main front without ammunition. Ochi was upset.

All Army Headquarters did was issue exhortations: "Exhibit all the brilliant fighting traditions of your division and attack!"[44]

Only luck had carried his men forward unharmed, Ochi felt at the end of this hot Friday 13th, with their Ichikawa Battalion in the lead, far ahead of their division. In the evening it was difficult to dig in because the hard earth was full of small stones. The more fortunate had acquired British entrenching tools, but even their dugouts were shallow and narrow. "It's like a coffin already," someone said.[45]

Just when the sun rose, like the devil with a red glint, the first morning shell exploded with strength. Some of those who had dug no holes were thrown through the air like matchsticks. Ochi happened to be in a hole four metres deep, five by ten metres wide, probably designed as a British tank trap, which saved his life. Every other minute a giant shell exploded in the same manner. "Daaawn!" was the first seemingly unrelated sound the bomb made when it was fired off far away. But almost at once the lethal black monster was upon them.

These were the "drum cans" Arai had been watching over at Buona Vista, guessing correctly that they were meant to stop the 5th Division's onslaught south of Bukit Timah. The deadly loads were armour-piercing shells propelled by cordite cartridges inserted into the breech behind the projectile by two gunners of the British Royal Artillery, from Battery Command Post atop Fort Siloso on Blakang Mati island.

"It's coming! Coming — it's here!!" Huge thuds and explosions ushered in 14 February. For two hours the shells kept pouring into their rubber tree positions. It was chaos; the communications specialists spoke frantically on the phones, trying to tell their own artillery about their positions.[46]

At mid-day six Japanese air fighters streaked across the cobalt blue sky. It was a magnificent sight, but why wasn't their own artillery shelling the British heavy gun emplacements?[47]

When the firing subsided, Ochi's troops resumed their advance in the direction of Singapore. The front line Ichikawa Battalion would soon be in a position to make a dash into town. But their 11th Regiment was running out of ammunition, with just four and a half cases left. That meant they had 2 minutes and 15 seconds worth of bullets for each of their two heavy machine guns.[48]

Ochi didn't mind that ammunition was very low. He had a knife. He wanted most of all to see the city with his own eyes. They had come this far. The prize was just over there! After that he didn't care if he died. He would have achieved his ambition, quenched his thirst. Wada and Morimoto were sharpening their bayonets on the edge of a stone. Ochi adjusted his helmet to see better ahead. "Well, then," Ochi imitated the voice of Captain Oue, "shall we slowly get a move on?" And as always the answer came: "We're running a little late," to the merriment of all and sundry.[49]

"Forward!"

Chikatan, chikatan, chikatan. Like a locomotive they rolled on. All were becoming battle smart, and Ochi was proud of his men. But again, two wounded. Dammit! At least they were not heavily wounded. Very soon they would be in Singapore! At the latest their ammo would be gone early next morning. Machine-gunners without bullets — ha! what clowns they were! But there was no other way than forge ahead. If only to see Singapore — even if only with one eye left! *Chikatan, chikatan, chikatan,* their steam engine pushed on.[50]

If they occupied this island, Japan would have won the first round of the war! The heavily-damaged US fleet in Hawaii would not dare to stage an attack across the Pacific. And if Japan got all the oil in the Dutch East Indies, Japan would be invincible. Of course, the Army would go further and also take Australia.

But the immediate war aim was the liberation of Asia! All they had to do for now, was to take Singapore sprawling before them. It was magnificent — well done! Japan would defeat the Malayan Lion at night in force. The night attack was their specialty. "The night is one million reinforcements," their manuals said. Anyway, without ammunition it was only at night that they could advance into enemy positions. Tonight would be the great break-through. The last minutes were ticking away. To eat or be eaten, to be or not to be — to win or die! Infantry and artillery were both at their very best, one smooth magnificent body. The artillery would hurl its last shell, and then beseech the gallant infantry: "Please carry on!"[51]

However, Saturday night was not their night to enter Singapore. Regimental Headquarters wanted a massed thrust into the city, all together.

Soon day would be breaking. Ochi was studying the object on the hill next to theirs, which on their map said: Hospital. From their slightly lower location, a building appeared perched up on the neighbouring hill, just barely visible in the darkness of the early morning hours. The hospital stood in the Okabe regimental war zone. Okabe's front line troops, however, were still far behind in the MacRitchie reservoir area, locked in battle. They could not possibly advance up to their line by morning. If the hospital wasn't taken by then, the enemy would have time to gather there and trounce the Ichikawa Battalion from above. Even though the hospital lay in another battalion's battle zone, commander Ichikawa felt strongly that they had to take the building since it was the highest elevation around and a tactical hazard.

Now was a good time, he decided, and ordered 11th Company under Capt. Taruoka to immediately press an attack against Hospital Hill while it was still dark. It meant action for Ochi's colleague Yasuda and his platoon of heavy machine-gunners attached to that company.

Company commander Taruoka set off with his men.[52]

After a while, however, and to everyone's surprise, the entire 11th Company returned unexpectedly. Capt. Taruoka reported to Ichikawa: "There are so many enemy soldiers up there...."

"Taruoka — HURRY!" the commander replied, looking at his watch, "by the time day breaks we'll be in trouble!"

Taruoka turned around and rushed up again to Hospital Hill.

Ochi had been fighting for many years now, but never had he seen a company return before the object was taken. Of course, this was also the first time that Taruoka had ever done this. Although his order was couched in vague terms: "The targeted object lies really in the war zone of 41st Battalion, but go and have a look at the situation," the real meaning of the order was "Hospital Hill must be secured!". They were absolutely not supposed to return.

Why had Capt. Taruoka come back? If people are endowed with a sacred intuition, a sixth sense, Taruoka had it. The fall of Singapore was at hand, with or without Hospital Hill, and his sense of premonition simply told him that rushing Hospital Hill was suicidal.

"2nd Lieutenant Ochi!"

"Is it Yasu?"

Ochi saw Yasuda, who had his right arm in a sling.

"How's the wound?"

"Almost healed."

"What about ammunition?"

"Each gun has twenty rounds."

"Sorry about the ammunition."

"Don't be silly, over there is Singapore already."

"That's right. And that white thing up there is a hospital. Perhaps if you find some pretty little nurses, please think of me and spare me one. But no native nurse, please. Spare me a white one, a tight lassie, please, one that fits your taste," Ochi tried to be funny.

"Take good care!"

"Good luck!"

"OK. Keep it up," Yasuda's white teeth glinted, as he mixed back in with the 11th Company soldiers and disappeared into the night.[53]

Ochi looked again at the topography on the map. Far behind them they could hear the gun sounds from 41st Battalion's war line. Furious firing could be heard. Did they have enough ammunition? Or was it only the enemy firing? Unable to sleep, Ochi stood and gazed ahead at Singapore city. Then he looked back up at the hospital.

Suddenly shots were fired up there. Shots from all directions, it seemed, fierce rapid fire: "Da, da, da, da, da, da, da, da!"

After three minutes it was all over. What had happened? Surely Yasu was in luck. He must have found some Eurasian nurses and was returning with one over his shoulder, Ochi mused, as he watched the southern night sky — he would soon be thrusting into the city together with his friend.[54]

Morning broke and Hospital Hill, across, looked no higher than their own position. Ochi was with Maj. Ichikawa, sitting cross-legged, and looking at the hospital, when Pvt. Aoyama came rushing in, wounded.

"11th Company came under attack, three dead ..."

"Ah, ah," Ichikawa sighed, "Dead."

"Ochi is going up to the Hospital," Ochi saluted and ran out east.

But he didn't get far. The Ichikawa Battalion simply could not move during the day. As soon as wind moved the high grass, their advancing position was revealed, and heavy fire concentrated on them. Probably Taruoka was in the same situation.

Because of the shortage of ammunition, an attack at noon would be impossible, Maj. Ichikawa judged. They decided to wait for the evening and tackle Hospital Hill in a major night attack. But what if Capt. Taruoka now needed reinforcements badly...? One loss after the other, Ichikawa kept pondering the situation.

Ochi tried again: "Shall we go up to the Hospital?" he asked for the third time. Just then they saw fires erupt at the grass patches on Hospital Hill, probably lit by gasoline set on fire by the enemy.

"What? Go there now?" mumbled the Major. "You'll be burnt!"

Ochi ran off, anyway. He came across ten sappers and quickly enlisted them with their spades. "Cut the grass!" he ordered them, to prevent the flames from jumping into the rubber forest. The Hospital's steep approach was already partially burnt.[55]

But it was strange to see neither enemy nor friend, although firing was still going on somewhere out there. Even if Taruoka's company had been defeated, some men surely would have survived, Ochi thought. Taruoka had around 130 men (of his original 220) when he set out. Plus Yasuda's platoon added another 20, so all together around 150 men. Surely not all had perished? If Ochi went round the south side of Hospital Hill, they could easily access the compound.[56]

It was only ten in the morning, and a rotten waste having to sit still here until night. But to advance was too dangerous. Please wait, those of you remaining from Taruoka's company! Hang on!

Feeling the competition of the 3rd Battalion, the only battalion advancing, Ichikawa could not help telegraphing Regiment Headquarters in the hope of receiving approval for a dash into Singapore: "Ichikawa Battalion is poised on the northern end of Singapore, preparing to forge into town. It is 10 a.m. One company is attacking Hospital Hill."

Back at headquarters, commander Watanabe was searching his map for Hospital Hill. He found it on the northeastern edge of Singapore town. If their regimental main forces tried to advance there at their present speed, it would take them one day. So he urged restraint: "Ichikawa Battalion — stay where you are and wait for the advance of the main regimental body. The attack into town is set to take place tonight."

The cautious reply from Regimental Headquarters discouraged Ichikawa. His earlier aggressive mood was gone and he now felt hesitant. He came under more pressure from his own men who, if they could not forge into Singapore, at least they wanted to do something about Hospital Hill.[57]

Lt. Itami pressed: "It's better to advance as quickly as possible." Ochi, too, thought mainly of helping Yasuda's 2nd Platoon in trouble. Commander Ichikawa agreed that 10th Company under Capt. Okawa should detour west around to Hospital Hill, together with Ochi's machine-gun platoon.

But at 2 p.m., Capt. Okawa was still with the battalion commander. Ochi went over to Headquarters to tell commanders Ichikawa and Okawa sitting there: "Hurry up! Let's move on!"

"Ummm, well, sit down, Ochi!" Ichikawa ordered Ochi, all the while staring at the map. It was so different from this morning when he'd chased Taruoka up Hospital Hill without a second thought. Perhaps he wanted no more blood on his hands. Okawa, too, felt little like moving. "Ochi, come here!" Ichikawa said finally, opening a flask of whisky, which he offered first to Okawa and then to Ochi. They took big gulps.

"Ah! Thank you!"

"Well, then, so long." Okawa stood up.

"Forward!"

"*Ganbare!*"

Itami and Ochi moved out.

"If you find Yasuda, shoot five or six flares."

"OK. Forward!" Ochi ordered. The platoon set in motion.[58]

Silently they moved forward towards the fate of 11th Company. After a while there was a sudden flurry in the forward ranks. Ochi stepped up to see what was the matter. From the Hospital Hill's southern side many men could be seen rushing down the slope.

"That must be the enemy!"

"Stop!" Captain Okawa shouted.

"Machine-gunners — forward!" Ochi was already running ahead. From the Hospital's southern valley they saw masses of people coming up to them. Ochi ordered his men to take up their machine-gun positions number one and two.

"Let them approach to around fifty metres before you shoot!" It was a desperate situation. So many enemies and so few bullets. Each position had only three rounds of shots, a total of 90 bullets for nine seconds of shooting.

"Yessir!" Ochi observed the movements of the masses approaching. It was a strange mass of men.

"Take aim!"

"No! — wait!! Don't shoot!" Ochi noticed that not one of the oddly-clad men carried a weapon. Tramping along and gesticulating with cries, they came straight ahead.

"Keep the safety lock on!!" Ochi shouted as he ran down the hill to the men. When he got close to them he spread his arms: "All men stop!" Twice he shouted at the top of his voice. From out of the mass appeared a white flag. At the same time a white flag was lowered out of the Hospital's second floor window.

"What's all this?" Ochi confronted the crowd. "What are you doing?"

"We are surrendering!" their leader, a corporal, said in broken Japanese, with an affable smile.

"Surrender?" Ochi couldn't believe it. He remembered a situation at Labis in Johor where British soldiers had hoisted a white flag and then attacked.

"Sit down!" Ochi said in a more relaxed voice. The leader gave the order and all sat down.

"Hand your pistols to 1st Platoon!"

As Ochi oversaw this operation covering close to 2,000 surrendering personnel, the white men looked on at Ochi, inquisitively.

Ochi looked at his watch. It was quarter past two in the afternoon. The cannons had ceased firing. There was an unusual quiet over the island.

"That hill, too?" Ochi pointed to the hospital. "Is it surrendering too?"

"Yes, it's a total surrender. Japan won."

Total? you fools, Ochi thought, aren't you soldiers? "Where are your officers?"

"At four o' clock the whole battle will stop. The officers won't come out until that time. We've all discussed this matter and decided to abandon the hill. At other places the Japanese army is still far from their target, but here we are very close. We don't know when you will attack."

(Unconditional surrender! Holy smokes! So it was ...)

"Are British soldiers still up there?" Ochi pointed to the hospital.

"No soldiers, only officers."

(It could be a lie, Ochi thought, let me go and see...)

"Ooooi! Call the Captain! The enemy has surrendered," Ochi shouted to his men above. The commander of 10th Company came down with his men.[59]

Ochi ran off down into the valley and up on the other side to find out for himself. The hill side was burnt to the roots.

"Aah!" said someone who looked like a Japanese from out of the burnt shrubs, with wild eyes.

"Aaah! Ochi dono, Sir!" was all the man could say.

"Are you wounded? Pull yourself together!"

"I am Nakamura from 2nd Platoon!"

"Yes!"

"Not wounded!" he said, trembling all over.

"What about Yasu San?"

"He's alive!" he uttered in a strangled voice. They reached the steep slope of Hospital Hill which was totally blackened by the burnt shrub and grass. Ochi left Nakamura and went on calling: "Yasu-San!" running straight up the hill's winding road.

There up in a thicket lay Yasuda holding his breath.

"Oi! Yasu San!" His face popped out of the bush, eyes glaring, with the look of a man gone crazy and about to kill. "Good, man, you're alive!" But Yasu only stared at Ochi with demented eyes.

Ochi shouted his name.

"Oh! 2nd Lt. Sir!" cried Yasuda and came out down on to the road with his revolver in his right hand.

"It's dangerous with a revolver. Won't you put it away?"

"Yes, yes," slowly Ochi approached Yasuda. He took his revolver. "What happened, Yasu?"

The machine-gunners had been climbing the steep slope of Hospital Hill. Just when they thought Taruoka's company must have arrived up at the plateau, heavy fire erupted with crying voices of desperation, broken calls, sentences stopped in death, calling each other. From the sound of their voices he knew that all were dead. It had happened instantly. Nothing could be done.

Taruoka wiped out? In only an instant, immediately? That couldn't be. Yet up above Ochi it was unusually calm.

When the firing had started, Yasuda and his men had jumped into the grass to crawl back to base. But whenever the wind blew the grass, concentrated fire came immediately at them. When day broke, Yasuda and his men could move no more. They had to dig in on the hillside and wait it out in their foxholes. Gradually wind and enemy fire strengthened, and all they could do was hold their breath. Whenever the wind blew and revealed any one of them, the man was doomed. Whoever moved, was shot.

When the valley started to burn with gasoline, Yasuda's platoon prepared for annihilation. But the fire avoided them and swept uphill, and the enemy never came out to attack. So Yasuda and his men had to dig in, while quietly above their heads the enemy waited, patiently, picking them out. At noon, Nakamura decided to make a dash and report back to headquarters; at 1 p.m. Fukuhara left; at 2 p.m. Yasuda gripped his revolver: "Tamura, try after me at 3 p.m., please. But if I don't return, send no one else. Have the rest remain here until the end!" With this, Yasuda had set off ... almost insane. At the end of his story, all Yasuda could say was: "Ochi 2nd Lt. Sir!" over and over again.

"Where is everyone now?" Ochi asked.

"Up there." He cried again.

"Yasu San, Nakamura is down there! Quick, go and report with him back to headquarters! The enemy has surrendered!"

Yasuda dashed down, alert again.[60]

"Ooi! 2nd Platoon anyone? The enemy has surrendered!" Ochi cried out loudly in the opposite direction, as he climbed the hill. "Put away your weapons!"

Ochi arrived on the top of Hospital Hill, which had become the barracks of the enemy machine-gunners. At the entrance of one building, in a half-circle, lay the bodies of one unit. Some still had the finger on the trigger. Their positions spoke of a sudden *blitz* attack. Eyes were all fixed upward on one particular point from where they must have been met with sudden fire. In the middle of the crescent lay 2nd Lt. Hamamoto. His body faced Ochi and he seemed to be smiling, with apple coloured cheeks and clear eyes.

"Hamamoto! The enemy has surrendered!" Ochi shouted at him.

But the crimson coloured young man didn't stir.

Are you dead? Ochi could not believe it. He tapped Hamamoto's cheek. It felt hard and cold. There was also the smell of blood.

Ochi looked around. He checked other soldiers. All were glaring at him.

"Ooi! Oooi! Ooooooi!" No one answered, only deep silence. So, all were dead. Ochi was inured to seeing dead men in battle. But this death scene was different. He would not forget it until the end of his life. It was inexplicable.

Until the moment when the bullets struck them, Hamamoto's men must have believed themselves invincible. There was absolutely nothing sinister in their final expressions. Rather, their faces were light and clear. It was good of you, Hama, to die with your men, Ochi felt. The bodies were positioned in their platoon formation, as if they were going to rise any moment and make a dash and finish their task, before their sudden death in a rain of a thousand bullets.

Ochi sketched the locations of all the fallen bodies. He found Capt. Taruoka stooped over with his back against a wall, feet stretched out, head collapsed forward on his chest. Two other platoons were poised left and right in attack positions, with the command group about to advance into the space between them. Commander Taruoka must have been standing on top of a small crest directing the attack of each of his company platoons. It was a perfect text book formation. The dead soldiers, too, lay as if they were just about to rise and carry out the attack. Capt. Taruoka appeared to have slipped and fallen on that small hill's back edge before he was killed. From there, it seemed, Taruoka was pulled by three of his soldiers, holding in one hand their weapon, with the other dragging their commander away from the fire of the enemy, about ten metres to the back, as they themselves perished in a hail of bullets. One soldier died still holding the left foot of Taruoka.

The forward-most platoon, too, lay in a crescent around the entrance of the inner building. The 2nd lieutenant of the Kariyama Platoon had collapsed in the middle of their formation on the concrete of the entrance, waving his sword in one hand high above his head. His mouth half open, with clenched white teeth, he must just have heard the deathly cackle "Ka!" of a dozen triggers, as he ducked to evade the bullets which killed him instantly. Ochi could only approach him in awe, uneasily. His head lay sideways on the concrete. Between his eyes and ears were holes from which blood still trickled.

Are there such things in this world? No one from the Company Captain downwards had survived. All of them had died in these lively attitudes and postures. One could easily believe that of one man, or of several — but for a hundred human beings all to die at the same time, in the same place — was it possible? Ochi couldn't get over it. It was an unbelievable scene. Nothing moved on Hospital Hill. All was silent. Only the sun shone hot on the green trees and the white building.[61]

"Taruoka!" someone cried out behind him. Ochi turned around. Several men in dirty uniforms had entered the scene and stood round Capt. Taruoka. Maj. Ichikawa, who had sent him to his death, held Taruoka in his arms, shaking him and swaying, hoping he was still alive.... "Taruoka!" the major's voice trembled loudly. "It was terrible for you!"

Ochi looked at Lt. Itami who looked out far away into the valley. Ochi turned around and raced down the hill.

The sun had gone down. Fires lit up. One lonely plane droned in the evening sky, its engine ebbing and growing, all alone, beginning to dive. It was an eerie situation, like in a faraway, different world.

"Well, has it already stopped, now ...?" asked Yamate. The war, he meant. The strain had not yet lifted from the men of Yasuda's Platoon who had survived Hospital Hill. Even now there were many weeping faces. There was so much to cry about. Silently they looked on into the fire. Like enlightened monks (*arhat*), with expressionless mien, huddled close together.

Ochi rejoined his men.

"Surrender — does it mean only this place?"

"No, the entire front."

"Don't be foolish! Over there, they're still superior, we've got a little ammo still...."

"Even if it were so, we've received orders to stop attacking."

"That's strange."

Just like Arai, and all the men in the 114th Regiment at the 18th Division's Keppel Harbour war zone, they, found it a strange ending. The front line men just could not figure it out. But from the hills behind them, as if part of a great wave, they could hear victory shouts of Banzai! come rolling on.

"Well, Sir, may we make a fire?" Sgt. Asahina asked.

"What ... fire?" Ochi did not get it immediately. He looked across at Lt. Itami who sat cross-legged, miles away, lost in thought.

"It's OK," Ochi said, "Go ahead, light fires."

Asahina guided the men to a hut with lots of wood to burn. Other companies followed suit and quickly they had several fires burning.[62]

"Company Commander, Sir — won't you propose a toast?" Sgt. Asahina asked.

"What? A toast? Kampai?" Lt. Itami looked up at Sgt. Asahina, his white cheeks shone on by the flames that lent him grace.

"Well, you see, I've brought a bottle of whiskey along and I thought..."

Lt. Itami, motionless, looked Asahina's face down to his heels, very slowly.

"Whiskey?" someone else said. "Are we allowed to have it?"

"Well, I'm not much of a drinker myself," Asahina said uneasily, "But in case we made it into Singapore alive, I thought I'd drink a whole bottle straight down; so although I threw away a lot of things during the battle, I held on to one little bit of whiskey...." All laughed.

"You brought it along with you?" the lieutenant asked. It was against company regulations. With a studied expression, Lt. Itami finally said: "OK. Well then, Sergeant Asahina. Bring out that bottle of whiskey!" All this with a straight face is top class, Ochi thought. Here is one good lieutenant.

Like a young cadet, obediently, Asahina trotted off to execute this order, returning in a moment with a square can in both hands. "What a stiff-necked, impudent, stubborn, intractable guy," Yamaguchi said. "Until this day he's been carrying this huge thing around with him!" Sanetomi's voice sounded full of regret.

"You Sanetomi — you must wait for the first drink until the first day into victory!" Everyone roared with laughter. But the momentary levity quickly died down in the flames, as whiskey was poured out in drops into tin mess cans. The officer went around to express his grief and extend his condolences to soldiers.

"Thanks to everyone's effort today, this Fifteenth of February, the fight for the conquest of Singapore is over. Here's a toast to the future of the Japanese Empire!" Lt. commander Itami raised his cup.

"Banzai!" "Banzai!"

It was a muffled, soft Banzai. It was gentle, an honest Banzai that could only be uttered at the very front. Not a sentimental Banzai shouted from the top of the voice somewhere behind the lines, in some backwater of the Empire, or in a raucous locality in downtown Tokyo. Theirs was a toast spoken in awareness of all that had happened and from the bottom of the heart.

At the same time an approaching emptiness seemed to cry out: "What's next?" No one had thought about that. Their one burning purpose had been to conquer Singapore.[63]

The crackling campfire cast its spell. Had it all just ended like this? And was it satisfying? All their comrades who were gone. Couldn't be brought back to life again. Over there, before them, lay Singapore. To conquer it, all together and alive, had been their hope and sole purpose. Never thinking of the cost. Only, we must storm it! ... but at what price.... Had it all been worth it?

"For His Royal Highness, the Emperor!" — it was all just dressing, and in Ochi's mind that included indulging in singing the anthem Kimigayo. What sentimental hogwash. The real thing was not that. "For the country, for one's descendants" was what "history" would make of it afterwards. Only they who had battled and lost so much could know the true feeling: "We opened the way for Japan!" The battle of the century had ended, and probably history from that day would undergo a great change. But let us never forget that the Malayan campaign, and the fall of Singapore, was neither "for the Emperor" nor was it won in a tactical "operation"! It had nothing to do with that. It had to do only with fighting spirit. That was all. It was so clear to the men who sat silently around the campfire that night. It was a very lonely mood.[64]

"Lieutenant Commander, Sir, I'm going to sing a war song," Ochi cut the silence.

"What? — ah, OK. Go ahead!"

"All together, now, Infantry, let's sing on our territory!" Ochi led them into the song "Damashii Yamato". Soon each company sang its songs, while on Hospital Hill burial squads were disposing of the bodies of Capt. Taruoka and his men. Waves of songs wafted over them as they worked, and a bright fire burnt late into the night.

Lt. Itami sang along, as he scrutinised his men, one by one, thinking deeply about each one of the soldiers, his men, who had departed.

"Is it all right to sleep?" someone asked.

"I want to sleep quickly."

"Sentries — don't put out the fires." One after the other, slowly they went off to sleep around the fire. But many could not. One could hear whispering and murmuring continuously.

"Ochi, 2nd Lieutenant, Sir." Yasuda sat down beside Ochi.

"The officers of 11th Company did it ... right?" Yasuda's eyes moistened, thinking again of Taruoka. On their way to Malaya in the transport ship's saloon, Capt. Taruoka in the middle, shoulder to shoulder with officers Kariyama, Akishina, and Hamamoto, the four of them, hop, hop, hop, had done a French dance and the company commander had sung a song, Ochi and Yasuda reminisced. Together they broke out in quiet laughs. Why had it happened this way? Disperse, disperse....

Strange. "Our platoon only suffered three lightly wounded." It was fortunate. But there was no need to chatter that much! Ochi thought, tears welling up inside.

"Yasu-San, let's go to sleep."

"Yes ... well, finally we can!"

"It was a dangerous place."

"Are you sleepy?"

"Well, a little."

"It was bitter for the Captain."

"Well, for all of them."

"Poor Taruoka..."

"Well, Yasu San, let's sleep."

"Yes." For a long time, both looked into the night sky, and then dozed off.

The Eurasian Asuta in Haadyai was calling Ochi in his dream. She had beautiful big hips which she could bend nicely. The Indian girl from Kuala Lumpur was there, too, with good hips. And the handkerchief of Asuta bandaged his light wound. All around them it was still as in the world of death. And from the shoulder wound bound with Asuta's handkerchief Taruoka's face peeped out fiendishly.[65]

* * *

After crossing the Straits, the Imperial Guards advanced quickly into the northeastern section of the Mandai ridge, just beyond the causeway, held by the Australian 27th Brigade. For seven days in February, Singapore Island was a gigantic chessboard on which the coloured invaders challenged the white defenders, inexorably pushing King George into a tight corner at Keppel Harbour, Hospital Hill, and finally also at Paya Lebar, in the eastern sector of Singapore Island, where the Imperial Guards were turning on the pressure.

Brig. Maxwell lost his front pawns, as the right wing of the 5th Kobayashi Regiment advanced on West Hill 145, and the middle, and left wings move against East Hill 60. After occupying Seletar airbase, Lt.-Gen. Nishimura ordered an advance west into the northern side of the reservoir area, and then south towards Bukit Timah to relieve the 5th and 18th Divisions. These zigzag movements caused some confusion for the 13,000 Imperial Guard troops, as they were sent first east and then west, but always in a southerly direction to split the island's eastern zone from Singapore city.

Moreover the pace of Tsuchikane's company attacks got faster, more hurried. There was no time to rest, just go forward, and again forward. Cannon smoke hung over their way amid the never-ending sound of guns. Enemy trucks, jeeps, and armoured vehicles obstructed their frantic passage, marked by corpses that lay neglected in grotesque positions that reflected the agony of their last moments. In the beautiful English gardens and on the lawns of superb villas, smashed cars and trucks were burning, upside down. Rubber, palm, and banana trees were in shreds. There was devastation everywhere: holes in the road, churned up rubble lying in great clods all round, tangled masses of telephone, telegraph and electric cables strewn across the street, and everywhere the smell of the blast of aerial bombs. Estates burnt down, and in the ghastly scene of destruction Tsuchikane felt pity.

Everywhere in the beautiful island's total chaos the panicked local people were dashing here and there, not knowing where to turn, balancing their belongings on long shoulder poles, running pell mell in confusion, going in circles, while Tsuchikane's battalion advanced inexorably throughout the night.[66]

The sugar cane field they were coming out of gave way to a rice paddy, and this paddy continued on for about 200 metres before reaching a patch of rubber. In the middle of the rice paddy ran a narrow water ditch, about one and a half metres wide, with a narrow footpath on its right side.

On this path, the soldiers now filed across the paddy one after the other. Made careless by the heat and the ease of advance, they carried their weapons slung over their shoulders. Nibbling merrily on cane stubs, and licking off the sweet juice, they filed over the footpath in one single row.

They were just about to reach the middle of the paddy, when the enemy opened up fire from inside the rubber forest. Taken completely by surprise, Tsuchikane's unit jumped into the ditch, sinking into the slush, burying their faces in the mud as violent machine-gun volleys grazed the footpath above their heads. One bullet passed through Tsuchikane's rucksack sticking out on top of him, giving his body a wild jolt.

This was it. The end. He'd come this far only to die. In an ever-changing panorama, the faces of his family appeared one after the other. He could neither lift his head, nor move. He lay immobile. Just like that. And breathed. It was the only way to be sure he was still alive. As time passed and nothing happened, he became a little easier. The enemy appeared to have been shooting from out of the front rubber forest's left side. In this situation how could they best move into an attacking position?[67]

His friend First Class Soldier Tomihari, right behind him, set up his light machine gun on the footpath of the ditch and activated the trigger. It worked, opposition fire stopped quickly. Tsuchikane, too, began to fire back. Gradually they were joined by fire from their front and back ranks.

From many places now they could hear groans. Tsuchikane realized that some of their group had been badly hit.

Then Tomihari cried out and his gun jumped out of his hands, all bloody. Tsuchikane reached for the towel he kept under his helmet. The towel was always there to keep the helmet on tightly, and also to keep some space between the helmet — which heated up — and the crown of his head. He pressed the towel against Tomihari's wound. It was tough on him, but all Tsuchikane could do in their awkward position. Then First Class Soldier Kayama, in front of Tsuchikane, called out: "Sergeant Tsuchikane, Sir, my stomach seems very hot. Please have a look at it," writhing in pain.

"Show me." Tsuchikane looked at him in a half-crouching posture. No blood came out of his abdomen. No traces of a bullet. "Show me your back."

In the ditch water he sat with his back exposed and his waist slightly elevated. Tsuchikane looked closer. In the middle of his belt was a small round hole. A bullet had pierced him, and come to a stop inside Kayama's stomach. If he told him that, Kayama might get so worried that he really would die.

"No. There's nothing. Absolutely nowhere you've been hit. It's OK. Let's get a move on."

"Yes Sir!" said Kayama who recovered miraculously.

"Sir, 1st Class Soldier Mori was hit too." He had been right behind Tomihari.

"I've been hit on the head," he said with a bloodied face, but comporting himself well. He still had a good, clear, strong voice. It looked as if a bullet had entered his helmet and grazed his head. He was lucky.

As well, First Class Soldier Ueno, just in front of Kamiyama, was dripping blood from the mouth. One couldn't understand what he said. On a closer look, he had been hit in the throat.[59]

The officers of the platoon and the company called out their soldiers' names to see who was alive. Slowly they established who was wounded and who dead. The huge popular company commander Otsuka was badly hurt on both arms. Platoon leader Kobayashi had got it in the legs. Many were dead. Tsuchikane didn't know how much time had passed. The sun was already setting into the rubber trees. Finally they heard their artillery respond to the attack, and the enemy's response.

But they still had no idea about the strength or whereabouts of the enemy and couldn't get out of the ditch yet. Calling each other's names, they encouraged their comrades to carry on and not to give up, as they waited for complete darkness to settle. The attack must have taken place around ten in the morning. Nine hours in the ditch had made their bodies go cold and purple.

When it was completely dark, they clambered back onto the dirt path to shake their limbs and sort themselves out. In Tsuchikane's platoon only four, including himself, had survived unharmed. Four more were lightly hurt and could go on. That made them eight. Other platoons, too, had suffered. It had been the worst possible place to be hit, and wiped out almost the entire strength of their company. A lieutenant had led them across the Straits; when he was wounded, a sergeant had taken over; now a second-year corporal became their leader. Responsibility was fast moving down the chain of command.

To their right, down a slope, stood some houses. There they brought their dead and wounded, and entered a house to rest and dry their clothes. The owners had left suddenly. A meal was still on the table, untouched, with hot food in a pan on the stove and piles of bananas in the room. They gulped it all down and began to feel good again.

First they administered to the wounded. For the heavily wounded they built stretchers to dispatch them back to rear quarters. The unfortunates on the verge of death got no stretchers. The more lightly wounded received medicine to administer themselves. The long time in the ditch had caused their limbs to swell and made walking difficult. In this condition they were useless as a fighting unit, and the commander decided to stay put for the night.

It would give them time to bury the dead (after first severing their wrists to return hands to their homes). But digging proved difficult, and after only 30 centimetres water appeared. So they did the opposite, they heaped earth to create a burial mound where they placed the corpses.

Fig. 10   Grave markers and offerings for Japanese soldiers killed in action.

With two others, Tsuchikane was then ordered to ossify the wrists and hands by burning them to the bone. In an adjoining house, after sealing it and making sure no smoke escaped outside, they washed the pan from which they had just eaten their hot meal and put it on the stove. First they took commander Miyamoto's hand from the mess tin and began to grill it. "Shuu, shuu," it sizzled in the pan, with lots of grease escaping from the hand. Strong smoke with a hideous stench soon filled the room. It got unbearably hot and the three stripped to their loincloths as sweat cascaded down their bodies. One wrist took ages. Their chopsticks got shorter, catching fire many times owing to their efforts of turning the flesh and then burning away the muscle from the bones. The bones picked from the charcoal were transferred to a British tobacco can and passed on to the men waiting outside. They, in turn, put the bones in a white cloth and stored the packages with great care in their service bags.

The soldiers had promised each other to enter Singapore together, even if it were only their remains. They had fought together until today, they had eaten the same rice, they had ducked under the same bullets, and they felt bonds no different from those between brothers. Perhaps the bonds were even stronger through their knowledge of man's fleeting existence they had experienced each day over the past months.[69]

Again the guns boomed and in the garden an explosion created a pillar of fire. Tsuchikane ran out of the house. "We're here! Come!" The order was shouted from a villa 50 metres away. Tsuchikane jumped over the shrubs, as the house he'd just been in came under concentrated artillery fire. After 20 minutes the attack died down.

Tsuchikane went back to count the dead and wounded and assess the new damage done. There were large holes in the garden, the papaya trees in tatters, and half the house where Tsuchikane and his mates had been working was blown away. The mound they'd built for their fallen comrades was also gone. One platoon of heavy machine-gunners who had sought refuge in an air-raid shelter in the garden had received a direct hit in the trench. All died.

Only a couple of hours ago they'd rejoiced over surviving one attack in the ditch, only to perish in the next one. The guns of February either struck or they didn't, as the wheel of fortune steadily reduced the strength of the company to a third of its original fighting strength.

Their unit of eight got underway early next morning, zigzagging inside the rubber forest, changing their path left, then right, frequently. They did this all day until the evening of 14 February.[70]

The next morning Tsuchikane's company discovered a rich cache of war vehicles and materiel, wool covers, uniforms, shoes, and food among the rubber trees. Trucks, jeeps, reconnoitering vehicles, all brand new, without a scratch on them. Their mileage showed that they'd been driven a couple of kilometres up to the front. Even their gasoline tanks were full. Just landed, the fresh war materiel must have been transported straight to the front, unused. All personnel changed into fresh uniforms, and after a good meal their spirits returned.

The company commander spread out a map and began a speech: "Our company is about eight hundred metres from the enemy's defensive positions. We shall shortly begin our attack. First we capture the defense positions and then, in one stroke, we advance on the road to the right which leads straight into Singapore."

They were noble words, worthy of any company leader. The only thing wrong was the fact that theirs was a company in name only. Their actual strength was that of a full-sized platoon. If they really went ahead this would be everyone's final attack.

They straightened their uniforms, tightened their belts, and for one last time went through the motions of jabbing the enemy with a bayonet.

Tsuchikane's buddy, First Class Soldier Kimura, who had been with him since Alor Star, said good-bye: "Corporal Tsuchikane, please take care of me when I'm dead." His time had come and he was preparing for the final moment on earth. "Yes, I will," said Tsuchikane, "and if it's my time, please look after me." The company deployed into the rubber forest and began its advance. No one said a word.[71]

Curiously, the violent rifle fire was weakening; even the cannon sounds were falling off. Then they could no longer hear even the machine-gun rattle, nor the ubiquitous crackle of pistols. The noise on the war front was giving way to an unsettling calm.

Faintly, from somewhere, they heard: "Banzai!" "Banzai!"

"That's a Banzai," someone said in a loud voice. All stopped and strained their ears.

"Yes, really, it is a Banzai!"

"We did it, we did it!" "We won!" Some did a happy little jig.

But the commander admonished them: "We have no official communication! Don't be careless! Until the attack on the front comes to a full stop, we don't know when we'll be attacked by the enemy."

For a while they stood by in the rubber forest, until their messenger returned from Headquarters, and the company commander announced the official surrender of the enemy.[72]

The soldiers took out small rising sun flags to attach to their gun barrels. Pvt. First Class Soldier Uchida broke out in tears. It was so good to cry. The sweaty, dirt covered, smelly warriors, embraced each other happily, and shouted over and over again in loud voices: "Banzai! Banzai!" as evening settled on the rubber forest. Many soldiers wept openly, some quite loudly. Tsuchikane, too, felt tears running down his cheeks, unable to hold them back.

First Class Soldier Fujimoto took out the remains from the cloth wrapping and, holding the wrist bones high up, he shouted to his war buddy: "Hey. Listen! Ooi! The enemy has surrendered! Do you hear? Singapore has capitulated, you know!!" Emotions reached a high, words became awkward, and then just blubbering and sobbing.

Fig. 11   British and Japanese military personnel honour dead soldiers at a Christian gravesite.

It was a grand moment, and when they had digested it, the company returned to the rich depot in the woods, from where they had started out on their final attack, this time filled with relief and merry laughter. It was time for war songs into the night, time to relax in the rubber forest, time to feast freely on the Churchill supplies and fill their bellies to their hearts' delight. There was also talk of the fallen comrades. The fire from the nearby tanks still burned madly, bathed all in a soft hue of red light. How long had it been since they'd enjoyed such a peaceful night? Tsuchikane leant against his rucksack and became absorbed in reminiscences of his hometown. Nearby he soon heard snoring.[73]

Early on 16 February, they drove into town with four of the new trucks decorated with flags given them by their friends when they had left their homes in Japan. All was quiet as they passed along the road into Singapore. Intact villas appeared. Beautiful homes. These must be the suburbs. And there, tall buildings — that must be Singapore city.

With a machine gun mounted on top, their trucks sped into town at 40 km/hour. They found no resistance along the rows of houses and then careened into the first curve, and saw their first Prisoners of War. The Japanese soldiers thought it safer to point their rifles at them. The prisoners walked in rows of fours, some without shoes, many half naked from the waist up. British, Indian, Australian, and other soldiers all mixed together. All were tired out, walking or hobbling along.

Tsuchikane felt no hostility towards these silently suffering men, despite the loss of so many of his comrades at the hands of these creatures. Rather, he felt pity: that's your lot when you lose at war, he mused as they passed many more on their way to the city centre.

But at what cost victory had come! Moving slowly into the town, many soldiers held the urns of their fallen comrades high over their heads, so that those who had fallen in the line of duty might join in the victory. Tsuchikane was 22 years old when he savoured this sweet moment. The strength of his company, 130 strong when they had left Indochina, now stood at 40, including the wounded. His 2nd Platoon now had just four members, including himself. Silently he bowed his head. The price to enter the city had been exorbitant.

Their trucks continued down Orchard Road, until they came to a stop in front of a tall Ferro-concrete building that looked like a bank.

Inside, Tsuchikane's entire company received the order to join the Military Police forces as auxiliary troops. They would be in the rare position to stay in the city to establish law and order in Singapore.[74] What an honour and superb crowning of his short and impressive career to redress the *status quo* among the big powers in the world.

Tsuchikane couldn't know it at the time, as not even the military police itself did, that before the week was up, they would have nothing left to be proud of. For it would be in connection with his new work, as an auxiliary trooper under Onishi and the Second Military Police Field Unit, that the huge Japanese victory would quickly slide into utter dissipation.

10

The Victory Dissipated

TSUCHIKANE, Ochi, and Arai had exhausted themselves fighting an enemy whom, since Johor Bahru, Onishi Satoru and his military policemen had continuously underestimated in their intelligence reports to Army Headquarters. On the second day of the battle for Singapore it was Onishi's turn to test the enemy's strength for himself. He was then still attached to the Imperial Guards Division, with orders to stay as close as possible to the front-line troops. The front-liners, however, gave them a hard time when Onishi and his men wanted to join their assault craft on the evening of 9 February. They had no room for policemen. As usual, Onishi had to plead with the staff division officer before finally being allotted space in one of the boats of the communication unit.[1]

During their crossing, the sky near the Mandai hills, where the main assault force was moving inland, was ablaze with the bombardments from both sides. Their boat headed for the Kranji River mouth immediately west of the causeway. When they landed at the far end of a rubber plantation, the entire area was still filled with smoke from burning oil tanks, which three hours earlier had contributed to the death of many in Tsuchikane's first assault wave. Even before their scouts returned, the troops started out along the narrow road of the rubber plantation. In the absence of feedback from the scouts, they wandered to the west, straying into the battle zone of the 5th Division, whose mop-up operation was still underway. Onishi found himself advancing on ground strewn with the corpses of newly-fallen Australian soldiers.[2]

By noon they caught up with a 5th Division unit near Tengah airfield, from where they advanced down Choa Chu Kang Road towards Bukit Panjang. To his great joy, Onishi came across Kempeitai Headquarters at two o'clock, and immediately reported to his commander Oishi, who was happy to have Onishi's unit back, unharmed.

"But this is not our battle zone," Onishi apologised to the commander, "we drifted too much into the Fifth Division's battle section. We shall immediately correct our course and catch up with our Imperial Guards Division."

"That won't be necessary," said Oishi, "I have received orders from Headquarters to have all Kempeitai units released from their respective divisions, and to reassemble and proceed as one unit on our own again." From the commander's voice, Onishi sensed vaguely that something was afoot. He could not say what, but made a mental note of it. Already in January, at Kluang, Oishi had apparently received orders to gather back his troops, once on the island.[3]

All day and the next the military police stayed close to the Japanese troops attacking Bukit Timah, the main obstacle to the conquest of Singapore, and important strategically because the two reservoirs on its eastern side were the main source of Singapore's water supply. Located to its north were the headquarters of the Australian 8th Division, commanded by Western Area commander Lt.-Gen. Gordon Bennett.

On the night of 10 February, the 18th Division from the west of Bukit Timah and the 5th Division from Bukit Panjang attacked the main Hill 225 of Bukit Timah, which they occupied on the evening of the 11th. The military police advanced on the other side and awaited further orders.[4]

When Army Headquarters knew that Singapore would fall, it began to worry about disgraceful acts troops might commit on forays into town. On 13 February it allotted the military police additional manpower and assigned them specific battle zones. The commanders were determined to maintain military discipline and public order. As a result, the Kempeitai would be part of the final assault. They would fight among the front line troops.

After receiving orders to this effect on the morning of 13 February, Col. Oishi immediately had his military police advance in the following formations: the left wing military police headquarters, under Lt.-Col. Yokoda Yoshitaka, would be led by Lt. Mizuno Keiji, Lt. Goshi Kosuke, and Lt. Onishi Satoru. Right wing headquarters, under Maj. Jyo Tomotatsu, would be led by Capt. Uezono Yoshiharu and Lt. Hisamatsu Haruji.[5]

Near the Bukit Timah crossroad, they came under heavy fire for one hour and forty minutes. A shell fragment hit Lt.-Col. Yokoda, but was deflected by a flashlamp on his belt. Chief of war operations, Col. Tsuji Masanobu, and his assistant, Maj. Asaeda Shigeharu, happened to be sheltering in the ditches along with the left wing unit. During a lull Tsuji said: "The advance of the Kempeitai is premature, just take shelter for the time being."[6]

Maj. Jyo's unit on the right, however, continued the advance. He sent out two truck loads of military police, headed by Second Lt. Nakashima of the attached infantry regiment, to scout the road. As they approached the south-west Bukit Timah crossroad, enemy fire killed Nakashima and his Malayan driver, and wounded two others.

Since it proved impossible to advance, they received orders from military intelligence to investigate the Mandai area. The entire military police was despatched in the night of 14 February, but they found nothing suspicious.[7]

What concerned commander Oishi and his lieutenants was a serious shortage of ammunition, something that could soon land them all in great trouble. By 14 February, the artillery was running precariously low on shells. Large numbers were available in Johor, but the invasion force could not spare men to collect them, or cope with the problem of bringing them to the front amid heavy British shelling. Some at Headquarters Staff Office even thought it better to stop the attack temporarily.[8]

At the surrender conference, Gen. Yamashita had agreed that no regular army units would be allowed into the city of Singapore; maintenance of law and order would be the sole responsibility of the Military Police, beefed up by extra troops drawn from the three divisions. That same evening, Col. Oishi gathered all his officers to assign them their garrison zones. He explained the various points where the Allies would surrender their weapons and elaborated on the general rules that would govern the occupation of the city, the disarming of enemy troops, the patrolling of the island, and the maintenance of public order.

Lt.-Col. Yokoda would supervise the eastern part of the city from the Kallang River in the east to the Singapore River in the west. This area was further divided into three zones handled by the Mizuno Unit, the Goshi Unit, and the unit of Lt. Onishi, which was assigned the crowded Jalan Besar area that bordered on Kallang River.

Fig. 12 Japanese troops on parade in Singapore.

Maj. Shiro was put in charge of the town area west of the Singapore River, patrolled by the Kamizono Unit and the Hisamatsu Unit.

Raffles College, where the British Army made its last stand, near the Bukit Timah/Adam Road junction, would be the general meeting place for agreements on detailed matters following the surrender of the British Army, and commander Oishi ordered Onishi to go there early next morning to disarm the enemy troops.[9]

The Onishi Unit entered Raffles College on Monday morning at six o'clock. Without an interpreter, Onishi forced his way past enemy troops lounging on their sides. A number of them were shaving. Onishi was slightly amused. To him, a bit more deference towards the victor seemed in order; probably the British troops had not given much thought to the fact that from now on they would be prisoners. They showed no feeling of shame, or of humility; they seemed to take it more like a sports event; they had lost one match. But for the Japanese who had given their life for this match, for whom felling the citadel of white colonial supremacy had meant everything, it created a strange impression.

"Did you sleep well last night?" Onishi engaged the brigade leader in genial conversation, praising the British military exploits. He quickly interviewed him and then directed that all weapons, other than those considered to be private property under international law, be piled up in the university square. Cavalier about it all and with exceeding frankness, the urbane British leader quickly complied with Onishi's directives, and commanded his troops to commence disarming. Following which, the British army was instructed to assemble at Changi Prison Camp.[10]

With this task out of the way, Kempeitai commander Oishi took Onishi's unit with him to requisition the central police station in downtown Singapore. They arrived there on 17 February at nine o'clock in the morning. The British station chief had left his post, and the only staff present were the local police and the night watch. Commander Oishi summoned the remaining police officers and explained to them that under the Japanese Army, they would be given better treatment than they had received under the British, and that the local police would continue to maintain public order in the city. The local officers thereupon immediately gathered together the rest of the station staff and ordered them to continue working as usual. The same instructions were relayed to each police station in the city.[11]

Another task was to free the Japanese residents of Singapore, around 40 of them, held at Changi Prison since the outbreak of war. Many of them became translators or guides, and assisted the army.[12]

While Military Police Headquarters was set up in Gen. Percival's battle command post at Fort Canning, the military police units established guard posts in their respective sectors of the city and settled down in the police stations. They were empowered to stop soldiers or civilians in military employ from entering the city, but owing to a lack of manpower it was difficult to carry out this task. A hundred things demanded their attention, and initially they had a difficult time assembling and transferring the surrendered troops, controlling conflagrations caused by accidental fires, and upholding public order. While they were able to prevent most looting by residents in the city, this proved more difficult in the outlying English residential areas.[13]

With the assignment of around 150 supplementary troops per military police unit, drawn from the three divisions, they were able to gain control of public order two or three days later. In the meantime, Onishi's Unit at the Kandang Kerbau police station began administrative activities. He moved into the White House Hotel, a popular pre-war drinking place for British soldiers, on the corner of Jalan Besar and Mayo Street.[14]

In those first days after the fall of Singapore, Gen. Yamashita gathered his troops at the campus of Raffles College on 20 February to pay tribute to those who had fallen in battle and at the same time to present awards to those who had done well. On this occasion, Campaign Manager Col. Tsuji gave a speech, entitled "Malaya, Singapore Operations" to the officers. Onishi was in the audience, and couldn't help being impressed by Tsuji's masterful direction of operations, his sharpness of mind, and the trenchant clarity with which he presented the countless factors that had contributed to the success. There was, however, some criticism of Tsuji among the high-ranking officers, for he spoke boastfully, as if he had handled the war operations all by himself. And even as he described the decisiveness which he had shown in directing operations to take the Bukit Timah high land, his disposition as a man of extremes was causing the Imperial Army to commit one of its gravest mistakes, an irrevocable error that would haunt the Japanese for generations to come.[15]

Three days after the surrender, on 18 February 1942, the 25th Army issued an order to purge those Overseas Chinese who were anti-Japanese in Peninsular Malaya and on Singapore Island. To carry out the order, duties were allocated as follows:

1. Responsible for Peninsular Malaya: 5th Division (Commander: Lieutenant-General Matsui Takuro).
2. Outside Singapore City: Imperial Guards Division (Commander: Lieutenant-General Nishimura Takuma).
3. Inside Singapore City: The Shonan[16] Garrison (Commander: Major-General Kawamura Saburo), which consisted of 200 military police and a supplementary military police force of two battalions, with a tank corps and one armored car corps.

It was vaguely known that the 25th Army had intentions of this kind before the attack of Singapore. Already at Kluang, where Army Headquarters was stationed from 28 January to 4 February, the Military Chief-of-Staff, Lt.-Gen. Suzuki Sosaku had told commander Oishi: "The army is considering purging the Overseas Chinese after Singapore is taken, therefore please prepare the Military Police to cooperate." And Oishi had told his subaltern Yokoda back at Kempeitai headquarters: "This is going to be serious business."[17]

Moreover, on 10 February, when Onishi had first come across his commander on Singapore Island, he had felt that something was up.

When their forces entered Singapore city and no urgent instructions were issued, Lt.-Col. Yokoda felt relieved. This feeling was to be short-lived.

On the evening of 18 February, an order came for officers above the rank of squad commander to assemble. The previous evening, Maj.-Gen. Kawamura Saburo (commander of the 5th Division's 9th Brigade) had been made garrison commander for Shonan. He would uphold safety with the 2nd Military Police Field Unit and two battalions of auxiliary forces.[18] When the officers arrived at Fort Canning, commander Oishi briefed them on how to carry out the inspection operation:

1. Date: On 19 and 20 February, assemble all Overseas Chinese at suitable places in the respective areas of assigned responsibility, and carry out the inspection from 21 to 23 February.

2. Target: Overseas Chinese volunteer forces, Communists, anti-Japanese members, those who made donations to China, rascals, and ex-convicts.
3. Information: The list of anti-Japan organizations.

The local Chinese population was estimated to number around 700,000. To inspect such a large number within three days by a small force of Military Police, unfamiliar with the local geography and not knowing the local languages, posed a serious problem. Commander Oishi was well aware of this, and immediately upon receiving the cleansing order had requested that the period of examination be extended to ten days. Army Headquarters, however, objected; too many days spent on this matter would adversely affect ongoing military operations.[19]

With reluctance, Oishi gathered the brains of his Military Police to devise the following outline:

1. Use locals to do the inspection. (Local police officers, private detectives, detectives and officers of the volunteers.)
2. Base yourselves on the available lists. (These were lists of anti-Japan organizations obtained during the operations at Ipoh, supplemented with name lists assembled with the help of detective bureaus, police and the Japanese released from prison.)
3. Examine the old, the young, females, and the ill first.
4. Pay special attention to communists, volunteers and guerrillas.
5. Regarding rascals and ex-convicts, refer to the testimony of the locals and the records kept by the police and the jail.
6. Take proper custody of vacated houses within the designated areas.
7. Issue "good citizen" cards to those who pass the examination.

The procedure would be speedy, and as accurate as the sordid circumstances allowed. It was given an air of thoroughness by having the people pass through three checkpoints. The first one would be manned by locals willing to cooperate. They would be hooded to protect their identity. All people would have to pass this checkpoint in a single line and the informer-cooperators would point out the suspects. At the second checkpoint, the Military Police would investigate the suspects, allowing the innocent to proceed. The third checkpoint was for further investigation of those kept at the second checkpoint. Finally, people without any problem were to be issued "good citizen" cards. In the end, however, because of a lack of preparation, there were not enough "good citizen" cards, and those free to go home received a red chop on their shirts, sleeves, on the arm, anywhere.[20]

Based on these Fort Canning instructions, the army issued the following public announcement on 19 February:

> Those Overseas Chinese residing on Shonan Island between the ages of 18 and 50, must assemble on 21 February at the following areas:
>
> The plaza at the junction of Arab Street and Jalan Besar.
>
> The area at the south end of River Valley Road.
>
> The rubber plantation at the junction of Kallang and Geylang Roads.
>
> Vicinity of the police station at Tanjong Pagar.
>
> Junction of Paya Lebar and Changi Road.
>
> Those who violate this order will be punished severely. You should prepare your own provisions and drinks.
> *The Military Commander of Great Japan*[21]

The announcement also appeared in the English-language *Shonan Shimbun* newspaper and in the Chinese edition of the same paper. It was a modern media affair, in which the unfortunate Chinese population responded to public announcements, press advertisements and radio messages to show up at various checkpoints for inspections.

Lt. Onishi was in charge of Jalan Besar, one of the five assembly points for the purge. Women and children were not exempted, but were examined first. The initial stage of inspecting young people, elderly, and the women went relatively smoothly. At Onishi's second checkpoint, there was a young woman in a man's suit. Relatives of the woman told one of the military policemen that she had dressed as a male for fear of an assault by the Japanese soldiers. When brought to his attention, Onishi led her to a private room and summoned an interpreter as a witness according to the criminal prosecution procedure. Owing to the language problem, the lady immediately took off her pants and showed him her genitals. Onishi was struck dumb by her act. She did this without embarrassment, in a state of extreme fear. Through the interpreter Onishi told her to get dressed and that there was no need to be afraid of the Japanese soldiers. He then sent her home.[22]

As the examination wore on, provisions became insufficient and the complaints increased. Some had ill feelings towards the Military Police and started to denounce them. But the Military Police continued the inspection with increasing assertiveness while the public suffered at being assembled in the heat under extremely congested conditions.[23]

One of Onishi's men recalls that there must have been about 10,000 people rounded up at their checkpoint. Sgt. Ishibe Toshiro based his investigations on the name lists. It was an unfortunate event, he says; the Kempeitai ordered the crowd around, and if there weren't enough numbers, they just grabbed some in a fuzzy way at random. The indiscriminate selection of so-called "anti-Japanese elements" was done based on individual judgement during a time of confusion after the surrender. Who could know who was good or bad!? Under normal circumstances, the whole affair would have been carried out in the span of one year. Then one might have investigated more thoroughly. But this screening had to be completed within two or three days! Ishibe really felt sorry for those who were selected and regretted the outcome. They were the unlucky ones. They could only give up and accept it as their fate.[24]

A mixture of innocent people, Dalforce volunteers (last-minute Overseas Chinese volunteer troops for the British), rascals, and ex-convicts were arrested, but Onishi was left with a feeling that some members of the communist party and anti-Japan organisations were still at large. Given the short time allowed for the inspection, it was very difficult to judge people, especially by using hooded local informers, as there were probably some who used this opportunity to gain personal revenge on their enemies.

During the screening the Vice Chief-of-Staff, Maj.-Gen. Manaki Akinobu, inspected the sites, and the Chief of War Operations, Col. Tsuji Masanobu, was highly visible. Along with Tsuji's aide, Maj. Asaeda, they gave directions outside their area of responsibility. Tsuji inspected each checkpoint, and on 21 February, in company of Lt.-Col. Yokoda, came to the Jalan Besar area, where he summoned Onishi.

"How many suspects have you got?" he asked Onishi.

"At present, seventy."

"What are you doing?" he shouted at Onishi loudly. "I intend to cut the entire population of Singapore in half!"

Of course this may not have been Col. Tsuji's real intention, but the utterance shocked Lt. Onishi. Their ranks were different, but the Army Chief-of-Staff was not the direct boss of the Military Police. And although Onishi had to follow the instruction he had been given, he continued at the same pace.[25]

Tsuji not only visited Onishi's location, but also inspected Hisamatsu's checkpoints and others, relentlessly dispensing instructions. Moreover, one night during the purge, Asaeda made an ostentatious visit to Military Police Headquarters at Fort Canning, where he unsheathed his sword and shouted angrily: "Wake up! Wake up! Isn't anyone around? Those who don't follow the policy of the army, even if they are Military Police, I'll kill them!" and issued firm instructions. Entering their dormitory, he intruded without permission into their rooms, shouting so that even mosquito nets shook. He was like a devil, who willfully pushed his own designs and forced the investigation and examined the people.[26]

Around noon on 23 February, Onishi received the order to have the auxiliary Military Police dispose of suspects selected through the inspection by "severe punishment", the Japanese euphemism for death penalty. What an unreasonable order it was! The Military Police was carrying out the inspection to maintain order, and it was a natural duty to remove outlaws and anti-Japanese elements. But to apply "severe punishment" so soon was far too harsh, illegal, and inhuman. Neither the military police, and still less the supplementary troops who would have to carry out the killings, felt keen about disposing of the men who had been detained at the third checkpoint during the interrogation process.[27] Moreover, Onishi was not sure whether the charges of the suspects could be cleared in three days' examination. Startled, he visited his direct superior, Lt.-Col. Yokoda, to suggest alternatives:

In my opinion to impose "severe punishment" immediately is rather strong. We haven't had time to really examine the suspects. We have no real proof that they are hostile anti-Japan elements. It's very inhuman to immediately kill them all. Since there are empty prisons, why not put them into prison first, for further inquiry, and only after thorough investigation get rid of the worst cases? Or at worst, expel them to the islands.[28]

Yokoda had the same thoughts, as did their commander Col. Oishi who submitted a report in that vein to the army.

But Army Headquarters was unbending, saying that it was a military operation and had to be handled this way. This was not the time to think of military laws, or hold conferences to discuss the for and against. Anti-Japanese elements of Chinese extraction were still around, and therefore unreliable elements had to be killed. Even though the purge took place after the surrender of Singapore, it was an extended mopping-up activity, and had to be treated as a military operation. For the prosecution of the war, those persons standing in the way had to be removed.[29]

Against this intractable attitude neither Kempeitai commander Oishi nor garrison commander Kawamura Saburo could do anything. They lacked the ability and the capacity to counter the grim order. Military orders were absolute. No one who held his life dearly would disobey such an order. To do so was insubordination, which carried an immediate death penalty. The more so if a military field policeman showed signs of insubordination. The soldiers could do nothing but go along. They had to carry out the order, even if against their will.[30]

When Kawamura, the newly-appointed commander of the Shonan Garrison objected to the army order,[31] Chief-of-Staff Officer Suzuki Sosaku replied: "There are all sorts of opinions regarding this operation. But since the army commander has decided it this way, the nature of this decision is a wipe-out operation." Despite all the disputes, the order was difficult to change now. Army Headquarters would not budge. Even Kawamura had no choice but to follow the order.[32]

The authority of Army Headquarters was then absolute. Had the Chief-of-Staff trusted military justice, or had persons such as Tsuji Masanobu not been around, Kawamura felt he might have been able to mitigate the order to a certain extent. But with such obdurate figures in charge, he was unable to do anything. Under the circumstances trying to change the order was more foolish than counting the age of a baby that had passed away. The only thing Kawamura thought he could do at that time was acquiesce and leave it to fate.[33]

The Military Police had no power to change or even to protest the order for a purge of the Overseas Chinese, although they opposed it from the outset. At the Military Police Academy they had studied various national legal systems as well as international law and were, accordingly, more knowledgeable than staff officers in matters of trial and penalty. To the police it was difficult to believe that those glorious warriors, who had just gained a stupendous victory, those prominent staff officers who had received the highest military education, would talk and behave so erratically, at a time of busy operations and when Malaya was in an unsettled state immediately after the stupendous British surrender.

Without influence and lacking assertiveness, Lt. Onishi returned to his Headquarters and conveyed the liquidation order to the captain of his auxiliary Military Police. The cruel task would fall on his company of auxiliary police. Neither the auxiliary forces nor the military police were eager to massacre the Chinese.[34] A company at that time consisted of around 60 soldiers equipped with rifles or light machine guns. They hauled the victims away on lorries and slaughtered them down by the beaches. One of his auxiliary Military Policemen, Yamaguchi, carried out the executions with the help of others, near Changi Road.[35] The number of victims is not known. The figure given by the Japanese was 6,000. The highest Chinese figure was 50,000.

Yap Yan Hong was one of those who went to Onishi's Jalan Besar checkpoint for screening. On the morning of the radio announcement, he put on a pair of new shoes and his best shirt. They were told to bring food and drink for three days. At the packed Jalan Besar Stadium he had a harrowing time, suffering from heat during the day, from exposure to cold at night, never knowing what to expect from one moment to the next. On the third day the women and children were told to go home. But the men were lined up and paraded before a high-ranking officer. As they passed him he flicked one index finger. If it was his left it meant the person must be detained; a flick of the right finger was a sign to go home. The fate of many thousands of people hung on the whim of a single person, on the wagging of a finger.

When asked by the military policeman at the third interrogation point where he had worked since the outbreak of war, young and naive Yap Yan Hong thought of the most innocent occupation.

"In the map drawing business," he replied. This could be a spy, the policeman thought. So Yap was detained for two days. Then he was tied with a rope as part of a group of six and made to mount a truck with two other groups. They were taken past Changi prison to the end of the island. It was already evening when his group was made to wade into the sea and was shot by the Japanese auxiliary military police forces. Yap was lucky. When his rope made contact with the sea water, it loosened and Yap, miraculously, was able to swim away, and survived to tell his story.[36]

On the afternoon of 21 February, Mr. Royal Goho, leader of the Singapore branch of the Indian Independence League, visited Maj. Fujiwara Iwaichi, who at his liaison agency (the Fujiwara-*kikan*) was successfully recruiting Indians to join the Indian National Army.

"Major, do you know that the Japanese soldiers are indiscriminately detaining Overseas Chinese and massacring them? One can barely face such cruelty. Has the Japanese Army lost its mind? The British had already surrendered and the war was supposed to be over!"

Busy overseeing the surrender of the 55,000 Indian POWs, Fujiwara was unaware of the incident.

Goho pleaded:

> The residents of Singapore and Malaya respected the Japanese soldiers' bravery and their fine policy to liberate and protect the natives. It is true that Indians and Malays were deeply hostile towards those Chinese who had been exploiting them to their hearts' content under the British. And it is true that some even rejoiced in the massacre of Overseas Chinese. However, upon witnessing horrifying scenes, their regard for the Japanese army has turned into fear. This is a sad thing for the Japanese army. Can't you do anything to stop it?

Fujiwara dispatched some members of his agency to investigate the situation. The result of the investigation was even worse than what Mr. Goho had recounted. Shocked by the seriousness of the matter, Fujiwara immediately went to see Chief-of-Staff Col. Sugita at Army Headquarters, and inquired if this really was an order from the Army.

With a pensive expression, Sugita lamented that his moderate position had been overruled by staff officers holding extreme opinions, and an order to carry out the massacres had been issued much against his wishes. Fujiwara countered that the result of this purge was a disgrace for the Japanese Army; it would only obstruct military administration and dash any hopes for winning the trust of the people. In particular it would hinder his recruiting of Indians, and he pressed Sugita to improve the matter. It would never be possible for the Japanese Army to counter the charge that they had carried out inhumane mass murders in which countless Chinese were executed indiscriminately on the beaches, in rubber plantations, and in jungles without investigation or trial. There was no justification for the massacres even if some Chinese had fought against the Japanese as volunteers and collaborated with anti-Japanese elements. The suppression of Overseas Chinese tainted the glory of the Malayan campaign. It also adversely affected the achievement of his mission with the F-Kikan.[37]

When it came to pinpointing the origins of the mass killings, Lt. Onishi at his checkpoint in Jalan Besar felt that even if the incident had the approval of Gen. Yamashita, and as an army mopping-up action was agreed on among those below the Chief-of-Staff, it was guided by Col. Tsuji. It was unmistakably Tsuji who had proposed the scheme. He was the originator of the incident.

Had there been proper guidance from the Central Military Authorities, the purge incident of Singapore might not have happened. But the central leadership procrastinated and neglected their responsibility to guide and supervise the soldiers. It has been said that the main factor lying behind Japan's defeat in war was her lack of talented men. More than that, Japan was clearly defeated on the humanitarian level. Japanese soldiers committed cruel atrocities of many sorts, the most extreme being the purge of Shonan. At that moment in February, Onishi felt that they had lost the war already as far as morality was concerned.[38]

The purge order also touched 5th Division machine-gunner Ochi. His front line unit (of the Ichikawa Battalion) had been included in the auxiliary forces assigned to garrison duties in the eastern end of Singapore, where around 50,000 prisoners of war were interned at Changi prison.[39] Ochi's unit was keeping an eye on the local people when the unexpected order reached them: "Get those Chinese who cooperated with Chungking China! You may inflict 'severe punishment'."

In response to this vindictive order, they picked up 11 suspects. Only one was actually found carrying a pro-Chungking China publication on him, and the battle-tested frontline troopers saw no reason to shoot any of them. But with military police and plainclothes policemen swarming the island, it was not easy to hide their lenient attitude. Ochi simply reported that "eleven persons were imprisoned and punished". Ten of them were not harmed, and the 11th they sent for temporary custody to 10th Company on Bintan Island. These decisions were made with the approval of battalion commander Maj. Ichikawa Tadashi.

Like Ochi's unit, Tsuchikane's Imperial Guard troops had almost reached the town when the fighting stopped on 15 February. They were also among those assigned as auxiliary troops to help the military police keep order.

Things were all right in the beginning, when Tsuchikane's 1st Company was made to man the checkpoints, in groups of five, on the trunk road between Bukit Timah and Johor Bahru. And the group was elated to receive an Imperial gift of tobacco, presented on rare occasions as a reward for special success. As each soldier accepted the beautiful white flat box from their commander, he raised the gift with both hands reverently above his head, and bowed low. Later, off duty, inhaling deeply, they smoked each cigarette, embossed majestically with the Emperor's seal, to the very end slowly, relishing each puff of this gift from heaven.

Then began Tsuchikane's descent into hell. Depending on the daily roster for their unit, they were sometimes used to round up Overseas Chinese under the order to punish and mop-up anti-Japanese elements. Tsuchikane was assigned a junior position in the first detachment of the auxiliary military police, and worked at Kempeitai Military Headquarters. The exact content of that job he would never be able to bear to talk about in detail for the rest of his life. It was not the job of an honourable front-line soldier. But under orders the young man was forced to commit atrocities and brutalities that were beyond the imagination.

Every day, so-called anti-Japanese elements of the local people were arrested and brought to military police headquarters. Inside an empty storehouse within police headquarters, the military police used interpreters to have them confess under dreadful torture. Tsuchikane was used as an aide to carry out these tortures. That abominable work created a wound that would never heal. The endlessly savage, unfair, and lawless cruelties and tortures meted out he would never be able to record one by one, or put into print in any form. Finally his duties as an auxiliary military policeman ended on 26 April, when the Imperial Guard Division moved to Sumatra.[40]

The Overseas Chinese purge took place in three stages, and it was during the third stage, in central Malaya, that reluctant Pte. Miyake Genjiro of the 5th Division became directly involved. Stationed in Kuala Lumpur, he had to go and wake up Overseas Chinese in the middle of the night. All suspicious people were to be examined. All thrown into jail. It was the continuation of the Singapore purge and the beginning of the Malayan massacre. They were going to kill even good people, those who had done no wrong, brought there from all over Malaya.[41]

After one week, the order went out: "Come with your trucks to the prison." Seventy people were loaded onto Miyake's truck, standing up. They had six trucks and in this way could pack 400 people.

They drove to a rubber plantation ten minutes away. There they led the captives into the rubber trees, where their commander stood already waiting for them. Sixty Chinese were assigned to Miyake and his comrades.[42]

"Now you must obey orders," the commander said. "You must now kill these Chinese." Kill. They had to kill them. Miyake and his colleagues harboured no hostility against their assigned group. They couldn't stir up any hostile feelings. They had been done no harm by the Chinese people, they had no reason to take their lives, no murderous intentions, they did not want to kill. These were human beings. People.

To raise their will to kill the people, the officer in charge of them said: "You are about to kill these people by order of the highest general, the Emperor." Then he proceeded to cut off the heads of two of them. He did it with his sabre. The blood came out in a hissing sound — "shooo!" — and spurted two or three metres into the air, spraying around.

Another 12 were beheaded, the rest stabbed. A ghastly stench of blood pervaded the rubber trees. All 400 were dumped into a big trench and buried. Miyake's impression was that about half of them were not yet dead, and buried alive.

"The emperor now orders you to kill these...," Miyake never ceased asking himself: Does the emperor have this right? Can he give such an order?[43]

11

Epilogue

FOUR months into the occupation, a weary passenger from India disembarked the *Kamakura Maru* at Singapore's Keppel Quay. It was his fourth visit to the port since the outbreak of the Pacific War, and this time the businessman got off the boat of his own volition. Japan had nothing better to offer Omori Kichijiro.

The Japanese civilian prisoners of war at Pranakila had learned about the fall of Singapore from newspapers. Omori was among the first batch to be released from Pranakila camp in July, when Japan and the Allied Forces concluded a Prisoners of War exchange agreement. It involved civilian prisoners all over the world sent out of the battle zones to concentration camps, from which their governments recovered them in repatriation schemes across the continents. Omori was repatriated from Bombay across the Indian Ocean via Singapore as part of a large-scale swap involving British and US civilian internees.

Now that Singapore was Japanese, Omori had high expectations of the flourishing crown colony he had known in prewar times. From Keppel Harbour he went straight to town. This was a different Singapore all right, Omori noticed on his way to his former Senda company office. The place was now called Shonan, and all the white people had disappeared off the streets.

Mr. Shinya, his superior, had returned to Shonan before him and had already found out from the Japanese Military Administration that their Renggam rubber estate had been requisitioned. All the former rubber merchants and Japanese owners of plantations in Malaya had, moreover, been gathered into the Shonan Rubber Union, a new body which supervised all matters concerning rubber. Omori and Shinya could not ask for the return of their property, nor would they have been permitted to manage it. They did have an opportunity to see the ledgers maintained by the Anglo-Thai Corporation, to whom Omori had entrusted their estate before the war. The books had been kept faithfully until 14 February — what tremendous book-keeping in burning Singapore, right up to the day of capitulation! What had happened to good people like Mr. Husband, and to companies like the Anglo-Thai corporation, Omori wondered. But his colleagues discouraged him from asking the military authorities: "Omori, never mention Englishmen as friends."

Since the attitude of the Military Police was incomprehensible, it was better not to do anything. Omori had expected changes to the Singapore he had known, but nothing so secretive and stifling as what he found. Most bizarre had been the interrogations by the Kempeitai of those who returned to Singapore. Why did they have to be examined at all? Weren't they all Japanese? Couldn't they be trusted? Soon they also heard about terrible things done to the Chinese. It was no surprise since the Japanese military ill-treated even their own countrymen.

It was not until after the war, from Japan in 1947, that Omori finally sent Mr. Husband a letter through the Anglo-Thai Corporation in Singapore, hoping that they would forward the letter to him. When a reply did come from Mr. Husband in England, it saddened Omori deeply. It was so unlike Husband to write such a letter because he had always been very kind to Omori. Husband wrote that he now regarded Japan as his enemy; he had been badly treated and was nothing but a skeleton, and expected to live only a few weeks longer. At a loss how to console him and apologise, Omori found no words to reply.[1]

Sgt. Arai Mitsuo was repatriated to Japan in the same year as Omori, in February 1946, but from China. Soon after the fall of Singapore, his 18th Division had been ordered to the Burmese front. When Arai's term of military service expired in July 1942, he returned to Japan, only to be re-drafted into the army and sent to North China, where he remained in the reserve forces until the end of the war.

Today Arai reminisces: "Yes, well, at that time we were all in the same boat. It's difficult to evaluate those years. Were they good or bad years? It was all fate; our fate. When I look back, now that I have reached 80 and I don't know how many years I've got left, when I come to think about death, I think I might have been better off to die together with those people who fell one after another around me at that time in the battle for Singapore. One has to die anyway. Is it not better to die at the time that one is required to die?"

"The fall of Singapore has a certain significance in world history."

"Oh, is that so?"

"Mr. Arai, how do you feel about it?"

"Well, I have no particular feelings about the fall of Singapore. In 1941, it was a matter of course that Japan had to attack Singapore. I'd been in the military for five years, and slowly we were running out of military doctors, medical treatment, and were at an impasse in China, and still we kept extending our battle fronts. That was a mistake. This is how we thought among soldiers. When we took Singapore, we didn't think much of it. It was a feeling of doing something unavoidably. All the while hushing up things and keeping everything secret, the military had been pursuing this war.... We were fighting under the circumstances of shortages of everything. Unless we conquered it quickly, the consequences would be unthinkable."[2]

Miyake Genjiro, who was ordered to carry out killings in Kuala Lumpur, feels worse. Fifty years later, he gains a livelihood in Shikoku in a small workshop, carefully crafting wooden rice ladles and spatulas, smoothing them with sandpaper. At 79, he is a slow carpenter, but his memory is good. He recalls only too well not only the guns of February but also the knives of March. And as he planes his wood, he mutters: "As a human being, I don't want to talk. Why? Because of shame. Our shame. It's too difficult to talk about. But I can testify to it in my own person." He does so in a video: "Aggression on the Malayan Peninsula: The War They Did Not Teach Us About." He spoke out to awaken the world, to explain what war is about.[3]

Memories of the Malayan campaign differ widely, often according to whether one had to participate in the purge of the Overseas Chinese following the surrender. Ochi, from the same division as Miyake, did not have to stab anyone on military orders. He is hence more sanguine about his record.

"Shonan was born before my eyes, and it died before my eyes, when once again it became Singapore."[4] Ochi had seen the Japanese heroes' monument erected on Bukit Timah Hill in 1942, and destroyed in 1945. The site is now occupied by a massive satellite installation for television. Their splendid Shinto shrine in the MacRitchie reservoir gardens, too, went up in flames at the end of the war, and several of Ochi's Regimental commanders put themselves to the sword, on Bukit Timah, the scene of their greatest victory.

There is a touch of bitterness when Ochi recalls how Gen. Yamashita had at least guaranteed Gen. Percival his life at the time of Britain's surrender. There was no reciprocation when Japan lost the war, and Gen. Yamashita was hanged. Such is the white man's so-called "humanism".[5]

After the war, at the complete mercy of the victors, Japan's younger generations imbibed "humanism", and were indoctrinated with democracy leavened with jazz.[6] Their elders were sidelined, impotent and at a complete loss. They had lost the power to sustain and teach the young. Perhaps the real victims of war were, after all, the young ones, the next generation.

"One thing needs to be said clearly. Japan did not invade Singapore for the sake of conquest. It was in the name of the Greater East Asia War." It was for self-preservation and self-sufficiency, and in that sense Ochi believes it was a good thing. Tremendous victories had marked the beginning. Japan did well, perhaps too well. Had the war proceeded at a slower pace in their favour, with gradual victories one by one, it would have been better for Japan.

Until the fall of Singapore, each soldier and general fought for all-encompassing victory of the entire army, without thought for self, and to the death. All the tiny little inter-service mistakes were not yet being blamed on each other. If such patriotism had continued to the end, the Greater East Asia War would have taken quite a different turn, and Japan's fate would have been different.

As it was, the Japanese carried within themselves their greatest deficiency. It was this. The attack on Pearl Harbour, the occupation of Singapore, the sea battle successes off Malaya, the occupation of one place after the other in Indonesia, and so on, each fed on the other and led to Japanese self-pride and conceit. Drunk as they were on their sole object of winning the war, generals were aiming at glory, their juniors at a rise in career, the people at a net profit out of the war. Each was seeking with characteristic impatience and a quick temper their own "net profit".

To quickly grow proud and arrogant after their small victories, and give free rein to self-interest and even public black markets, was truly deplorable. If such Japanese had controlled and reigned over Asia, it would have become a miserable and pitiful place.

The Japanese had not yet evolved into a constitutional people. So there was really no reason to challenge the United States or Great Britain, which were already constitutional peoples. The biggest reason for Japan's defeat was her backwardness. It was good that Japan was defeated. Japan can now completely reform and remodel itself and its cultural standards. It's the young that must do this. Only the young can complete and achieve this.[7]

Probing more deeply, former military police Lt. Onishi Satoru regrets there never was any thorough re-examination of the cause of the Greater East Asia War. He tried to find his own answers by writing a book 22 years after the conflict. A direct participant, an ordinary man who followed the orders of his country, he writes as one put in the singular situation of having had to make life and death decisions over 10,000 people in his custody in late February 1942.

> It was a big mistake to start the reckless war without taking fighting capability into consideration while being contemptuous of the enemy and solely depending on spirit and the gods' protection. Moreover, Japanese soldiers committed cruel atrocities in all sorts of respects: Shonan was the extreme. We lost this war already as far as morality was concerned.[8]

No one was made to feel the moral loss in a symbolically more telling way than Imperial Guards Division Cpl. Tsuchikane Tominosuke. Back in Alor Star, at the beginning of the Malayan campaign, his Indian friends had given him a silver bracelet as a farewell gift. The Southeast Asians had had confidence in their new Japanese friends; they were going to liberate the coloured peoples in British Malaya. The gods had been smiling on Japan and her soldiers.

But then the Japanese soldiers did not pass the test. Dying for the emperor and committing atrocities in his name proved in the end a horrific hoax. Everyone needed their eyes opened to see this.

Tsuchikane experienced the disillusion and loss of trust in a poignant act at the end of the war, as a prisoner of war, when an Indian soldier noticed the silver bracelet on Tsuchikane's arm and took it away. Surely it was loot. Tsuchikane was mortified.[9]

The gods had retrieved their token. They were angry. The Japanese Army did not deserve rewards. It had had an opportunity to liberate

Southeast Asia. But after partially fulfilling this destiny, the army quickly dissipated its achievement in a mindless massacre. A stigma would henceforth attach to Japan's brilliant victory. After having fought a courageous battle, the Japanese General Staff in the end did not show magnanimity and foresight, only petty mindedness, fear, and hatred towards the Chinese in Singapore.

The ruthless purge nullified what otherwise might have been remembered as one of the great conquests of the century. It might have found acceptance in the world, and been written up in Japanese history textbooks, remembered in the same way as the heroic Battle of Hill 203, when Japan had defeated Russia in Manchuria. When Onishi and his policemen had stopped at Port Arthur on their way to the Malayan war theatre in 1941 and visited the battlefield where Japan under the legendary Gen. Nogi won a huge victory over Russia in 1905, they hoped that soon they would be involved in a similar success, one that might even surpass the victory over Russia.[10]

At first these hopes were realized. Singapore was Port Arthur and Dairen all over again. If anything, it was even more spectacular. But in the end it was nothing to be proud of. The Army erased its glory as soon as it had gotten it. And ironically it was the zealous architect of the glorious capture of Singapore, Tsuji Masanobu, who obliterated the heroism of the campaign by insisting on and organising the Overseas Chinese purge. Although the Singapore victory was more brilliant even than the Port Arthur victory, in the end victory and defeat, fame and shame, could be refracted in the person of Tsuji Masanobu, a man of extraordinary strategic brilliance, courage, frugality, and discipline, but also a man who held human rights in low esteem, and was vainglorious, cruel, and infamous.

Every year, on the day of surrender, the Singapore Chinese Chamber of Commerce commemorates the sacrifices of Singaporeans at the civilian war memorial at the corner of Beach Road and Bras Basah. The four huge obelisks were financed through US$17 million of "quasi-reparations" paid by the Japanese Government in 1967 after the discovery in 1962 of a mass grave in Singapore containing the remains of several hundred people apparently killed during the occupation. Onishi Satoru suffers when he sees this construction, which he describes as a spiked tower of 120 metres that looms high in a plaza overlooking the city, along the coastal avenue to the side of the Raffles Hotel and east of the City Hall building.

The four sharp obelisks pierce his heart. They will stand forever as a reminder of Japan's biggest mistake at the beginning of the occupation.

> The incident of the purge of the Overseas Chinese in Shonan will remain in the people's mind until the erosion of this tower which will take a long time. As one of the persons involved in this incident, I feel as if stabbed by a knife, aware of my responsibility towards the victims, to whom I offer my sincere and deep condolences. As a person who was deeply involved [in the purge], I am not trying to justify or to excuse ourselves. The purge was a cruel act committed by the Japanese army. It constitutes truly shameful behaviour, and remains a most disdainful act in the Great Eastern War.[11]

At sunrise on 15 February 1992, bagpipes opened the Fifty Year Commemoration at the Allied War Cemetery at Kranji. More than 4,000 war veterans, family members, and spectators poured into the memorial gardens. No Japanese were invited. It was not yet time for reconciliation. On the same day at noon, however, when the Singaporeans held their annual ceremony at the four obelisks, they had for the first time invited the Japanese ambassador and members of the Japanese community. It was a large community, and a substantial presence. Singapore was home to the largest Japanese school outside of Japan, and major Japanese department stores occupied prominent retail space on the island. After 50 years, the Chinese community offered a degree of reconciliation. They were willing to shake hands, not forgetting the past but at least offering to begin to understand one another, and to forge a new relationship.

The fall of Singapore is remembered today mostly in negative terms by the soldiers who once defended the impregnable fortress, and saw the vanity of the pretensions of the military authorities who ran it and watched it slip from their grasp. The city itself has been rebuilt from the rubble, a vindication of sorts for the primary victims, the Overseas Chinese, who have constructed a resplendent high-tech city and a teeming corporate hub. The island has an airport that is a paragon of its kind, built on landfill at Changi, by the beach, resting on the bones of the slain.

Notes

Introduction

1. *From Singapore to Syonan-to 1941–1945* (Singapore: National Library Singapore, 1992).
2. A.B. Lodge, *The Fall of General of Gordon Bennett* (Sydney: Allen & Unwin, 1986); Mark Clisby, *Guilty or Innocent: The Gordon Bennett Case* (Sydney: Allen & Unwin, 1992).
3. Erstwhile bystanders in the war, and armed only at the end to help the desperate British delay the surrender, the Chinese vanished into a limbo of suspicion as the Japanese sought to castigate them and keep them in line through massacres on a large scale in Singapore and Malaya in February and March 1942.
4. Annelies Crone-Arbenz, *Singapore Saga* (Canberra: Thomas Rowland Publishers, 1988).
5. See "Malaysia" in Ota Hirotake, "Nanpo ni okeru Nihon gunsei kankei no bunken mokuroku" [Bibliography on the Japanese military administration in the southern regions], *Gunji Shigaku* [*The Journal of Military History*], ed. *Gunjishi Gakkai* [The Military History Society of Japan] 28, 3 (Dec. 1992): 91–3.
6. Sir Winston Churchill, *History of World War II: The Hinge of Fate* (London: Cassell, 1951).
7. In English this volume first appeared as *Singapore: The Japanese Version* (Sydney: Ure Smith, 1960). The cited material appear on p. xxi. Oxford University Press reissued the book as a paperback retitled *Singapore 1941–1942: The Japanese Version of the Malayan Campaign of World War II* (Singapore: Oxford University Press, 1988).
8. The *sook ching* operation (in Japanese the *shuku sei* operation) was planned by the Operations Staff of the 25th Army and carried out under an order issued in the name of Gen.

Yamashita, the directive being transmitted from Yamashita through his chief-of-staff, Lt.-Gen. Suzuki Sosaku to Defence headquarters under Maj.-Gen. Kawamura Saburo, commander of the Syonan-to garrison, who in turn delegated the task of carrying out the purge to the *kempeitai*. See Yoji Akashi, "Japanese Policy Towards the Malayan Chinese 1941–1945", *Journal of Southeast Asian Studies* 1, 2 (Sept. 1970): 66–8.

9.   Mamoru Shinozaki, *My Wartime Experiences in Singapore* (Singapore: Institute of Southeast Asian Studies, 1973), Oral History Programme Series No. 3, p. 15.

10.   Mamoru Shinozaki, *Syonan — My Story: The Japanese Occupation of Singapore* (Singapore: Asia Pacific Press, 1975; republished by Times Book International, 1982, reprinted 1984, 1992).

11.   Watanabe Wataru, *Shosho (Malaya, Singapore) Kankei Shiryo* (Tokyo: Ryukei Shosha, 1988), 5 vols., 11,407 pages, and "Daitoa senso ni okeru Nanpo gunsei no kaiko: Naki Yamashita shogun o shinobu" [Recollections of the military administration in the southern region during the Greater East Asia War: Remembering the deceased General Yamashita], *Gunji Shigaku [The Journal of Military History]*, ed. *Gunjishi Gakkai* [The Military History Society of Japan] 28, 3 (Dec. 1992): 69.

12.   Ibid., p. 66.

13.   Ibid., p. 82.

14.   The writer thanks Dr Paul Kratoska for kindly pointing out and providing copies of the relevant monograph material.

15.   Boei-cho, Boeikenshujo, Senshishitsu [Self-defense Agency, National Defense College, War History Office], *Nanpo no gunsei* (Tokyo: Asagumo Shinbunsha, 1985), Vol. 104.

16.   Three other volumes in the series deal partially with the Malayan campaign: *Hito/Maree homen kaigun hinko sakusen* [Naval offensive operations in the Philippines and Malaya], Vol. 24, *Nanpo shinko rikugun koku sakusen* [Offensive operations of the Army Air Force in the southern areas], Vol. 34, and *Nansei homen rilcugun sakusen: Marei Ran'in no boei* [Army operations in the Southwest: Philippines and Malaya naval offensive operations], Vol. 92.

17. London, 1957.

18. "Kakyo taisaku yoko" [Outline of policy toward the Chinese], in ibid., p. 108.

19. Yoji Akashi, "Japanese Policy Towards the Malayan Chinese", "Bureaucracy and the Japanese Military Administration, with Specific Reference to Malaya", in William H. Newell, *Japan in Asia* (Singapore: Singapore University Press, 1981), pp. 46–82; "Japanese Cultural Policy in Malaya and Singapore, 1942–45", in *Japanese Cultural Policies in Southeast Asia during World War 2*, ed. Grant K. Goodman (New York: St. Martin's Press, 1991), pp. 117–2; "Japanese Military Administration in Malayan: Its Formation and Evolution in Reference to the Sultans, the Islamic Region and the Moslem Malays, 1941–45", *Asian Studies* 7, 1 (Apr. 1969). Lt.-Gen. Fujiwara Iwaichi, *F-Kikan: Japanese Army Intelligence Operations in Southeast Asia during World War II*, trans. Akashi Yoji (Hong Kong: Heinemann Asia, 1983).

20. Shingaporu Shisei Kai, *Shonan tokubetsu-shi shi: Senjichu no Shingaporu* (Tokyo: Nihon-Shingaporu Kyokai, 1986).

21. For an extensive annotated bibliographic survey on published and unpublished memoirs of many more Japanese participants at this level, see Akashi Yoji, JCC *Bulletin*, Japan, Japan Cultural Centre, Kuala Lumpur (The Japan Foundation) 23 (May 1994): 1–4; JCC *Bulletin* 24 (Aug. 1994): 1–7.

22. One must read him with care, though. In his other books Tsukushi, who seems to have been an army aviator, gives the impression he was a participant in the events he describes, although he was apparently not involved in actual fighting but based his accounts on hearsay. The writer gratefully acknowledges this comment on his paper from Professor Hata Ikuhiko at the Forum on the Japanese Occupation of Malaya and Singapore, 22 Oct. 1994.

23. Completed on 10 March, Tsukushi Jiro's *Shingaporu koryaku ki* (Tokyo: Jidai Sha) was published on 8 May 1942, the day that Japan's southward advance met its first reversal in the Battle of the Coral Sea.

24. Ibid., p. 58.

25. Ibid., pp. 134–6.

26. Tsuchikane Tominosuke, *Shingaporu e no michi: aru Konoe hei no kiroku* (Tokyo: Sogeisha, 1977), 2 vols.

27. Ibid., pp. 129–30.

28. Arai Mitsuo, *Shingaporu senki* (Tokyo: Tosho Shuppan Sha, 1984), pp. 31, 40, 45–6.

29. Ibid., pp. 49–50.

30. Ibid., p. 130.

31. Onishi Satoru, *Hiroku: Shonan Kakyo shukuseijiken* (Tokyo: Kameoka Shuppan, 1977), pp. 144–50.

32. Lee Geok Boi, *Syonan: Singapore Under the Japanese 1942–1945* (Singapore: Landmark Books, 1992), p. 121.

33. Oral History Department of Singapore. Interview with Tsujimoto Sanosuke, Accession No. B 000119/03.

34. Oral History Department of Singapore. Interview with Nagase Takashi, 8 June 1987, Accession No. 000789.

35. Ienaga Saburo, *Senso sekinin* (Tokyo: Iwanami Shoten, 1985).

36. Kobayashi Masahiro, *Singaporu no Nihon gun* (Tokyo: Heiwa Bunka, 1986).

37. Shu Yun-Ts'iao and Chua Ser-Koon (eds.), *Nihon senryo Jo no Shingaporu*, trans. Tanaka Hiroshi and Fukunaga Hei (Tokyo: Aoki Shoten, 1986).

38. *Xin Ma Hua Ren Kang Ri Shi Liao* (Singapore: Cultural and Historical Publishing House, 1984). The materials are from the collection of Col. Chuang Hui-Ts'uan.

39. Takashima Nobuyoshi and Hayashi Hirofurni (eds.), *Maraya no Nihon gun: Negri Sembiruan ni okeru Kajin giakusatsu*, trans. Murakarni Ikuzo (Tokyo: Aoki Shoten, 1989).

40. Writer's impression during the "6th Study Tour to Research Japan's War Experience on the Southern Part of the Malayan Peninsula" at the gravesites in Sungei Lui, Negri Sembilan, 10 Aug. 1991.

41. Senso giseisha o kokoro ni itonamu kai hen (Society To Engrave In Our Hearts The Victims Of War), *Nihon gun no Mareesia jumin gyakusatsu* (Tokyo: Toho Shuppan, 1989), Vol. 3. The Society convened the first forum in Osaka on 15 August 1986, and publishes the conference results every following July.

42. Fujiwara Akira, Writer, and Hayashi Sota, Illustrator, *Kogane iro no Kaze*, War Series Vol. 3 (Tokyo: Sodo Bunka, 1991).

Fujiwara Akira, Writer; Yatsurugi Hiroki and Kichijoji Kazuya, Illustrators, *Jufa no sora*. War Series Vol. 4 (Tokyo: Sodo Bunka, 1991).

43.   Torninaga Kenko and Ito Shunichiro, *Shingaparu koryakusen: Shashin de miru Taiheiyo senso*, Vol. 2 (Tokyo: Akita Shoten, 1972, 1982).

44.   Haji Abu Hurairah Habu Abdullah (Habu Yoshiki), *Nihonjin yo! Arigato: Mareesia wa koshite dokuritsu shita* (Tokyo: Nihon Kyoiku Shimbunsha, 1989, 3rd printing 1990).

45.   Nakajima Michi, *Nitchu sehso imada owarazu: Maree "gyakusatsu" no nazo* (Tokyo: Bungei Shunju, 1991).

46.   Ibid., pp. 127–40.

47.   Hayashi Hirofumi, *Kakyo gyakusatsu:Nihongun shihaika no Maree hanto* (Tokyo: Suzusawa Shoten, 1992).

48.   *Shiryo: Maree ni okeru Nihongun nojumin gyakusatsu* [Documents: The Japanese army's civilian massacres in Malaya] (Tokyo: Travel Association to Think About Southeast Asia, 1988).

49.   Video production by Eizo Bunka Kyokai, *Shinryaku-Maree hanto: Oshierarenakatta senso* [Aggression on the Malayan Peninsula: The war they did not teach us about] (Tokyo, 1992), 110 mins.

Chapter 1

1.   Onishi Satoru, *Hiroku: Shonan Kakyo shukusei jiken* [Secret document: The purge of Overseas Chinese in Shonan] (Tokyo: Kameoka Shuppan, 1977), p. 24.

2.   Ibid., pp. 19–23.

3.   Ibid., pp. 1, 19–23, 281. Ishibe Toshiro, Interview, 4 June 1994.

4.   Onishi Satoru, Interview, 28 May 1994.

5.   See Boei-cho, Boeikenshujo, Senshishitsu [Self-defense Agency, National Defense College, War History Office], *Maree shinko sakusen* [The Malaya Campaign] (Tokyo: Asagumo Shinbunsha, 1966), Vol. 1 in Japan's official 104-volume history of the Pacific War [hereafter BBS], p. 1.

6.   Onishi, *Hiroku*, pp. 24–5.

7. Arai Mitsuo, *Shingaporu senki* [Singapore War Diary] (Tokyo: Tosho Shuppansha, 1984), pp. 7–9.
8. Arai Mitsuo, Interview, 10 Oct. 1993.
9. Arai, *Shingaporu senki*, p. 14.
10. Ibid., pp. 16–7.
11. Tsuchikane Tominosuke, *Shingaporu e no michi: aru Konoe hei no kiroku* [The Road to Singapore: Diary of an Imperial Guard Soldier] (Tokyo: Sogeisha, 1977), Vol. 1, p. 101.
12. Tsuchikane, *Shingaporu e no michi*, vol. 1, p.102.
13. Ibid., pp. 103–4. Official war history account in BBS, pp. 157–9.
14. Ochi Harumi, *Maree senki* [Malaya War Diary] (Tokyo: Tosho Shuppansha, 1973), pp. 51–2.
15. Miyake Genjiro, Video production by Eizo Bunka Kyokai, 110 mins. with commentary, *Shinryaku — Maree hanto: Oshierare-nakatta senso* [Aggression on the Malayan Peninsula: The war they did not teach us about] (Tokyo, 1992), pp. 65–7.
16. Omori Kichijiro, Interview, 5 Sept. 1993, Singapore Oral History Project, Singapore National Archives, transcript, pp. 3–4.
17. Editorial note by Brian Farrell: When the civil and military authorities in Singapore declared an official State of Emergency on 1 December 1941, Straits Settlements Police were directed to intern Japanese citizens as soon as the military authorities reported any hostile Japanese action. The roundup began within hours of the first Japanese aerial attack on Singapore in the early hours of 8 December and was largely successful and incident-free. Any interception of Omori or other Japanese nationals the day before would not have been authorised by executive authority.
18. Omori, Interview.
19. Ibid., transcript, pp. 2–4.

Chapter 2

1. Tsuchikane, *Shingaporu e no michi*, vol. 1, p. 104.
2. Ibid., pp. 11–4.
3. Ibid., p. 16.
4. See Hillis Lory, *Japan's Military Masters: The Army in Japanese Life* (New York: The Viking Press, 1943), pp. 9–10.

5. Tsuchikane, *Shingaporu e no michi*, vol. 1, pp. 14–5.
6. Ibid., p. 16.
7. Ibid., pp. 17–8.
8. Ibid., pp. 19–20.
9. Ibid., pp. 22, 28–30.
10. Ibid., pp. 23–6, 31.
11. Ibid., pp. 26–8.
12. Ibid., pp. 41–2.
13. Ibid., pp. 42–3.
14. Ibid., pp. 44–6. Editorial note by Brian Farrell: On 2 July 1941 the Imperial Liaison Conference — the Cabinet, Army, and Navy General Staffs all meeting in the presence of the Emperor — made the fateful decision to exploit the German attack on the Soviet Union by "advancing south" to seize the resources of the Dutch East Indies. It was accepted that this step meant probable war with the United States and United Kingdom and direct preparations for that war began from this date. One such measure was a strict clampdown on news of all ship and troop movements, a reversal of previous policy to stir up public commitment to the war in China by fanfare surrounding such movements.
15. Miyake, *Shinryaku — Maree hanto*, pp. 65–6.
16. Ibid.
17. Ibid., p. 66.
18. Ochi, *Maree senki*, pp. 134–5.
19. Ibid., p. 136.
20. Onishi, *Hiroku*, p. 11.
21. Ibid., pp. 14–5.
22. Ibid., p. 16.
23. Ibid., pp. 16–7.
24. Ibid., p. 18.

Chapter 3

1. Omori, Interview, transcript, p. 1.
2. Wong Lin Ken, "Commercial Growth Before the Second World War", in E.C.T. Chew and E. Lee, eds., *A History of Singapore* (Singapore: Oxford University Press, 1991), p. 42.
3. Ibid., p. 52.

4. Paul H. Kratoska, *The Japanese Occupation of Malaya 1941–1945* (London: C. Hurst, 1998), pp. 20–1.
5. Ibid., p. 21.
6. Noel Barber, *Sinister Twilight* (London: Arrow Books, 1968), pp. 17–9.
7. Brian Montgomery, *Shenton of Singapore: Governor and Prisoner of War* (London: Leo Cooper, 1984), p. 49.
8. James F. Warren, *Ah Ku and Karayuki-San: Prostitution in Singapore 1870–1940* (Singapore: Oxford University Press, 1993), pp. 380–1.
9. Great Britain, Colonial Office, CO 273/659/50661, 14 Nov. 1939.
10. Jan Ruff-O'Herne, *50 Years of Silence* (Singapore: Toppan Co., 1996), p. 33.
11. Noel Barber, *Sinister Twilight* (London: Arrow Books, 1968), pp. 21–3.
12. Omori, Interview, pp. 1–3.
13. Ibid.
14. Ong Chit Chung, *Operation Matador: Britain's War Plans against the Japanese 1918–1941* (Singapore: Times Academic Press, 1997).
15. Omori, Interview, p. 5.

Chapter 4

1. Tsuchikane, *Shingaporu e no michi*, vol. 1, pp. 47–9; BBS, p. 128.
2. Editorial note by Brian Farrell: From the summer of 1940 on the Imperial Japanese Army conducted 10 significant training exercises to prepare for jungle and tropical warfare. The 5th Division was involved in several of them, operating in semi-tropical southern China, and specialized in amphibious operations from the mid-1920s.
3. Tsuchikane, *Shingaporu e no michi*, vol. 1, pp. 47–9. After nine months in the field, troops already regarded themselves as "old soldiers". At this stage, they were found most combat effective.
4. Ibid., pp. 49–50.

5. Chalmers Johnson, *Peasant Nationalism and Communist Power* (Stanford: Stanford University Press, 1962), pp. 57–9; Barbara W. Tuchman, *Sand Against the Wind: Stilwell and the American Experience in China 1911–45* (London: Papermac, 1991), p. 216.

6. Tsuchikane, *Shingaporu e no michi*, vol. 1, pp. 57–9.

7. Ibid., pp. 59–61.

8. Ibid., p. 62.

9. The decisions were reached in the crucial "Fundamentals of National Policy" and "Guidelines for Imperial Diplomacy" of the Four and Five Ministers' Conferences of 7 August 1936. See Henry Frei, *Japan's Southward Advance and Australia* (Honolulu: University of Hawaii Press, 1991), p. 136.

10. See Navy position paper "Study of Policy toward French Indochina" submitted to Army and Foreign Ministries, 1 August 1940, in *Gendai-shi shiryo* [Source material on contemporary history], vol. 10: *Nitchu senso* Tome 3 (Misuzu Shobo, 1964), pp. 369–71.

11. Ochi, *Maree senki*, p. 8.

12. Ibid., p. 12.

13. BBS, pp. 51–4; Masanobu Tsuji, *Singapore 1941–1942: The Japanese Version of the Malayan Campaign of World War II*, ed. H.V. Howe, trans. Margaret E. Lake (Singapore: Oxford University Press, 1988), p. 9.

14. Ochi, *Maree senki*, p. 8.

15. Editorial note by Brian Farrell: From 1938 the Imperial Japanese Army began to change the structure of its infantry divisions, from a four unit formation based on two brigades each containing two regiments to a three unit formation of three regiments. At the same time divisions began to receive higher scales of equipment. The idea was to increase firepower while decreasing numbers, to make divisions leaner and more mobile, yet harder hitting. But two of the divisions assigned to attack Malaya, the 5th and 18th, retained the old organisation because they had remained on almost continuous active service in China. When assigned to the 25th Army they were left unchanged, to allow them to form detachments that could operate independently in accordance with the

operational plan. From late 1940 the Imperial Japanese Army made further changes in the organisation and equipment of divisions. Hitherto most formations operated relatively few vehicles, relying heavily on horse-drawn transport. Many were now substantially re-equipped with motor vehicles and bicycles, including the 5th and the Imperial Guards. Such formations were known as Order 16 or *juroku-rei* divisions. One spur to such changes came from reports filed by Lt.-Gen. Yamashita Tomoyuki arising from a liaison mission to Germany, pointing to German success in Europe and arguing for still more tactical mobility and firepower at the division level. The limiting factor was the ability of the Japanese economy to supply the necessary equipment. Ironically, the army spent years preparing to fight the Soviet Red Army against which such a redesign would have been appropriate, as demonstrated by a heavy defeat suffered at Soviet hands in the summer of 1939. But now it turned towards another foe in another theatre, in which this new design was less useful. This further underlines the fact that Japan's leaders did not launch a long and elaborately prepared war against the West, as is still widely believed, but in fact turned towards such a conflict impulsively and in some disarray.

16. Ochi, *Maree senki*, pp. 9–10.
17. Ibid., pp. 11–2.
18. Ibid., p. 12.
19. Ibid., pp. 12–3.
20. Onishi, *Hiroku*, p. 20.
21. Ibid., pp. 21–2.
22. Ibid., p. 12.
23. See Hillis Lory, *Japan's Military Masters: The Army in Japanese Life* (New York: The Viking Press, 1943), p. 88.
24. Editorial note by Brian Farrell: Yamashita was in fact given another division as well, the 56th, but decided to leave it in reserve in Japan, to enable his inadequate pool of shipping to carry more supplies. The Imperial Guards Division moved overland to the border with Thailand, while the other two embarked by ship.
25. Tsuji, *Singapore 1941–1942*, pp. 24–5.

26. Editorial note by Brian Farrell: This march was similar in length to that later undertaken by elements of the 25th Army through Thailand and Malaya.

27. Arai, *Shingaporu senki*, pp. 7, 10; Arai, Interview.

Chapter 5

1. Tsuchikane, *Shingaporu e no michi*, vol. 1, p. 65.
2. Ibid., pp. 67–8.
3. Ibid., p. 70.
4. Ibid., pp. 71–3.
5. Ibid., pp. 74–6.
6. Ibid., pp. 77–8.
7. Ibid., pp. 78–9.
8. Ibid., pp. 80–1.
9. Ibid., p. 83.
10. Ibid., pp. 86–8.
11. Ibid.
12. Ibid., pp. 88–9.
13. Japan emulated Germany's famous paratroop blitz over Crete in May 1940 with its successful airborne landing in Palembang in Sumatra to seize Dutch refineries intact in March 1942.
14. Tsuchikane, *Shingaporu e no michi*, vol. 1, pp. 95–7.
15. Ibid., p. 98.
16. Ochi, *Maree senki*, pp. 10–1, 13, 16.
17. Ibid., pp. 16–7.
18. Ibid., pp. 18–20.
19. Tsuji, *Singapore 1941–1942*, p. 72.
20. Ochi, *Maree senki*, pp. 23.
21. Ibid., pp. 25–6.
22. Ibid., pp. 20–1, 24.
23. Ibid., p. 23.
24. See BBS, pp. 191–208, 217–32, 289–97.
25. Ibid., pp. 75–6.
26. Tsuchikane, *Shingaporu e no michi*, vol. 1, p. 106.
27. Ibid., pp. 107–9.
28. Ibid., pp. 110–1.
29. Tsuji, *Singapore 1941–1942*, p. 184.

30.   Tsuchikane, *Shingaporu e no michi*, vol. 1, p. 110.
31.   Ochi, *Maree senki*, p. 8.
32.   Ibid., p. 73.
33.   Ibid., pp. 76–81.
34.   Tsuji, *Singapore 1941–1942*, pp. 124–5; Ochi, *Maree senki*, pp. 110–8.
35.   Ochi, *Maree senki*, p. 138.
36.   Tsuchikane, *Shingaporu e no michi*, vol. 1, p. 111.
37.   Ibid., p. 114.
38.   Ibid., p. 115.
39.   Ibid., pp. 116–7.
40.   Ibid., pp. 118–9.
41.   Ibid., pp. 119–21.
42.   Ibid., pp. 121–2.
43.   Ibid., pp. 122–3.
44.   Ibid., pp. 124–6.
45.   Omori, Interview, transcript, pp. 4–5.
46.   Onishi, *Hiroku,* p. 26.
47.   Ibid., pp. 27–8.
48.   Ibid., p. 29.
49.   Ibid., p. 30.
50.   Omori, Interview, transcript, pp. 5–6.
51.   Arai, *Shingaporu senki*, p. 15.
52.   Ibid., pp. 18–9.
53.   Ibid., pp. 20–7.
54.   Ibid., p. 28. The description of half-naked local people is a fantasy. Neither the Thais nor the Malays in southern Thailand dressed in this way.
55.   Omori, Interview, transcript, pp. 6–9.

Chapter 6

1.   Ochi, *Maree senki*, pp. 141–2.
2.   Tsuchikane, *Shingaporu e no michi*, vol. 1, pp. 126–8.
3.   Ibid., pp. 128–30; Onishi, *Hiroku*, p. 40.
4.   Tsuchikane, *Shingaporu e no michi*, vol. 1, pp. 132–3.
5.   Ibid., pp. 133–6.
6.   Ibid., pp. 123–4.

7. Ibid., p. 136.
8. Ibid., pp. 137–8; Russell Braddon, *The Naked Island* (London: Pan Books, 1952), p. 86.
9. Tsuchikane, *Shingaporu e no michi*, vol. 1, p. 138.
10. Ibid., pp. 141–2.
11. Ibid., pp. 143–6.
12. Ibid., pp. 149–50.
13. Braddon, *The Naked Island*, p. 100.
14. Tsuchikane, *Shingaporu e no michi*, vol. 1, pp. 151–4.
15. Braddon, *The Naked Island*, p. 85.
16. Tsuchikane, *Shingaporu e no michi*, vol. 1, p. 155.
17. Ibid., p. 157.
18. S. Woodburn Kirby, *The War Against Japan: The Loss of Singapore*, History of the Second World War, United Kingdom Military Series, vol. I (London: HMSO, 1957), pp. 320–7.
19. Editorial note by Brian Farrell: Tsuchikane cannot have seen Australian corpses in Batu Pahat, for no Australian unit fought there. Very likely his unit moved through the Bakri and Parit Sulong areas, some 20 km away, where two Australian battalions did put up a staunch but costly fight against the Imperial Guards.
20. Tsuchikane, *Shingaporu e no michi*, vol. 1, pp. 155–6.
21. Ibid., pp. 159, 169.
22. Onishi, *Hiroku*, p. 30.
23. Ibid., p. 40.
24. Ibid., p. 41.
25. Ibid., pp. 41–2.
26. Ibid., pp. 42–3.
27. Ibid., pp. 43–4.
28. Ibid., p. 44.
29. Ibid., p. 45. Editorial note by Brian Farrell: That Onishi could be surprised that occupied civilians were too frightened of possible consequences to complain to the Japanese military police about mistreatment says a great deal about the perceptions of the men on the ground. On the other hand the Japanese were not the only Second World War army that sometimes dealt with non-fatal abuse of civilians by nothing more than a "stern warning".

30. Onishi, *Hiroku*, pp. 46–7.
31. Arai, *Shingaporu senki*, pp. 29–30.
32. Ibid., p. 31.
33. Ibid., p. 36.
34. Maj. Kunitake Teruto, Interview, 28 Nov. 1993, Waseda University Library.
35. Editorial note by Brian Farrell: 18th Division headquarters and the 114th Regiment, led by Lt.-Gen. Mutaguchi Renya in person, embarked in transports intending to assault the east coast of Johor, and were diverted to Songkhla only after a heated argument between Southern Army staff, which wanted the invasion to proceed, and 25th Army headquarters, which concluded the defenses near Mersing were too daunting to assault without unacceptable losses. The diversion was settled on 19 January. The developing breakthrough further west confirmed rather than caused the decision.
36. Arai, *Shingaporu senki*, p. 36.
37. Omori, Interview, transcript, pp. 11–2.

Chapter 7

1.   Ochi, *Maree senki*, p. 254.
2.   Ibid., p. 255.
3.   Editorial note by Brian Farrell: These figures, which come from Tsuji, are slightly misleading. The figure of 35,000 Japanese troops covers only those in combat units; adding support elements brings the total close to 60,000. The figure for Commonwealth armies includes these elements, but omits reinforcements that arrived too late to fight on the mainland.
4.   Ochi, *Maree senki*, p. 256; Tsuji, *Singapore 1941–1942*, pp. 213–5.
5.   Ochi, *Maree senki*, pp. 242, 256.
6.   Ibid., p. 257.
7.   Ibid., pp. 257–8.
8.   Ibid., p. 259.
9.   Ibid., pp. 260–1.
10. Ibid., p. 261.
11. Ibid., pp. 262–4.

12. Ibid., pp. 265–6.
13. Ibid., pp. 267–9; Tsuji, *Singapore 1941–1942*, p. 232.
14. Ochi, *Maree senki*, pp. 269–70.
15. Ibid., p. 272.
16. Ibid., pp. 270–1; Tsuji, *Singapore 1941–1942*, pp. 234–7.
17. Ochi, *Maree senki*, p. 270; Tsuji, *Singapore 1941–1942*, p. 233.
18. Editorial note by Brian Farrell: During the previous year, Maj.-Gen. H. Gordon Bennett, general officer commanding the 8th Australian Division, had struck up a friendship with the Sultan of Johor. Sultan Ibrahim had made an effort over the years to cultivate his imperial protector, including a substantial donation to help cover the costs of the coastal defences of Singapore. Bennett's representations thus fell on receptive ground when Malaya Command told its gunners not to target the Sultan's palace, the Istana Bukit Serene, in order not to alienate His Highness. Yamashita ensconced himself in the tower, which still stands, enjoying an excellent view of the battle he unleashed.
19. Tsuji, *Singapore 1941–1942*, p. 229.
20. Ochi, *Maree senki*, p. 272; Tsuji, *Singapore 1941–1942*, pp. 228–9.
21. Ochi, *Maree senki*, p. 275.
22. Ibid., p. 276.
23. Ibid., pp. 276–7. Ochi's etymology of the Malay word *perempuan* (woman) is completely spurious.
24. Ibid., p. 277.
25. Ibid., pp. 277–9.
26. Ibid., p. 280.
27. Ibid., p. 281.
28. Ibid., p. 282.
29. Tsuchikane, *Shingaporu e no michi*, vol. 1, p. 181.
30. Ibid., pp. 182–3.
31. Ibid., p. 184.
32. Ibid., pp. 185–6.
33. Ibid., p. 187.
34. Ibid., pp. 188–9.
35. Ibid., pp. 190–1.
36. Ibid., pp. 191–2.

37.   Ibid., pp. 193–4.
38.   Ibid., pp. 195–7.
39.   Ibid., p. 198.
40.   Ibid., pp. 199–200.
41.   Ibid., pp. 200–2.
42.   Ibid., pp. 203–4.
43.   Ibid., p. 205. The present of a "silver bracelet" suggests that the Indian family was Sikh, and the present a steel bangle of the sort worn by Sikh men.

Chapter 8

1.   Arai, *Shingaporu senki*, pp. 76–93.
2.   The Australian engineer in charge of demolition had opened the valves of the oil tank, let the oil run out to sea, and set it ablaze. See Kirby, *The War Against Japan*, p. 382.
3.   Arai, *Shingaporu senki*, pp. 138–9.
4.   Ibid., p. 140.
5.   Ochi, *Maree senki*, pp. 296–9.
6.   Arai, *Shingaporu senki*, pp. 123–4, 130–2.
7.   Ochi, *Maree senki*, pp. 301, 304.
8.   Arai, *Shingaporu senki*, p. 94.
9.   Ibid., pp. 101, 121, 132.
10.   See S. Woodburn Kirby, *Singapore: The Chain of Disaster* (London: Cassell, 1971), p. 240.
11.   Kirby, *The War Against Japan*, pp. 373, 399.
12.   Arai, *Shingaporu senki*, pp. 147–8; Ochi, *Maree senki*, p. 316.
13.   Arai, *Shingaporu senki*, p. 145.
14.   Ibid., p. 146.
15.   Ibid., p. 135.

Chapter 9

1.   Kirby, *Singapore: The Chain of Disaster*, p. 245.
2.   Percival, *The War in Malaya*, p. 289.
3.   Ibid., pp. 291–2.
4.   That morning Gen. Percival received information that the water supply would not last for more than another 24 hours,

that military food reserves had been reduced to a few days, and that they had practically no petrol except what was in vehicle tanks. See ibid., pp. 291–2. The momentous meeting is captured in lifelike figures at the very same Fort Canning Headquarters, which the Singapore Government has turned into a high-tech museum.

5. Onishi, *Hiroku*, p. 60; Kirby, *Singapore: The Chain of Disaster*, p. 248.

6. Onishi, *Hiroku*, pp. 60–1.

7. Oki Shuji, *Ningen Yamashita Tomoyuki* [Yamashita the Man] (Tokyo: Nihon Shuhosha, 1959; 6th ed. 1961), p. 235.

8. Onishi, *Hiroku*, p. 61; Kirby, *Singapore: The Chain of Disaster*, p. 250.

9. Onishi, *Hiroku*, p. 61.

10. Arai, *Shingaporu senki*, pp. 119, 149.

11. Ibid., pp. 118–9.

12. Ibid., p. 120.

13. Ibid., p. 149.

14. Ibid., p. 152.

15. Ibid., p. 153.

16. Ibid., pp. 153–4.

17. Ibid., p. 157.

18. Ibid., pp. 157–8.

19. Ibid., pp. 158–9.

20. Ibid., p. 159.

21. Ibid., p. 160.

22. Ibid., p. 156.

23. Ibid., pp. 164–5.

24. Ibid., p. 168.

25. Ibid., p. 170. Editorial note by Brian Farrell: Readers familiar with the Allied narratives of the battle will be surprised by this casual description of the much remarked last stand of C Company, 1st Battalion The Malay Regiment, ultimately led by 2nd Lt. Adnan Saidi. The company was surrounded overnight and forced to fight it out, only four men escaping. The battle is commemorated today by a heritage centre on Bukit Chandu, operated by the Singapore National Heritage Board.

26. Ibid., pp. 171–3.

27.   Ibid., pp. 172, 174.
28.   Ibid., p. 175.
29.   Ibid., p. 176. Editorial note by Brian Farrell: Arai exaggerates the situation. Fort Siloso was not strongly fortified; the two 6" guns and smaller ordnance found there made it a standard size coastal defence position. Fort Siloso is preserved today as a museum of coastal defence and of the British military presence in Singapore.
30.   Ibid., pp. 178–9.
31.   Ibid., p. 180.
32.   Ibid., pp. 181–2.
33.   Ibid., p. 183.
34.   Ibid., p. 184.
35.   Ibid., pp. 185–6.
36.   Ibid., pp. 187–8, and Arai, Interview.
37.   Arai, *Shingaporu senki*, pp. 192–3.
38.   Ibid., p. 194.
39.   Ochi, *Maree senki*, pp. 311–5.
40.   A.E. Percival, *The War in Malaya* (London: Eire & Spottiswoode, 1949), p. 278.
41.   Editorial note by Brian Farrell: Ochi no doubt felt he was on the receiving end of a full-scale counter-attack, but the assault was nothing more than a half-hearted probe launched by elements of one battalion, trying to regain the reservoir. Malaya Command never managed to deliver a major counter-attack on the island.
42.   Ochi, *Maree senki*, pp. 318–9.
43.   Ibid., pp. 320–1. Editorial note by Brian Farrell: There was in fact no chance the campaign could at this stage have reversed itself and ended in a rout of the Japanese. Their powerful air and naval forces totally dominated the entire region and were at hand to reinforce the attack on Singapore if necessary, while Percival's army was on its last legs and the water supply was failing fast. But Ochi's memory of an apparently desperate situation is shared by other Japanese present at the time, including staff officers at division headquarters.
44.   Ochi, *Maree senki*, pp. 322–3.
45.   Ibid., p. 324; Arai, *Shingaporu senki*, pp. 167–8.
46.   Ochi, *Maree senki*, pp. 324–5.

47. Ibid., pp. 329–30.
48. Ibid., p. 331.
49. Ibid., pp. 333–5, 338.
50. Ibid., p. 338.
51. Ibid., pp. 338–9; Meirion and Susie Harries, *Soldiers of the Sun: The Rise and Fall of the Imperial Japanese Army* (London: Heinemann, 1991), p. 328.
52. Ochi, *Maree senki*, p. 339.
53. Ibid., pp. 340–1.
54. Ibid., pp. 341–2.
55. Ibid., pp. 342–3, 345.
56. Ibid., p. 346.
57. Ibid., p. 348.
58. Ibid., pp. 349–51.
59. Ibid., pp. 352–3.
60. Ibid., pp. 354–6.
61. Ibid., pp. 357–9.
62. Ibid., pp. 359–60.
63. Ibid., pp. 362–3.
64. Ibid., pp. 364–5.
65. Ibid., pp. 365–7.
66. Tsuchikane, *Shingaporu e no michi*, vol. 1, p. 206.
67. Ibid., pp. 206–7.
68. Ibid., pp. 208–9.
69. Ibid., pp. 210–2
70. Ibid., pp. 213–4.
71. Ibid., pp. 214–5.
72. Ibid., p. 216.
73. Ibid., pp. 217–8.
74. Ibid., pp. 218–21.

Chapter 10

1. Onishi, *Hiroku*, p. 55; Onishi, Interview.
2. Ibid., pp. 55–6.
3. Ibid., p. 56.
4. Ibid.
5. Ibid., p. 57.

6.   Ibid., pp. 57–8.
7.   Ibid., p. 58.
8.   Ibid., p. 59.
9.   Ibid., p. 62.
10.   Ibid., pp. 62–3.
11.   Ibid., pp. 63–4.
12.   Ibid., p. 64; Mamoru Shinozaki, *My Wartime Experiences in Singapore* (Singapore: Institute of Southeast Asian Studies, Oral History Programme Series No. 3, 1973), p. 13.
13.   Onishi, *Hiroku*, pp. 64–5.
14.   Ian Ward, *The Killer They Called a God* (Singapore: Media Masters, 1992), p. 119.
15.   Onishi, *Hiroku*, pp. 136–7.
16.   A day after the surrender, Singapore was renamed Shonan, "Resplendent South".
17.   Onishi, *Hiroku*, pp. 68–9; Malaya Occupation Forum, eds., *Nihon no Eiryou Maraia: Shingapooru senryo 1941–45* [Singapore and Malaya Under Japanese Occupation 1941–45] (Tokyo: Ryukei Shyosha, 1998), p. 178.
18.   Hayashi Hirofumi, *Kakyo gyakusatsu: Nihongun shihaika no Maree hanto* [The Overseas Chinese Massacre: The Malaya Peninsula Under Japanese Occupation] (Tokyo: Suzusawa Shoten, 1992), p. 42.
19.   Onishi, *Hiroku*, pp. 69–70.
20.   Ibid., pp. 70–1.
21.   Ibid., pp. 72–3.
22.   Ibid., p. 71.
23.   Ibid., p. 72.
24.   Ishibe Toshiro, Interview, Osaka, 4 June 1994; Reel 2.
25.   Onishi, *Hiroku*, pp. 73–5.
26.   Ibid., pp. 75–6.
27.   *Nihon no Eiryou Marai*, p. 180; Onishi, interview, 7 July 1994, Waseda University.
28.   Onishi, *Hiroku*, pp. 73–4; *Nihon no Eiryou Marai*, pp. 178–80; Onishi, interview, 7 July 1994.
29.   Onishi, *Hiroku*, p. 74; *Nihon no Eiryou Marai*, pp. 179, 183; Onishi, interview, 7 July 1994.
30.   Onishi, *Hiroku*, p. 74; *Nihon no Eiryou Marai*, p. 180; Onishi, interview, 7 July 1994.

31. Editorial note by Brian Farrell: There is no record of the Military Police making any objection to the order to carry out the purge of Singapore Chinese other than this claim by Kawamura that he did so.

32. Onishi, *Hiroku*, p. 74; Kawamura Saburo, *Jusan kaidan o agaru: senpan shokeisha no kiroku* [Going Up Thirteen Steps] (Tokyo: Atoshobo, 1952), p. 164.

33. Kawamura, *Going Up Thirteen Steps*; Onishi, *Hiroku*, pp. 78–9.

34. *Nihon no Eiryou Marai*, pp. 178–9; Onishi, interview, 7 July 1994.

35. Onishi, *Hiroku*, pp. 74–5.

36. Yap Yan Hong, in *Sook Ching* (Singapore: Oral History Department, 1992), pp. 11–5.

37. Fujiwara Iwaichi, *F-Kikan: Japanese Army Intelligence Operations in Southeast Asia during World War II*, trans. Akashi Yoji (Hong Kong: Heinemann Asia, 1983), pp. 192–3.

38. Onishi, *Hiroku*, pp. 97–9. Editorial note by Brian Farrell: Perhaps the *sook ching* massacre in Singapore was the worst atrocity Onishi himself was involved in, but it pales in comparison to the December 1937 Rape of Nanking, the Bataan Death March, and the Death Railway in Thailand, to name but three extreme acts of barbarism perpetrated by the Imperial Japanese Army.

39. Ochi, *Maree senki*, pp. 374–5.

40. Tsuchikane, *Shingaporu e no michi*, vol. 1, pp. 221–2.

41. Miyake, *Shinryaku — Maree hanto*, pp. 67–8. Editorial note by Brian Farrell: Miyake, the reluctant warrior, raises a point that is often overlooked. The purge of Malayan Chinese is normally seen as having taken place only in Singapore, while in fact there were organised roundups in the larger towns on the mainland as well, particularly in Penang, Ipoh, and Kuala Lumpur.

42. Miyake, *Shinryaku — Maree hanto*, p. 68.

43. Ibid., p. 69.

Chapter 11

1. Omori, Interview.

2. Arai, Interview.

3. Miyake, *Shinryaku — Maree hanto*, p. 65.

4. Ochi, *Maree senki*, pp. 321, 376.
5. Editorial note by Brian Farrell: Yamashita was tried by an Allied Military Tribunal in Manila in connection with the wholesale massacre of civilians during the battle for that city in February 1945, committed by troops nominally under his command but in fact beyond his reach and disobeying his orders. His conviction and subsequent execution was widely condemned after the fact as judicial lynching, and the issue was even referred to the United States Supreme Court. On the other hand Yamashita was certainly responsible as the command authority for the brutal massacres committed by his army at Parit Sulong and at the Alexandra Hospital in Singapore, and during the *sook ching* operation. He would have been executed by a British military tribunal had he faced one. Ochi's suggestion that Percival had done anything whatsoever to deserve being executed and therefore needed Yamashita's protection is absurd.
6. Ochi, *Maree senki*, p. 377.
7. Ibid., pp. 321, 376–8.
8. Onishi, *Hiroku*, pp. 239–41; Onishi, Interview.
9. Tsuchikane, *Shingaporu e no michi*, vol. 1, p. 126.
10. Editorial note by Brian Farrell: Provided Japan lost the war, a safe assumption, the Malayan campaign would still have been stigmatised in the eyes of all but the Japanese, even without the *sook ching*, for three reasons: the unprovoked aggression Japan launched on Southeast Asia, the massacres committed by the army, and the subsequent behaviour of the Japanese as an occupying power. The campaign is regarded as an impressive military victory, but the general behaviour of the Imperial Japanese Army in all its Pacific War and China campaigns forever destroyed its reputation beyond any hope of its military exploits finding "acceptance in the world".
11. Onishi, *Hiroku*, p. 132.

Bibliography

Arai Mitsuo. *Shingaporu senki* [Singapore War Diary] (Tokyo: Tosho Shuppansha, 1984).

Barber, Noel. *Sinister Twilight* (London: Arrow Books, 1968).

Bennett, (Lt.-Gen.) Henry Gordon. *Why Singapore Fell* (London: Angus and Robertson, 1944).

Boei-cho, Boeikenshujo, Senshishitsu [Self-defense Agency, National Defense College, War History Office]. *Maree shinko sakusen* [The Malaya campaign] (Tokyo: Asagumo Shinbunsha, 1966).

Braddon, Russell. *The Naked Island* (London: Pan Books, 1952).

Chew, Ernest C.T. and Edwin Lee. *A History of Singapore* (Singapore: Oxford University Press, 1991).

Frei, Henry. *Japan's Southward Advance and Australia* (Honolulu: University of Hawaii Press, 1991).

Fujiwara Iwaichi. *F-Kikan: Japanese Army Intelligence Operations in Southeast Asia during World War II*. Trans. Akashi Yoji (Hong Kong: Heinemann Asia, 1983).

Harries, Meirion and Susie. *Soldiers of the Sun: the Rise and Fall of the Imperial Japanese Army* (London: Heinemann, 1991).

Hayashi Hirofumi. *Kakyo gyakusatsu: Nihongun shihaika no Maree hanto* [The Overseas Chinese Massacre: The Malaya Peninsula Under Japanese Occupation] (Tokyo: Suzusawa Shoten, 1992).

Johnson, Chalmers. *Peasant Nationalism and Communist Power* (Stanford: Stanford University Press, 1962).

Kawamura Saburo. *Jusan kaidan o agaru: senpan shokeisha no kiroku* [Going Up Thirteen Steps: Record of a War-Criminal's Punishment] (Tokyo: Atoshobo, 1952).

Kirby, S. Woodburn. *Singapore: The Chain of Disaster* (London: Cassell, 1971).

_____. *The War Against Japan: The Loss of Singapore*. History of the Second World War, United Kingdom Military Series, Vol. I (London: Her Majesty's Stationery Office, 1957).

Kratoska, Paul H. *The Japanese Occupation of Malaya, 1941–1945* (London: C. Hurst, 1998).

Lory, Hillis. *Japan's Military Masters: The Army in Japanese Life* (New York: The Viking Press, 1943).

Malaya Occupation Forum, eds. *Nihon no Eiryou Maraia: Shingapooru senryo 1941–45* [Singapore and Malaya Under Japanese Occupation, 1941–45] (Tokyo: Ryukei Shyosha, 1998).

Miyake Genjiro. Video production by Eizo Bunka Kyokai, 110 mins, with commentary, *Shinryaku – Maree hanto: Oshierarenakatta senso* [Aggression on the Malayan Peninsula: The war they did not teach us about] (Tokyo, 1992).

Montgomery, Brian. *Shenton of Singapore: Governor and Prisoner of War* (London: Leo Cooper, 1984).

Ochi Harumi. *Maree senki* [Malaya War Diary] (Tokyo: Tosho Shuppansha, 1973).

Oki Shuji. *Ningen Yamashita Tomoyuki* [Yamashita the Man] (Tokyo: Nihon Shuhosha, 1959; 6th ed. 1961).

Ong Chit Chung. *Operation Matador: Britain's War Plans against the Japanese, 1918–1941* (Singapore: Times Academic Press, 1997).

Onishi Satoru. *Hiroku: Shonan Kakyo shukusei jiken* [Secret document: The purge of Overseas Chinese in Shonan] (Tokyo: Kameoka Shuppan, 1977).

Percival, A.E. *The War in Malaya* (London: Eire & Spottiswoode, 1949).

Ruff-O'Herne, Jan. *50 Years of Silence: Comfort Women of Indonesia* (Singapore: Toppan, 1996).

Shinozaki, Mamoru. *My Wartime Experiences in Singapore* (Singapore: Institute of Southeast Asian Studies, 1973), Oral History Programme Series No. 3.

Chew, Daniel and Irene Lim, eds. *Sook Ching* (Singapore: Oral History Department, 1992).

Tsuchikane Tominosuke. *Shingaporu e no michi: aru Konoe hei no kiroku* [The Road to Singapore: Diary of an Imperial Guard Soldier] (Tokyo: Sogeisha, 1977).

Tsuji, Masanobu. *Singapore 1941–1942: The Japanese Version of the Malayan Campaign of World War II*, ed. H.V. Howe, trans. Margaret E. Lake (Singapore: Oxford University Press, 1988).

Tuchman, Barbara W. *Sand against the Wind: Stilwell and the American Experience in China 1911–45* (London: Papermac, 1991).

Ward, Ian. *The Killer They Called a God* (Singapore: Media Masters, 1992).

Warren, James F. *Ah Ku and Karayuki-San: Prostitution in Singapore 1870–1940* (Singapore: Oxford University Press, 1993).

Wong Lin Ken. "Commercial Growth Before the Second World War", in *A History of Singapore*, ed. E.C.T. Chew and E. Lee (Singapore: Oxford University Press, 1991).

Interviews

Arai Mitsuo, Kokura, Kyushu, 10 October 1993.

Ishibe Toshiro, Osaka, 4 June 1994.

Kunitake Teruto, 28 Nov. 1993, Waseda University Library.

Omori Kichijiro, Tokyo, 5 September 1993, Singapore Oral History Project, Singapore National Archives.

Onishi Satoru, 7 July 1994.

Index